THE
BOMBER AIRCREW
EXPERIENCE

Dealing Out Punishment from the Air

PHILIP KAPLAN

Skyhorse Publishing

Skyhorse Publishing books may be purchased in bulk at special discounts for sales promotion, corporate gifts, fund-raising, or educational purposes. Special editions can also be created to specifications. For details, contact the Special Sales Department, Skyhorse Publishing, 307 West 36th Street, 11th Floor, New York, NY 10018 or info@skyhorsepublishing.com.

Skyhorse® and Skyhorse Publishing® are registered trademarks of Skyhorse Publishing, Inc.®, a Delaware corporation.

Visit our website at www.skyhorsepublishing.com.

10 9 8 7 6 5 4 3 2 1

Library of Congress Cataloging-in-Publication Data is available on file.

Cover design by Rain Saukas
Cover photographs courtesy of Philip Kaplan

Previously published as *Bombers: The Aircrew Experience*

Print ISBN: 978-1-5107-0262-2
Ebook ISBN: 978-1-5107-0263-9

Printed in China

CONTENTS

"War is a nasty, dirty, rotten business. It's all right for the Navy to blockade a city, to starve the inhabitants to death. But there is something wrong, not nice, about bombing that city."
—Marshal of the Royal Air Force Sir Arthur Harris

The tumult and the shouting have died away. The B-17s and the B-24s will never again assemble into strike formation in the bitter cold of embattled skies. Never again will the musical thunder of their passage cause the very earth to tremble, the source of sound lost in infinity and seeming to eminate from all things, visible and invisible. The great deep-throated engines are forever silent . . .
—from *Heritage of Valor* by Budd J. Peaslee, USAF (Ret)

DELIVERY

Bomb-Boogiie, of the 401st Bomb Squadron, 91st Bomb Group, Bassingbourn, England.

Colonel Peaslee, air commander of the Schweinfurt attack of 14 October 1943, wrote those words in tribute to the men of the Eighth U.S. Army Air Force who participated in what many historians consider the most savage air battle in history, the second mighty U.S. bombing raid on the

Vereinigte Kugellager Fabrik (VKF), Kugelfischer AG (FAG), Deutsche Star Kugelhalter, and the Fichtel and Sachs ball and anti-friction bearing works at Schweinfurt, Germany.

Why did allied planners conclude that these targets at Schweinfurt were of such importance to the war effort

that a maximum effort attack had to be mounted that October day, even though the Eighth Air Force had suffered its worst losses ever when attempting a similar strike on the German town just two months earlier? Virtually all aircraft, tanks, warships,

submarines, machines, and precision instruments were utterly dependent on anti-friction bearings in their performance. Like the weather, friction was a formidable enemy, as surely as any declared political foe. Germany's entire war machine (like the Allies') literally ran on these bearings, and it consumed them by the multi-millions.

It was known to the planners of Eighth Bomber Command that most manufacturers of Germany's military industrial complex maintained only a small on-hand stock of finished bearings. They knew too, that an effective attack on the German bearings industry would undoubtedly result in one effect of particular importance to the Eighth Air Force itself . . . a nearly immediate and crippling disruption of German fighter aircraft production. The American planners found that the German anti-friction bearings industry was highly concentrated geographically, with some 73 percent of her entire bearings output generated by plants in just six cities. Schweinfurt alone produced 42 percent of all bearings utilized in the German war effort, and, as a target, was irresistible.

On 17 August 1943, one year to the day after the first U.S. Eighth Air Force B-17 operation of the war, the first major American bombing raid on the German bearings industry was mounted as part of a two-pronged attack. A combined force of 376 B-17s took their bombs to Schweinfurt, and to Regensburg, where the target was a large and vital Messerschmitt fighter factory. On that day, 315 of the bombers successfully attacked their targets, delivering a total of 724 tons of bombs. Thirty-six heavy bombers of the Regensburg force and twenty-four from the Schweinfurt force (a total of 600 American airmen) fell to enemy

flak and fighters, for a staggering 19 percent loss to the attacking force. Bombing results at Regensburg were judged good, with every significant building in the manufacturing complex badly damaged. The Schweinfurt effort, however, was not as successful, and those responsible for target selection at Eighth Bomber Command knew that the Yanks would have to go back to that town and try again.

The effort of 17 August, while useful and fairly effective, had resulted in losses that were clearly unsustainable. For nearly two months the heavy bomb groups of the Eighth lay incapacitated, unable to bring war to German targets. Grievously wounded, the Eighth slowly regathered strength and, by the second week of October, prepared to return to the fight with a renewed will and greatly increased firepower. On the morning of 8 October it sent a force of 399 heavy bombers to attack targets at Bremen and Vegesack with a loss of thirty aircraft. On the 9th 378 B-17s and B-24s were dispatched to hit targets at Danzig, Gdynia, Anklam and Marienburg, with a loss that day of twenty-eight of the heavies. It was followed on the 10th with an attack (the third major U.S. raid in as many days) by 236 bombers on the city of Münster where another thirty aircraft were lost. Then came a three-day rest, a breathing spell in which the crews of the Eighth could regroup for what they were to face on 14 October. The survivors would always remember it as "Black Thursday."

"On arriving at our equipment room we were issued our Mae West life vest, parachute and harness, goggles, leather helmet, gabardine flying coveralls, heated suit, and a steel helmet that had hinged ear flaps to cover

The crew of this B-17G is delighted to be safely back on their base in England after a mission deep into enemy territory.

Refueling a B-17G for a bombing mission over
Nazi-occupied Europe in 1944.

our radio headset. We were also given felt heated inserts to cover our feet inside our sheepskin-lined leather flying boots and silk insert gloves to wear under our heated heavy leather gloves. We also picked up our escape kits which contained a silk map which was highly detailed and could be folded quite small to take up very little space. The kit also held a razor, high-energy hard candy, a translation sheet in Dutch, Flemish, French, and German, and a plastic bottle and water purification tablets. We left behind our .45 calibre Colt Automatic and shoulder holster which had been issued to us to protect us from the German civilians and the SS. Intelligence had learned that our crew members who carried the weapons were sometimes shot because the presence of the gun gave the enemy an excuse to shoot them. In addition to all of our other gear, we brought our oxygen masks, headsets, and throat microphones, all of which were kept in our footlockers. After picking up our flight equipment, a six-by-six truck took us as a crew to our dispersal area and the hardstand where our B-17 was parked. It was about a five minute ride from the hangar and our equipment room. On the way out to dispersal, everyone was quiet. We all had our own thoughts."
—Roger Armstrong, 91st Bomb Group (H), Eighth USAAF

The decision to return to Schweinfurt on 14 October was made by General Frederick L. Anderson at Eighth Bomber Command Headquarters, code-named Pinetree, at High Wycombe, Buckinghamshire. It was referred to simply as Mission 115. Anderson and his little committee of specialist officers had many factors to consider in its planning: the

importance of the target relative to all others, the routes and timings of their attacking force, the German anti-aircraft and fighter defenses en route, the relative vulnerability of the target factories, the predicted weather for England, the weather for the routes to and from the target area itself, the types and categories of the bombs to be delivered, and the size and nature of the fighter escort needed to shepherd the heavy bombers both outbound and back.

Once Anderson had made the decision to attack Schweinfurt for a second time in a maximum effort, a Warning Order was issued to the Air Divisions of the Eighth Air Force across England, alerting them to begin preparations for the raid.

At twenty-five minutes to midnight on 13 October, Field Order 220 clattered from teletype machines at the various Eighth Air Force heavy bomber stations in the English Midlands and East Anglia. The message received at Great Ashfield, Chelveston, Polebrook, Podington, Thurleigh, Grafton Underwood, Bury St Edmunds, Bassingbourn, Alconbury, Molesworth, Kimbolton, Hardwick, Horsham St Faith, Ridgewell, Horham, Snetterton Heath, Thorpe Abbotts, Knettishall, Framlingham, and Wendling detailed the times for briefing and take-off for the crews who would fly the mission that day. In the early hours of the 14th, additional field orders arrived which defined the mission requirements in greater detail for the participating bomb groups. Earlier orders had instructed the groups as to the bomb loads they were to take and the other items essential to such strategic attacks.

Ground crew personnel were occupied for the next several hours in fueling the B-17s and B-24s taking part

in No 115. In addition to aviation gas, the bombers had to be supplied with ammunition, oxygen, extra clothing and shoes, sandwiches, first-aid kits, and maps.

At Debden and Boxted, at Bodney and Raydon, the P-47 Thunderbolt fighters of Eighth Fighter Command were alerted and readied shortly after two in the morning of the 14th for their vital escort role. To have much chance of returning safely to their English bases from this complex, demanding, and extremely hazardous operation, the bombers would require substantial protection by their little fighter friends.

By 2:00 a.m. every bomb group commander was in possession of the complete combat order for Mission 115. The order provided them with the information that would be the core of the briefings their crews would receive in a few hours, including, but not limited to, the schedules for starting engines, take-offs, assembly times and altitudes, the Initial Point, Mean Point of Impact, Rally Point, routes, bomb loadings amd weights, the anticipated enemy flak, and fighter opposition.

Lieutenant Raymond W. Wild was a B-17 pilot with the 92nd Bomb Group (H) stationed at Podington, Northamptonshire in the autumn of 1943. Ray was one of the first Eighth Air Force veterans I met and in the course of our many long conversations, he was exceptionally articulate in relating his vivid, colorful memories of his missions against German targets in what was the most difficult and dangerous period for the American bomber crews in the European Theatre of Operations. Mission 115, the second great Schweinfurt raid, was the third mission of Wild's tour of duty.

"We arrived at Podington and the 92nd Bomb Group in September 1943 and they had us shoot some landings right away. At Podington the runways were built right into the farm, and the farmer was still farming it. The farmer was there and the farmer's daughter was there. He'd be there farming when we left on a raid, and he'd still be farming when we came back.

"They checked out our crew and assigned us to a squadron, the 325th. They had a wall with names on it— twelve missions, fourteen missions— and MIA, KIA. None of us knew what that meant. They showed us that and then they took us to the ready room, and there was a certain kind of dust in there; I don't know what the hell it was, but I sneezed eleven times in a row. We took our crew out flying formation for a short period of time,

according to how fast they needed replacement crews to fly missions.

"When I got to Podington one of the first things I did was to look up an RAF pilot who had been a classmate of mine during training in the States. He and I went out and had a couple of beers with some of his buddies. They felt that we Americans were out of our minds. They had tried daylight bombing and it just wasn't feasible. They said we'd get the hell shot out

B-17 Flying Fortress bombers of the 381st Bomb Group at Ridgewell, England.

of us. But those Limeys did something that sure would scare me—night bombing. They'd come in over a target a minute apart, one guy this way, another guy from another point in the compass. This would scare me to death. They had tremendous intestinal fortitude. They were also realistic in that they couldn't bomb by daylight. Those Lancs were built to carry bombs, not to protect themselves, while we could. So long as we stayed in tight formation, we could throw a lot of lead out in the right direction at the right time.

"The frightening times of a raid for me were before take-off and after you got back down. In the ready room you were with a bunch of other guys, and you were wise-cracking to ease the tension. I remember that just before my first raid—the one where you are really frightened to death—I went into the john in the operations tower. Didn't have to go, but just went in and sat on the john. That was when the song 'Paper Doll' had just come out and somebody had written all the words on the wall. Just through nothing but being nervous I sat there and memorized those words. The mission was the 8 October 1943 raid, and it was a tough one. This day I was being sent as co-pilot with Gus Arenholtz, a helluva nice guy who later became a good friend of mine.

They were sending me to be oriented by him. We took off in the foulest weather and, when we got over the middle of the Channel, and I was really scared, Gus said to me, 'Take it a minute.' I said, 'OK' and took the wheel. We were flying in formation and he reached down and put on flak gloves, a flak suit and a flak helmet, and said, 'OK, I've got it.' So, I reached down and said, 'Where the hell is mine?' He said, 'Didn't you bring any?' I said, 'You're breaking me in!' 'Well, don't worry about it,' he said. 'It's gonna be an easy raid.' I said, 'OK, I'll hold it a minute. You take that stuff off. If it's gonna be an easy raid, give it to me.' 'Like hell I will,' he said. Our ship got back with a two-foot hole in one side, one engine shot out, three of the six elevator control cables shot in two, and our radio operator wounded. Because we got back safely and all the crew survived, from then

The crew of the B-24J *Arise My Love and Come with Me* at Horsham St Faith. The command pilot is Captain Howard Slaton.

on I sat in that same john every mission morning, and I still know every word of 'Paper Doll.'

"Many of my mission memories are associated with particular odors. The first time it hit me was in that ready room. It was damp and musty—had probably been that way for months. Then when we went into that briefing hut, and the briefing officers checked you out, you would always smell shaving lotion on those guys. It bothered the hell out of me. You had these heavy boots, heavy pants and jackets, and you opened them up and there was body smell then—not really unpleasant, but not pleasant, because it was connected with the raid. Then we might sit, waiting in the airplane for thirty, forty minutes, and there was a heavy smell of gasoline, but there was a ready room smell in there too, every time. I guess it was the smell of fear. On the runway, and for the first

The cockpit panel of a B-24 Liberator bomber.

thousand feet or so, there'd still be the gasoline, and the smell of burnt cordite from the Channel on, from the test-firing of our guns. The cordite smell was so strong that you'd keep asking the top turret and ball turret gunners to check the engines because you thought of fire. There always seemed to be a kind of haze in the airplane, from the guns going off. But it probably wasn't true.

"Everything was connected to emotion, I guess. You hated to get up in the English fog. You hated to be briefed. You hated to be told where you were going. You wore heavy woolen socks 'cause your feet perspired and they turned to icy-cold sweat if you didn't. You climbed in the truck and they took you over to the officers' mess and there was the odor of powdered eggs. God damn, that was horrible! If you were flying you got fresh eggs. The guys who weren't flying got the powdered eggs.

"The cold at altitude was incredible. The gunners wore electric suits—blue bunny suits—which they plugged in at their stations, but sometimes the suits would short out and then they were in trouble. Up front we had a heating unit which didn't work too well. At altitude you were nervous and frightened and you would perspire. If you didn't wear gloves the throttles would freeze and get slippery. I used thin kid gloves. They also had fleece-lined gloves, but they were impractical for flying. Coming back we'd take off the oxygen mask and smoke a cigarette, and there was that smell, and always the cold sweat smell, until we got back on the ground. But after we landed, there was no gasoline smell, no cordite, no sweat—nothing that wasn't nice. It was all connected with fear and non-fear, I guess."

14 October: "Believe me, I never hope to go through anything comparable to this again and live to write about it. If anyone were to sneak up behind me and bellow 'Schweinfurt' I would probably run screaming down the road. Those of us who were lucky enough to return know now how much body and soul can endure. When you have enough people trying to take that last little hold you have on life away, you really get down to some honest to goodness fighting and will use any measures to strengthen your grip.

My friend, James 'Tripod' McLaughlin, said to Budd Peaslee who was the Eighth Air Force commander in the air for this Schweinfurt raid, 'I don't think we're going to make it.' In his heart, I think he knew he was going to make it, or he wouldn't have gone. If someone tells you to get in an airplane, you're gonna bomb Schweinfurt today and you're not coming back . . . Jones is, Smith isn't, Brown isn't . . . hell, you wouldn't go! Who would go? If they'd say, 'Two out of three of you guys will not be coming back today,' you'd look at the guy on your left and the guy on your right and you'd say, 'You poor guys.' That was the whole concept it was built on. Pride made you get into the airplane, more than anything else. Certainly not bravery.

"You were either stood up or stood down. Stood down meant get drunk because you weren't flying the next day; your name wasn't on the list, which would go up at 9:00, 10:00, or 11:00 p.m. the night before a raid depending on when the word came through from Eighth Bomber Command. You went on the weather over Germany, not the weather over England. Your weather could be really bad, but if the weather over there

was good for visual bombing, you went. Sometimes, of course, it wasn't good for visual bombing and you did it by radar.

"Normally, we would be awakened at, say, 1:30 a.m. When you got up and knew you were gonna fly a mission, you hadn't slept all that well. Some will tell you they had, but they hadn't. The deepest sleep you'd get was five minutes before they would wake you up. We'd put on our coveralls and shoes and then flying boots over them. We wore our fur-lined flying jackets in to breakfast, as well as our 'hot-shot Charlie' hats—the garrison hat with the grommet removed to give it the 'fifty-mission crush' look. They would tell us that the truck would be outside in twenty minutes, and we'd go eat breakfast at 2:00 and be at the briefing at about 2:45. Then we'd go down to the ready room and the navigators went to their own briefing, which was much shorter than ours. After that, our co-pilot went down with the crew and shaped them up for the mission; made sure they all had their Mae Wests, parachutes and other gear; that the plane was ready to go. He had two to three hours on his hands in which to check things. The pilots just hung around the ready room, shootin' the bull and hoping the mission would be scrubbed and they wouldn't have to go. Then, we'd be told that take-off would be at, say, 5:00 a.m., the start-engines and taxi times when we all went out and weaved around through the taxi strips, following a certain airplane according to the order for take-off.

"When your turn came to take off, you lined up so that one guy would take off from this side of the runway, and the next guy from the other side. That way you had a better chance of avoiding each others' prop wash.

"The B-17 was a very consistent, dependable airplane. You went down the runway, you hit a hundred and ten, you pulled the wheel back and it would take off. You'd come in over the fence at a hundred and ten, it would stall out at ninety-two or ninety-three. Shot up or in good shape, they were pretty consistent. It was amazing, but it was also a tremendous feeling of comfort.

"The throttle quadrant on a B-17 is shaped like an 'H' with a closed top. The top two are the outboard engines; the bottom two are the inboards. There is a circle a few inches in diameter where half on the right is the number three engine, bottom right is the number four, top left is number one and bottom left is number two . . . so you could just roll 'em going down the runway.

"And boy, did it take punishment. It would fly when it shouldn't fly. There was no reason for it to fly and it would fly. Everybody in the '17 knew that the plane would get back. If they could stay in it, and stay alive, they knew they'd get back. We all had tremendous confidence in the airplane. My crew were convinced there was no other airplane like the B-17, and I could be the worst pilot in the world and they were convinced I was the best. What they were doing, I guess, was convincing themselves that they'd get back.

"I called every B-17 I flew *Mizpah*, Hebrew, meaning 'May God protect us while we are apart from one another.' The name was actually only painted on the first plane I flew. I flew a total of nine different B-17s. If you got one shot up, maybe they'd repair it or use it for spare parts, and the next day you'd be flying a different airplane. It could have flown ninety-two missions, or this could be its first, but

the ground crews were so great, it didn't make much difference.

"They would truck us to the ready room where we would yak, go to the john fifteen times and pick up our Mae Wests, parachute back or chest packs. Most of the pilots and co-pilots wore chest chutes because movement in the airplane was so restricted. You kept your harness on but stowed your chute right behind your seat so you could grab it and hook it on just before you had to get out. You also picked up your flak suit, which was like a baseball catcher's chest protector. Every time we would change planes, my engineer would change the armor plating under the seats because most of the flak would

come up from underneath. A lot of the wounds were castration, so we'd put armor plating under our bodies. Some guys wore a flak helmet. I didn't. I took the inner lining shell out of an infantry helmet and used that. I carried a .45. All the officers . . . the bombardier, navigator, pilot and co-pilot, had .45s. The chief engineer had a tommy gun and the other five enlisted men had carbines. We took them but I was against them because we had been told that if you got knocked down, you shouldn't give up to civilians because they had probably lost a mother, father, brother, sister, in a bombing raid and would pitchfork you to death. If you saw military and were caught, you should give up to them.

"There isn't anybody that wants to get killed. You'd go into the briefing room and you'd get the weather officer, intelligence, flak positions, and so forth. They'd pull the curtain back and you'd see this line going to the target and you'd think, 'Oh boy, I'm not going on this; this'll kill me.' And then you'd say, 'What I'll do is, I'll wait a while and then I'll go on sick call and get out of it.' Then you'd go down to the airplane and you'd figure, 'Well, I'll go on sick call later.' And then you'd see everybody get in their planes and you'd know they were just as frightened as you were, and you'd think, 'What the hell. I'll go about a hundred miles and find something wrong with the airplane.' But they had this tradi-

tion that an Eighth Air Force sortie never turned back from the target. So, in the end, you didn't dare turn back. Pride made you go.

"On instruments, we took off a minute apart; visually thirty seconds apart. On instruments we would take off and go straight ahead until we broke clear. The weather reports were real bad because we had so little information. The Germans weren't gonna give us any. But most of the time, the reports were fairly close, and when we broke through we did a circle and looked for the colored flares of the squadron and group leaders. We'd form on the squadron first, then the squadron commander would form on the group.

"We were off to a comparatively early start Thursday, October 14th. We reached altitude and got over the French coast. Somehow, we failed to pick up the low group of our wing. As we were lead wing, the Colonel decided we had better fall in with another group. We did a three-sixty over the Channel and, seeing a 'bastard group' of fifteen planes ahead of us that didn't seem to be attached to anyone, we just tagged along with them. We picked up enemy fighters at just about the time our own escort had to leave due to fuel consumption. We had P-47s and they could only take us a certain distance in, and you could see the Hun fighters circling out there, waiting for our escort to leave. From that moment, it was an unbelievable horror of fighting. For at least three hours over enemy territory, we had between 300 and 400 enemy fighters shooting tracer and rockets at us. You could see those rockets coming. They were about eighteen inches long, and when they hit they would explode and set a plane on fire. Some twin-engined jobs at about a thousand feet above us were dropping bombs on the formation. There was no way they could aim at any one bomber— they were just dropping bombs into the group. And they were dropping chains or cables to foul our propellers.

"We were riding Ray Clough's left wing when he got hit. He dropped out and, I believe, burst into flames because twenty seconds later I looked under my left wing and saw a burning

Views of B-24 Liberator bombers at war.

Under the cover of their fighter protection,
B-17E bombers of the 390th Bomb Group,
based at Framlingham, England.

B-24 Liberator waist gunner Staff
Sergeant Clarence Johnson.

wing floating lazily downward. Oliviero was riding Brown's wing when Brown got hit by a rocket and disintegrated; a great sheet of flame and then a hole in the formation.

"At this point I took over the lead of the second element just prior to going over the target. Major Ott was riding on three engines and had to drop behind. I never saw him again. Even over the target, the enemy fighters came on through the flak. It was one of the few times they did that. They were really first team, those guys. They had guts and they were damned good fliers. They'd come in close, and if you straggled by as much as fifty yards, you'd had it. You'd get hit by three or four guys. The German fighters normally attacked you from the best position they could get in, usually from above. At Schweinfurt, most of them came in from the front, forty or fifty abreast. They'd peel off and another forty or fifty would come in from the front, fire and peel off. They were close . . . real close.

"I called out 'friendly fighters' by mistake one time. I couldn't identify an airplane. God, I was horrible at it. Gene Logan, my co-pilot, was real good at identifying them. Many times they would barrel-roll through the group. About 90 percent of the time they weren't shooting at individual airplanes, just going through and pouring into the group . . . unless you straggled. Then they would come get you. The one exception was our lead plane. They always tried to knock down our lead plane because there were usually only two bombsights in a group . . . the leader and the deputy lead plane, and I guess they knew it. I'd look up and see these guys coming in and I'd scrunch down behind the skin of the airplane, which seemed like about 1/10,000th of an inch thick.

They'd come in and the rate of closure would be between 400 and 500 miles an hour and I would always wonder if they were gonna break or collide with us. They'd come in shooting. You could always see the wings 'blinking' and you knew they weren't saying 'Hello, Charlie' in Morse code. It was worrying because you'd think, if they hit my wingman then I've got to do something about that, but at the same time my oil pressure is up and my cylinder head temperature is up, and I just have too many things to worry about to be frightened . . . except I WAS. That rate of closure. They were coming in through a hail of lead, and they'd keep on coming. You'd see a wing break off one and he'd spin in, but the rest of them kept on coming. 'My God, he's not gonna break off, he's not . . .' Then, finally, he'd barrel-roll and go over or under us. They pressed home real good.

"The most frightening thing about the enemy fighters was not so much their pressing of the attack, but knowing that, having pressed in once, they would peel off, go out to the side, line up and press in again!

"As soon as you hit the coast of France, the first burst of flak would be right off your nose. I don't know how the hell they knew where you were going to be, but they knew. A flak burst that was a near miss produced a sound like pebbles bouncing off a tin roof, and you'd hear a crackling through the airplane where you were getting shrapnel coming through. In an actual hit, you wouldn't be there. With a near miss, there would be a 'whoomf' sound, and the blast effect moved the airplane. Mostly, we only heard the sound of our own engines, except for the whoomf of the near-miss flak bursts and, of course, the sound of our guns firing. They were

REAL loud. Going over the Channel, I'd tell the crew to clear their guns, and this would really break you up! Especially the chief engineer's turret right behind us. We'd feel that. There was a lot of conversation over the intercom . . . 'twelve o'clock level,' 'three o'clock high' etc. You couldn't talk across to your co-pilot without using your throat mike. It was even tough when you were down low. The B-17 engines were slightly behind you, but boy they were noisy.

"The German 88mm guns which were, I think, mostly used for flak . . . they were tremendously accurate, just fabulous. They used two types. One was predetermined; the other was box barrage. In barrage there'd be a flock of guns and they'd shoot at one spot in the sky and keep shooting at it. In predetermined, they were aiming at planes. The most frightening was the indeterminate one where they were shooting at a spot in the sky. You had to get through that spot when they weren't shooting. Emden, Kiel, Wilhelmshaven, Munich, Berlin . . . I think they did both at all five of those targets. But Schweinfurt was murder. I'm sure they shot barrage because they had so damned many guns. The German fighters stayed pretty much out of the flak, but on Schweinfurt they did come through it. It's one of the few times they flew through their own flak, but they were probably under orders. They were expending themselves. There was no reason for it, really.

"Evasive action? I don't think you can do it against flak. Certainly not against the barrage type. Where are you going to go? Off the target? You can't win, except through luck. Now, for the group as a whole flying up to a flak barrage, if the leader says 'Use evasive action' as the group is starting to get hit, and the group turns off a bit, that's 'evasive action,' but I don't think that the people in the low squadron would believe it. Still, for the group it's the best thing you can do.

"That indeterminate flak that was coming up, there was nothing you could do about it. You could take no evasive action against a box barrage. This was something that was gonna happen. It was impersonal as hell. There wa only one way to counteract it, and it began, 'Our Father, who art in heaven . . .'

"The main thing was, the lead bombardier did a beautiful job on the target. You were flying on the code of the day, to be at certain points at certain times . . . the Initial Point and then the Mean Point of Impact. You had to fly straight and level for six, seven minutes . . . I've seen it up to twenty-two minutes. You flipped on the automatic pilot and the plane flew wherever the bombardier aimed his bombsight . . . he was flying the plane, really. If the bombing altitude was to be 25,000 feet and the speed 150 indicated, all you did was control the throttles and altitude and he controlled the direction. There was no evasive action. The point was to drop the bombs on the target, and the Germans knew it.

"About three minutes after dropping our bombs we got hit in number three engine. Due to a loss of the prop governor control, we couldn't feather it and we began to sweat. We had to use maximum manifold pressure and 2,500 revs to stay in formation. A flak burst just off my side of the nose cracked my windshield into a million pieces. A piece of flak about an inch long and a half inch wide was right in line with my face, but fortunately we had a bullet-resistant windshield and it stuck in the glass. I had the engineer dig it out for me after

we landed. We limped home with the formation as far as the Channel and started to let down into the nearest field. We got into Biggin Hill, southeast of London. Seven Forts set down there and they were all shot up. Several had wounded aboard and one had a dead navigator. We had fifteen holes in the ship and only about sixty gallons of gas left.

"There were always runways somewhere in the neighborhood. If you were coming back from a raid in trouble and needed a field in a hurry, or if you were in soupy weather and couldn't find one, you'd just fly a circle while saying 'Hello Darky, Hello Darky' three times, and give them the code and call letters of the day on your radio. Then this English voice would come on and say 'Hello, Yank! How was it?' He'd be kidding you about it but within thirty seconds he'd have you on radar and would say something like, 'Fly 270 degrees for ninety seconds, then left for thirty seconds on 180 degrees, and there will be an airfield right under you.'

"The papers said we lost sixty Forts on this Schweinfurt trip. At one time all you could see were burning airplanes and parachutes. But then, we knocked a little hell out of them too. My crew got two fighters, giving us a total of three. After Schweinfurt, I thought the rest of our missions would seem easy."

"The tension of waiting to fly was obvious in everyone and suiting up in the crew room gave a clear indication of the stress everyone felt. I think most aircrew were superstitious. I know I was. We dressed in the same order for each trip. The right flight boot must be put on first. The same heavy socks must be used. Personal pieces of clothing, like a girlfriend's

scarf, must be carried. A rabbit's foot or a stuffed toy would be pushed into pockets. Each had his own talisman. Mine was a hockey sweater that I had worn playing for a Toronto team. I wouldn't fly without it. I still have it today and my children wonder why I keep this ragged thing around. Most crews had a ritual of things they did while standing around the aircraft waiting. Many urinated on the tail wheel for good luck. Others chain-smoked. Some checked the bricks and bottles they would throw out over Germany as their individual contribution to Hitler's woes. Bottles were supposed to make a screaming noise as the fell, and so scare the hell out of the Germans below."
—from *Boys, Bombs and Brussels Sprouts* by J. Douglas Harvey

Over storm-torn clouds' reflected livid glow, At cold wastelands of dead darkness down below. That his hellfire may consume this night of horror, He pours pitch and brimstone down on their Gomorrah.
—from *War* by Georg Heym

Major-General John M. Bennett, Jr was a commander of the 100th Bomb Group (H) as a colonel in the Eighth Air Force, based at Thorpe Abbotts, Norfolk, in World War II. During his stay there he wrote a series of letters about his war experiences to his father in Texas. These formed the basis of his book *Letters From England*. According to Harry Crosby, former group navigator of the 100th and author of *A Wing and A Prayer*, an excellent book about that group, Bennett "came in and quietly but with a glint of steel explained how it was going to be. We would maintain the discipline, on the ground and in the air. New crews would be checked out

left: A wounded gunner returns from combat; here: Protection afforded by the flak vest worn of this American bomber crew member.

before they could fly. Stood-down crews would have practice missions every day. Pilots who could not fly formation would become co-pilots. Gunners who did not do their duties would become latrine orderlies. Passes, promotions, and medals would be given as rewards, not as routine. Back at Thorpe Abbotts, we never understood him. I never saw him take a drink. He never took part in the bragging and flight talk in the Officers Club. I don't think he ever took the grommet out of his hat. He even sat erect."

Major-General Bennett: "The telephone in my quarters rang at five o'clock. I stumbled out of bed and groped my way across the room. 'Briefing at six o'clock, sir.' That was the Duty Officer who had been instructed to call me one hour before briefing. This was my first combat mission so my feelings were rather confused. I was very anxious to make the trip, but I was pretty nervous about the whole idea. I put on my heavy underwear and my heavy GI shoes. These shoes are very important in case you have to jump. They won't pop off when your chute opens. In case you land in an occupied country and are fortunate enough to escape capture, there will be plenty of walking to do. Breakfast at the Combat Mess is difficult to remember. I recall passing some inconsequential remarks with other fliers around me, but don't believe I ate very much. This is unusual, as breakfast is my favorite meal.

"The briefing room is right next to Operations. It resembles a crude theater with benches lined up one behind the other. There is a guard at the door who checks each individual who enters to see that he is authorized to be there. The end wall of the building is covered with a huge map of Europe. One can see a great deal of detail as the scale is one inch to eight miles. The Intelligence Section has marked in red those areas where anti-aircraft guns are located. Cities like Berlin, Hamburg, and others show up as large red spots. However, the largest red area on the whole map is the highly industrial Ruhr Valley. Naturally, the Germans are making every effort to protect this important district from Allied bombing.

"Up until this time the map is not visible to the combat crews as it is covered by a curtain. There is coughing and shuffling of feet as the crews make themselves comfortable. Suddenly the room comes to a dead silence as the Group Intelligence Officer pulls back the curtain covering the map. Outlined in tape on the map is our course to and from the target for today. The suspense is broken by a groan from all sides. The target is right in the middle of the Ruhr Valley.

" 'Happy Valley,' as it is called by the Eighth Air Force, has a greater concentration of anti-aircraft guns than any other area of equal size in the world. This explains the general sound of disapproval which was expressed at the briefing. Our only comfort was that this was to be a Pathfinder Mission. This means that the target would be covered with clouds and the anti-aircraft gunners cannot actually see you. Of course, they still have their radar-controlled guns which are plenty accurate. Our target was to be the synthetic gasoline plants at Gelsenkirchen.

"After the intelligence officer finished, the operations officer, Lieutenant-Colonel Jack Kidd, gave us the time for take-off and instructions for group, wing, and division assemblies. He also went over our route into the target and out again, explaining where we would meet our fighter escort for invasion and withdrawal. Next the weather officer gave us complete data on clouds, direction of winds at various altitudes and temperatures. This was followed by

the communications officer who gave us the various frequencies and channels to be used on the radio: group frequency, wing frequency, division channel, fighter to bomber channels for air-sea rescue, and many others. You really need a blonde switchboard operator in a Fortress. All of this is followed by the warning, 'Don't use any of these unless absolutely necessary for the success of the mission.' Colonel Harding, the group CO, then gave a few final words of advice about flying in close formation and how to exercise the supercharger regulators in order to keep them from freezing up at 27,000 feet, our bombing altitude.

"The next two hours were the toughest part of the raid. I believe the Bard of Avon expressed it, 'Thus conscience does make cowards of us all.' One is inclined to think of all the terrible things which might happen. Since this was my first raid, I was to fly with Ollen Turner whose home is in Dallas. The engineer-gunner was Sergeant Bennett from Terrell, Texas. He was very proud of his ship, 'Skipper.' I was told that this was the thirteenth trip for Turner and Sergeant Bennett and also for the airplane. The tail gunner, Sergeant Weatherly from Amarillo, was making his twenty-fifth raid. Since this was my first mission, we struck an even balance, one man finishing, one man starting, and two men about half way through. The rest of the crew were non-Texans (almost foreigners in the Eighth Air Force). These two hours were spent in checking the airplane, collecting personal equipment, and putting the guns in the turrets. Everyone is nervous and almost over-polite in attempting to be considerate of the feelings of others.

"It's now 7:40 so we start the engines and at 7:45 we start taxiing.

We line up in proper position and at last, at precisely 8:00, the first ship, the Pathfinder, starts rolling. The group assembly is good and we start to climb to altitude. All of this climbing is done over England. As leader of the high squadron, we are in good position to observe the formation. With a heavy bomb load it takes almost one hour and a half to reach 27,000 feet. I have kept myself busy by checking the oxygen of all crew members at 2,000-foot levels above 10,000 feet. This is done by calling on the interphone. Each man checks in, beginning with the tail gunner. If someone doesn't call in, you have to get the 'walk-around bottle' of oxygen and go and see what happened, maybe he has passed out. Today everybody seems OK. The rest of the time I spend checking the settings on the turbo-superchargers. These babies are rather temperamental at high altitudes when they get cold. Occasionally I relieve Turner at the controls. However, he does most of the flying. I think that he does not like my formation flying.

"After what seems like years, we reach our altitude. The lead ship fires some identification flares and we assemble with two other groups to form a wing. The wing, in turn, gets into position with the other wings in the division. The division leader likewise must find his proper place in respect to the other divisions. The Eighth Air Force is really out today. Now we are on our way.

"We leave the English coast just three minutes ahead of time. The sun is shining brightly and the sky is filled with bombers as far as you can see in all directions. This must be what Seversky means by 'Air Power.' As we near the Dutch coast, clouds begin to form beneath us. That's good protection from the anti-aircraft; just as we were told by the weatherman.

"High above us at about 35,000 feet, we can see small specks in groups of four. Each of these tiny dots has a white tailfeather. This is the most beautiful sight in the world, because we realize they are Thunderbolts, our fighter escort. The white plumes are vapor trails. We truck drivers really love these boys. They do a swell job. Their rendezvous with us is right on time. In their groups of four they skate across the sky above us, weaving back and forth. Unfortunately, for them, there's not very good hunting today. Occasionally a fighter dives down to about 20,000 feet to have a look below. He either sees nothing, or frightens away the enemy because he zooms back up to join his brothers.

"We are now over the Zuider Zee, having flown just north of Amsterdam to avoid the flak. Josh Logan, '31, wrote the book for the Triangle Club show, *Zuider Zee*. Well,

no time for Princeton memories now. We are turning to the southeast which will take us into Happy Valley. Something is wrong; cloud cover below is opening up. Hell, it's clear weather ahead. The anti-aircraft gunners will be able to see us plainly. 'Not tho' the soldiers knew, someone had blunder'd.' Tennyson's famous lines do not apply, because we know all right; only too damn well.

"The clear weather becomes artificially cloudy at our altitude. A huge black cloud, made up of smaller ones, boils up in front of us. This is barrage-type flak. The enemy guesses our target and makes some calculations. He figures where we will have to fly to release our bombs to hit the target. He then aims all his guns at this bomb-release point and fires as rapidly as possible. They seem to be throwing up every bit of scrap iron in the Ruhr. There is a burst directly in front of us and the sound of hail on a tin roof. The bombardier has

been knocked down by a jagged piece which does not penetrate his flak suit. The cockpit is filled with smoke and smell.

"Things are beginning to happen in rapid succession. Tha Pathfinder has been hit and knocked out of the formation. Our No 2 supercharger has started to run away. There is a whirring sound like a siren. I quickly grab the throttle of number two engine. We are now flying on only three engines. We are deputy leaders so we have to take over. Where the hell is the target? The navigator says we have passed it. During the confusion of changing lead ships, we have missed our aiming point. Turner calls the bombardier to aim at any town or industrial center in the Ruhr. This is our secondary target. Bombs are away. We are now making a turn to the left. 'Let's get the hell out of here,' shouts Turner. With three engines laboring, and by losing a little altitude, we can maintain our airspeed. The

The flying goggles of a U.S. Army Air Force gunner.

tail gunner reports that another plane in our squadron has been hit, has an engine on fire and is diving out of the formation. A few minutes later, far down below us, eight parachutes are reported opening.

"We are now out of the Ruhr. I have flown through the 'valley of the shadow of death.' The 23rd Psalm notwithstanding, I feared plenty of evil. Maybe I should go to church more often."

Dan DeCamp was born in Oakland, California in 1960, the son of a navigator who had flown for World Airways and later for Flying Tiger Airlines. As a teenager he knew that he wanted to be a U.S. Air Force pilot, and joined the Civil Air Patrol where he learned to fly light aircraft and quickly soloed. In 1978 he began studies at the U.S. Air Force Academy at Colorado Springs where he received a degree in aeronautical engineering. From Colorado he moved on to Sheppard AFB, Texas, where he earned his wings in the Euro-NATO Joint Jet Pilot Training organization. Instruction at Sheppard was provided by pilots from nearly all the NATO member nations and Dan trained with student pilots from Germany, Norway, and the Netherlands.

His first assignment after pilot training was to the A-10 Thunderbolt program, initially at Holloman AFB, New Mexico, and then at Davis-Monthan AFB, Arizona. He flew the A-10 for four and a half years including a posting to RAF Bentwaters/Woodbridge in Suffolk, England, and finished on that aircraft at Suwon, Republic of Korea. While at Bentwaters/Woodbridge Dan became aware of the F-117 stealth program and his interest in joining it was sparked. He was later selected for it and his initial

training in the program was at Tucson, Arizona on the A-7, and from there to the Tonopah Test Range base (TNX) in Nevada, to begin flying the F-117.

DeCamp: "By the time I arrived at TNX, the program had started to emerge from the black world [of Air Force secrecy] into the grey world. In October of 1988 the Air Force had released the first grainy front quarter photo of the F-117, had given some limited details about the airplane and it had acknowledged the existence of TNX as a USAF base.

"Training in the F-117 was a well-conducted affair with civilian instructors presenting the systems classes, as well as about twenty-five hours in the simulator, which culminated in a check-ride. After that, the basic syllabus involved nine rides in the airplane including four basic aircraft handling and instrument sorties for familiarization, one air-refueling ride, and four surface attack rides in which we practiced the core mission of the aircraft: medium altitude laser-guided bomb delivery. These nine sorties were all flown in daylight [unlike in the earlier history of the plane] and accompanied by a T-38 chase plane. With only a few minor exceptions, the F-117 flew very well, with its fly-by-wire control system.

"On 30 November 1990 I was on my way to Langley AFB, Virginia, to meet up with our jets and continue on to King Khalid AB, Khamis Mushait, Saudi Arabia. Khamis Mushait is in the high desert of Southwest Saudi Arabia about seventy-five miles north of the Yemeni border. There, we were outside of Saddam Hussein's SCUD missile range, and well away from Riyadh and Dhahran. Our base was state-of-the-art. The hardened aircraft shelters were pristine, having

just been finished by the Dutch contractor. They had not yet been turned over to the Saudis when we occupied them. Each group of shelters included living space, showers, large briefing rooms, and common areas as well as the aircraft shelters and maintenance areas. One of the shelters housed all the administrative functions of the Wing including the Wing Operations Center, Intelligence, and the Mission Planning Cell where I spent all of my extra time.

"I was half asleep when I was awakened and told that I didn't have to worry about the remainder of my alert shift. The Mission Planning Cell was getting quite busy and I began to realize that we were definitely going [to war], and the Air Operations Center (AOC) headquarters in Riyahd for all Desert Storm was obviously going [to war] because we were suddenly faced with numerous target changes.

DESERT STORM—NIGHT TWO
"My first turn and it was a failure. It should be noted that all F-117 missions were flown in strict radio silence and I like to think it was much tougher the second night as we had made the Iraqis very angry the previous evening. About half-way between my pre-strike refueling and the target, a security apparatus building on the east side of Baghdad, I had an apparent fuel transfer malfunction which would have left me with no fuel just at the point of crossing the border. I immediately turned southeast and headed directly to the tanker. My biggest fear was that I was now no longer following the planned route and that someone on our side might decide that I was a possible hostile. I climbed into our sanctuary block, the airspace block between 22,000 and 24,000 feet, in which our guys were not to

Framlingham-based B-17s in a strike on
Marienburg, Germany.

The 100th Bomb Group B-17 *THE BIGASSBIRD II* and her crew at Thorpe Abbotts, England.

engage during the time of our ingress to egress, and hoped for the best. I climbed and slowed down a bit, and the tank started feeding again, leaving me feeling quite sheepish. By this time, however, I was so far out of the flow that there was no longer any hope of turning back and trying to make it to the target.

"My second mission was a comedy of errors. I found the tanker and then headed for the border. The weather en route was horrendous. I spent most of the flight in formation off the number four engine of the KC-135 tanker while the rest of that big airplane intermittently disappeared in the heavy cumulus build-ups. It was the best way for an F-117 to get through areas of thunderstorms or heavy precipitation, as we had no special radar for flying through heavy weather.

"Dodging weather, and accomplishing my last fuel top-off delayed my getting started on the mission. My wingman, who was flying the same route and going to hit the same target group, was supposed to be about seven minutes behind me. I was flowing through the target area with about five other airplanes, all of them flying different routes, but all assigned to hit targets in the same general area.

"Before the mission I had selected an update point on the route at which to correct any navigational errors that might accumulate in the two hours of flight time to the target. I had typed these new coordinates into my inertial navigation system (INS) during the pre-flight of my aircraft. Somehow I had mis-typed the update point by a full degree, or about sixty miles north of the intended point. I finally discovered the error when I was about half-way between the group I was supposed to be flying with and my own wingman. My error put me

three minutes behind the group. As they attacked the target, the Iraqi anti-aircraft artillery (AAA) opened up and continued to shoot for about five minutes. I got the full force as I came across the target and was lucky to get away with it. I was doing the same thing to my wingman who was now just three to four minutes behind me instead of the five to seven minutes as briefed. I'd screwed up, and probably deserved to face the music.

"The target was a C2 bunker near the town of Abu Gurayb. I was then to make a 100-degree left turn followed by forty-five seconds of wings-level time before hitting a second target, another bunker near Taji. The AAA began to die down just as I overflew the target, but then my engine noise triggered it again. I glanced to the rear through each side window and saw what looked like a boat wake of AAA fire spreading out behind the aircraft. In spite of the various distractions, the target was easy to find, and I put the cursors on the Desired Mean Point of Impact which was about ten meters from an entryway to the bunker. I got the weapon off and tracked the target for the terminal guidance phase of the laser-guided bomb, and watched the thing go about twenty meters beyond the cursors and miss the target completely.

"With no time to dwell on the miss, I selected the next waypoint and started that big turn toward the next target. It was a fairly steep banked turn and while in it I looked through the canopy at the barrel of what seemed to be a 37mm gun blasting away at me. I was mesmerized by the sight and thought that turn would never end. I checked my head-up display and it appeared that I had turned about twenty-five or thirty

degrees past the correct heading. In a weapons-delivery mode, the airplane will follow the turrets of the infra-red (IR) targeting system, wherever they are looking. They should be directing at wherever the inertial navigation system thinks the target is. The target was ninety-plus degrees to my left and, when I changed to the next waypoint, the IR system attempted to look all the way to the left and it jammed in that position. The airplane would have flown in circles all night, so I knocked off the autopilot and turned the plane back toward where the INS said the target was.

"I turned off the offending upper turret and, like magic, the target area popped up in the sensor display through the lower turret, with about ten seconds to go until release point. This target was not so easy; a dirt-covered bunker in an area of dirt with no distinguishing road patterns. I let fly with a 'wish bomb,' wishing that the target would show up between release and when the weapon required guidance before impact. Another miss. In retrospect, it was a pretty callow thing to do, but it was not a populated area, and I was a little jangled having just been shot at for the first time in my life.

"The same crummy weather I had experienced on the way in had now moved up into our post-strike refueling track. Luckily, I found the tanker and got into contact position while popping in and out of the clouds. Just then another F-117, apparently looking for any port in a storm, stumbled on to our tanker and stayed with me for the rest of the mission. My poor wingman, meanwhile, had to make an emergency fuel divert. Fortunately, he then met another tanker en route and was able to make it back to Khamis."

Flying from their base at Snetterton Heath, England, B-17s of the 96th Bomb Group bring their bombs to a German target in 1943.

B-24 bombardier Captain Ross Measner relaxes after a mission in 1944; left: A painting of 2nd Lt Gilbert S. M. Insall, VC, MC, RFC, by Edward Newling.

LEAFLET WAR

"Are you aware it is private property? Why you'll be asking me to bomb Essen next."
—Sir Kingsley Wood, British Secretary of State for Air, on plans to set fire to the Black Forest, September 1939

"War will not come again . . . Germany has a more profound impression than any other of the evil that war causes; Germany's problems cannot be settled by war."
—Adolf Hitler, August 1934

With the German invasion of Poland in September 1939, U.S. President Franklin D. Roosevelt made an ardent appeal to the nations involved in the war, and to those about to become involved, to avoid the bombing of undefended cities and towns, and of any targets where civilian casualties might result. Britain, France, and a few weeks later, Germany, all agreed and gave their assurances. RAF Bomber Command found itself encumbered by a bombing policy that was, to say the least, bizarre. It was ordered to refrain from attacking targets of any type on German soil due to the nearly impossible challenge of identifying the purely military ones, and thus avoiding any possibility of hitting civilians. What they could attack were German naval ships moored in harbors or steaming at sea, though not those in port alongside a wharf. They were also allowed to operate over Germany in order to drop propaganda leaflets prepared by the Political Intelligence Department of the British Foreign Office. So, they could hit the German fleet when they could find it, providing no civilian lives were at risk,

Warum in den letzten Tagen des Krieges sterben?

SCHLUSS MACHEN!

Examples of leaflet types dropped by the American and British air forces during the European air offensive in World War II.

and they could practice psychological warfare. A joke making the rounds at the time had bomber crews being warned to be sure to untie the leaflet bundles before dropping them lest they hurt someone below. Still, for the leaders in Bomber Command, this odd approach to military engagement came with a silver lining of a sort . . . it bought them time to build strength in manpower, aircraft, and ordnance and to attain some vitally needed reconnaissance and training experience.

Bomber Command desperately required intelligence about the German enemy and set out to make the best use of this period during which they were prohibited, for the most part, from doing what they were designed to do. They began, instead, on the first night of the war to carry

out long-range reconnaissance flights to Germany, and they continued this intelligence-gathering activity throughout the bitter winter of 1939-40. Fliying deep penetration sorties into the German homeland, Armstrong Whitworth Whitley bombers, as well as some Vickers Wellingtons and Handley-Page Hampdens, were utilized to obtain and confirm information about potential bombing targets such as industrial factories, aerodromes, air defenses, power stations, roads, and rail centers. These trips provided invaluable training and experience for the aircrews in extremely demanding conditions over what for them was largely unknown terrain. The missions were ostensibly for the purpose of distributing anti-Nazi propaganda leaflets over selected

German towns. After a week of this pamphleteering, the British public expressed its anger over the policy of bombing the Nazis with leaflets while the Nazis were busy bombarding Poland with the real thing. The reaction brought the leaflet campaign to a swift halt. It was resumed a few weeks later, however, though by that point the British government had concluded that its bombing offensive would have to be cranked up a notch or two. The degree to which the leaflets influenced German public opinion is debatable, but not so the importance to the Royal Air Force of the military intelligence and aircrew experience gained through the missions.

In the effort to deliver some 74,000,000 of the leaflets, the Whitley crews found and brought back urgently needed reconnaissance data. This data, combined with that obtained by the Advanced Air Striking Force in its own reconnaissance over western Germany, greatly aided those who would plan and organize the major attacks that Bomber Command was soon to launch. Operationally, they helped to show that even target cities in the most distant parts of Germany could be reached and hit by the British bombers. RAF navigators faced the challenge of finding their way to and from a range of target sites with a foretaste of the troubles they would encounter many times on future raids. Crews had to operate frequently in dense cloud cover, extreme cold, the murky German black-out, the nerve-wracking enemy searchlights and anti-aircraft fire. They contended with these difficulties but suffered most from the icy effects of that particularly savage winter. They found that ice would collect to a thickness of six inches on wings and windscreens. As it accumulated, it gradually caused controls to stick, sometimes rendering

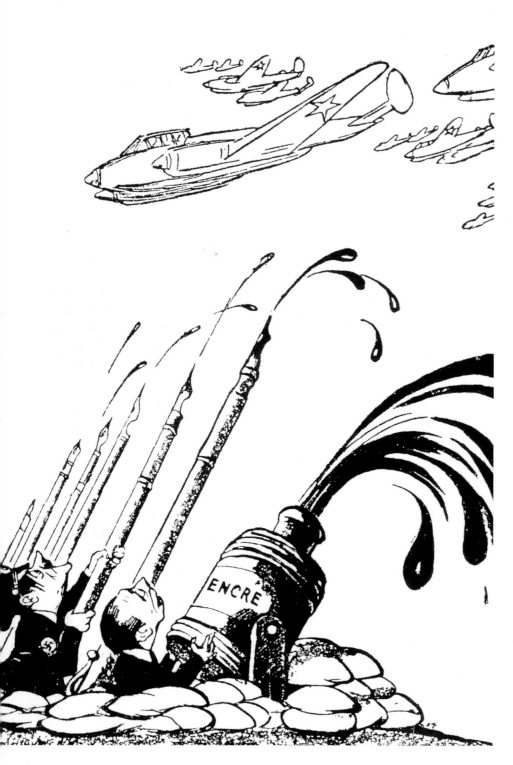

the aircraft uncontrollable. They were equipped with de-icing gear but it was often ineffective in the conditions they experienced. Equally ineffective was the heating equipment provided in the aircraft. Added to this was the strange phenomenon of fine, rime ice that would penetrate the aircraft, covering the crew with a white powder that froze on their clothing and equipment. Flight instruments became encrusted with the opaque crystalline ice and frequently froze up.

Another aspect of the leaflet raids was the level of endurance they demanded of the crews. Flown at night and in varying conditions, the raids lasted between six and twelve hours and were unequaled as tests of both navigation and endurance.

According to an Air Ministry account of the leaflet offensive, nearly all of the Whitley bomber crews experienced one common problem: it was all but impossible to lower the turret from which the pamphlets were discharged due to the intense cold. The temperature varied between minus twenty-two and minus thirty-two degrees centigrade. In one aircraft the starboard engine had to be shut down when it caught fire. The Whitley was then in heavy cloud and approximately six inches of ice had formed on its wings. The aircraft went into a dive and it required the strength of both pilots to pull it out at 7,000 feet. They then found that the elevators and rudder were immovable. The wireless operator sent a signal to say that one engine was on fire, and tried to get an immediate "fix" but could not be certain that he was actually transmitting as the glass covering his instruments was thick with ice.

At this point the Whitley was relatively stable but losing altitude at the rate of 2,000 feet a minute. The port engine was stopped and the crew estimated that about four inches of ice was protruding from the inside of the engine cowling. The propeller, the wing leading edges and the windscreen all had a thick ice coating. The pilot ordered his crew to abandon the aircraft but he got no reply from either the front or rear gunners and immediately cancelled the order. It was later discovered that both gunners had been knocked unconscious in the dive and subsequent recovery.

The plane then began a shallow, high-speed dive and the pilots opened the top hatch and a side window to see where they were going. The Whitley broke from the cloud into heavy rain at a height of only 200 feet. The crew saw only thick forest with a small grey patch in the middle, for which they were heading. They skidded the bomber through the treetops and managed to drop it into the small clear field. It careened through a wire fence and skidded broadside into the trees at the far side of the clearing. The engine fire was now extreme and the crew quickly got out of the fuselage and attempted to put out the flames. The pilot found that the extinguisher they carried in the cockpit had discharged in the crash-landing. The wireless operator attacked the fire with the extinguisher from near his crew station.

The bomber had come down in France and, after spending the night in their airplane, the crew was cared for by local inhabitants.

"The entry of the United States into the war is of no consequence at all for Germany. The United States will not be a threat to us for decades—not in 1945 but at the earliest in 1970 or 1980."
—Adolf Hitler, 12 November 1940

Another Whitley on the leaflet mission that night developed a defect in its oxygen system, creating a shortage of supply to the crew. They successfully dropped their propaganda but by that point both the navigator and the wireless operator were suffering from insufficient oxygen and had to lie down and rest on the floor of the fuselage. The cockpit heating was inoperative and the entire crew was suffering from extreme cold and distress. The pilot and the navigator were experiencing the agonizing onset of frostbite as well as a lack of oxygen. On the homeward journey they descended to 8,000 feet, but the icing grew worse. All windows were covered. The crew heard ice as it was whipped off the propeller blades against the sides of the nose. The pilot had to move the controls continuously to keep them from freezing up. Still, they made it back to base and the bomber landed safely.

A third Whitley on this particular night raid also made a forced landing in France. It was an especially heavy landing and the rear gunner was badly shaken. He emerged from the aircraft and made his way to the nose to have a word with the pilot and found that he was alone. The rest of the crew had bailed out on command of the pilot. Evidently, the intercom had failed and the rear gunner had not heard the order to abandon the airplane, which had somehow landed itself with no one at the controls.

The gunner made his way to a nearby village and came upon his entire crew safe in a café there. They talked about their experiences and the front gunner told how he had been unconscious during his parachute descent. He regained consciousness on his back in a field among a herd of curious but friendly cows. The wireless operator, too, managed to land

in a field—of curious and definitely hostile bulls. In full flying kit, the radio man rapidly made for and cleared a four-foot fence. The pilot landed unhurt and the navigator incurred only a sprained ankle. After their reunion in the café the crew were taken to a French hospital where they were treated and released. They were returned to their unit that same day.

Clearly, the principal danger faced by the crews on these early leaflet raids was weather, but there was the occasional interference by a German night fighter. In an incident where a Me 109 closed to within 500 yards of a Whitley whose leaflets were about to be dropped, the rear gunner reported the presence of the enemy fighter to the pilot. The pilot instructed the rear gunner to hold his fire while the navigator and wireless operator completed the leaflet drop. After a bit the rear gunner reported that it would no longer be necessary for him to take action against the 109 as it had flown into the cloud of released leaflets and had dived away.

Flight Lieutenant Tony O'Neill was one of the first RAF pilots to participate in the leaflet raids. R. D. "Tiny" Cooling, a former Wellington pilot, described O'Neill's first propaganda attack: "With the outbreak of war not yet twelve hours past, Bomber Command had already launched penetration raids over Hitler's Reich. The first, by a Blenheim IV of No 139 Squadron, was a photo-reconnaissance mission to Wilhelmshaven. That same night ten Whitley crews were briefed for sorties to Hamburg, Bremen, and the Ruhr; their task to drop thirteen tons of paper, some six million leaflets, on these cities in northwest Germany. In part, it was a propaganda mission, in part a demonstration to the population

ITALIA FARÀ DA SE

that the Royal Air Force could roam freely through German skies notwithstanding Hermann Goering's boast that no enemy bomber would ever penetrate the airspace of the Fatherland.

"Preparation began three days before. A runway was being laid at Linton-on-Ouse, home to No 58 Squadron's Whitley Mk IIIs, so ten aircraft (three from No 51 Squadron and seven from No 58) were detached to Leconfield to take on their paper load. Code-named 'Nickels,' these leaflets would become familiar to bomber crews in all theatres of the war. In obscure Oriental languages they would flutter down over Japanese-occupied territories, over North Africa and the Western Desert they would invite Axis troops to surrender; over occupied Europe they took the form of mini-newspapers like La Revue de Monde Libre or its equivalent in Dutch, Flemish, and German. On 3 September it was a warning addressed to the German people, a forecast of things to come.

"The Whitley was a twin-engined bomber which had entered RAF service in 1937. The Mark III was powered by Armstrong Whitworth's 845 hp Tiger engines which had a disconcerting habit of blowing off cylinder heads, even complete cylinders, punching holes in the long chord cowlings. Deliveries of the later and much more reliable Merlin-powered Mark V had only begun days before in August.

"Briefing was in the late afternoon, take-off at dusk. The route ran from Leconfield to Borkum, an island off the estuary of the Ems, south along the frontier of Holland to Essen, and then along the Ruhr Valley, scattering bundles of leaflets through the flare chutes of the bombers. The weather forecast, unaffected by security, stemmed from observations less than twelve hours old. Intelligence was a different matter. Information about searchlights, guns, and balloons was based on conjecture and deduction. Navigation would be by dead reckoning aided by any trustworthy radio bearings coaxed from the atmosphere. Release height was set at 16,000 feet. Into the gathering darkness the Whitleys crossed the Yorkshire coast and headed out over the North Sea on their way, for the first time, to Germany.

"The island of Borkum lay below, a black shadow fringed with a grey lace of surf. Cloud covered the German coast, spreading across the hinterland. An unpracticed searchlight crew probed their beam through a distant break in the stratus sheet. Flight Lieutenant O'Neill sat watching the instruments glowing green in the dark, glancing at the port engine and its spinning propeller. Gradually, G-George climbed to the selected height. The crew were in their oxygen masks, which were uncomfortable but bearable, and it was cold.

Four hours out and the Whitley was over the Ruhr. A few heavy shells burst in tiny red sparks in the distance. Inside the gloom of the long metal fuselage the crew began posting bundles of leaflets through the flare chute. There was no oxygen in its vicinity and there were no portable oxygen bottles. In less than ten minutes the two men were exhausted. Two others took their place while those relieved went forward to plug into the main oxygen supply and refresh themselves for a further spell. It was then that the port engine showed the first signs of failure.

"The choice was clear. Two hours to the southwest lay France and friendly territory. There was no point in risking aircraft and crew in a flight through hostile airspace, steadily losing

PIÙ DI 1.000 BOMBARDIERI IN UNA SOLA NOTTE SULL' ITALIA

422nd Bomb Squadron CO Lt Col Earle Aber and two crew members awaiting their D-Day takeoff at the Chelveston, England base.

height, then to face the North Sea on a single engine. O'Neill headed toward Rheims, discharging the last few bundles of leaflets as he went. Unfortunately, the route lay across neutral Belgium, but an aircraft in trouble could expect more consideration than one deliberately violating the frontiers of a non-combatant nation, and total cloud cover beneath would help them.

"The Whitley droned on across the Belgian border, past Liege, into France, descending slowly. Then the port engine failed completely, its propeller windmilling in the slipstream (the day of the feathering airscrew still lay in the future). The starboard engine now began showing signs of strain. A landing could not long be delayed, but it was still dark. The cloud layer stretched above them now and ground detail was almost invisible. O'Neill launched a flare. In its light he identified one field large enough for a wheels-up landing. It was nip-and-tuck to line up and creep in over the hedge. A railway embankment loomed up but he was committed. With a loud thump, and the tearing of metal, G-George skated across a vegetable patch. Group Captain O'Neill, DFC, now retired, recalled cabbages bouncing about the cockpit like short-pitched cricket balls as the broken bomb-aiming window sheared them off like a harvester's knife. The crew emerged unharmed. They had been in the air for seven and three-quarter hours.

"The silence was profound, almost oppressive. An erratic ticking from metal contracting within the cooling engine and the subdued voices of the crew were the only sounds. As the daylight increased, some men emerged from the darker edges of the field and approached cautiously.

"G-George lay inert. The Whitley's tailplane was festooned with leaflets in German gothic script where the slipstream had trapped them. It was some time before the group of French farmworkers could be persuaded that it was the Royal Air Force which had dropped in on them. From then on the warmth of the welcome became overwhelming. They had landed close to the village of Dormans, near Epernay in the heart of the Champagne country. As news spread, the village was en fete. Eventually transport was found to ferry the fatigued crew to Rheims where a telephone call to Linton notified the squadron of their situation. Finally, the bliss of bed and sleep. On 5 September a De Havilland Rapide flew Lt O'Neill and his crew to Harwell and they were soon back at Linton. Only G-George did not return.

"On 9 April 1940 German forces invaded Denmark and Norway; the 'Phoney War' was almost over. Since that first sortie the number of leaflet raids had risen to sixty-nine. Fourteen aircraft were lost. Severe weather caused a four-week break in operations, and over ten days around Christmas and the New Year, Bomber Command flew only shipping searches, but on the night of 12-13 January 1940, Whitleys carried nickels to Prague and Vienna. At the same time Wellingtons and Hampdens joined the fray, in their initial night operations. On 10 May the Western Front erupted as the Luftwaffe savaged Rotterdam. On 11 May Bomber Command carried the first bombs to mainland German targets. Leaflets now took second place. But these operations had been immensely valuable. At low cost a basic cadre had been created upon whose experience the development of the bomber offensive was to build. That warning

MESSAGE URGENT

du Commandement Suprême

des Forces Expéditionnaires Alliées

AUX HABITANTS DE CETTE VILLE

carried by Tony O'Neill was to prove justified.

"On the night of 8-9 September 1942, I was flying as navigator in Wellington 1342. The target was Frankfurt. Crossing the city we were coned in searchlights and came under intense anti-aircraft fire. We were hit and the starboard engine lost power. We were unable to maintain course. We were hit again and found that we were losing fuel rapidly. We could not maintain altitude and it was obvious that we wouldn't make England and our base. We crossed out over the coast and took up ditching positions. The wireless operator sent out a distress signal on the Mayday wavelength and clamped down his key. Shortly thereafter, as we were still airborne, he went back to his seat and tapped out the SOS again. I reminded him to bring his Very pistol [flare gun] with him. While climbing over the main spar he slipped and must have squeezed the trigger as a couple of stars shot past my face, burnt through the aircraft fabric and, in so doing, set fire to some leaflets which had blown back during the dropping operation. Between us, we beat out the flames and again took up our ditching positions.

"It was quite misty, and, while holding off just above the water, the starboard engine suddenly cut out; the wing dropped and struck the water, and the poor old Wimpy broke her back. The lights went out and the IFF blew up in a blue flash. I was trapped, but eventually managed to struggle free and was washed out of the fracture in the middle of the fuselage. As I emerged, a couple of packages floated up beside me and I tucked them under each arm and pushed off on my back.

"In my hand was a Woolworth's torch which was switched on. I heard voices calling but I couldn't tell from which direction. The pilot, bomb aimer, and wireless operator had got into the dinghy and, guided by my torch, came alongside me. The wireless op seized me by the hair and the others hauled me into the dinghy. Apparently the rear gunner had gone down with the tail.

"It was now 4:30 a.m. and quite dark. We baled water from the dinghy and made ourselves as comfortable as possible. At about 6:30 we heard the sound of an engine and saw a launch in the distance. Not knowing whether it was one of ours or a German, we fired off a marine distress signal. We assumed the launch hadn't seen us or our signal, as it turned and disappeared from view. Five hours later we again heard and saw a launch. The bomb aimer tried to fire another distress signal, but the igniting tape broke so he used his thumb to ignite the flare, and burnt the palm of his hand in so doing. The launch saw our signal and headed towards us. As it approached we saw the RAF roundels on the hull. The launch crew put out a scramble net over the side and with assistance we climbed aboard. They told us that when we first saw them at 6:30, they were recalled due to a naval action taking place in the vicinity (about ten miles from the Channel Islands). When they got back to their base, their CO sent them out again. They had plotted our position from our Mayday signal. We were given dry clothes, rum, and hot coffee by the launch crew as we headed for the Needles on the Isle of Wight."
—John Holmes, Nos 102 and 142 Squadrons, RAF

"The bus made its way slowly to Madingley along the winding country roads, through villages undisturbed by the passage of time, full of mellow stone and thatched cottages. It was raining fitfully and as I peered through the raindrops on the bus window, my mind was straining to remember the events that led up to fifteen Cheddington airmen being buried in that military cemetery, and two more being listed on the Wall of Missing. Nine of those still buried there

had been from my unit, the 406th Bombardment Squadron, Eighth U.S. Army Air Force.

"There was Lieutenant Colonel Earle J. Aber, Jr, our squadron commander. I don't think anyone who had been in the squadron will ever forget how his remains had come to be buried in this hallowed ground, which had been donated by Cambridge University to the American Battle Monuments Commission. Just as the bus arrived at the cemetery, the rain stopped and the sun broke through and shone brightly on the 3,811 white crosses and Stars of David headstones marking the graves of American servicemen from every state, the District of Columbia, Puerto Rico, and the Philippines.

"As I wandered along the paths, looking at each perfectly manicured plot for the graves of the airmen who had been stationed at Cheddington, I found that my task had been made easier by the thoughtful cemetery superintendent who had marked all fifteen graves with a miniature U.S. flag. I found the simple white cross with the inscription EARLE J. ABER, JR. LT COL., 406 BOMB SQ., 305 BOMB GROUP (H), WISCONSIN, MAR. 4, 1945. What it didn't say was that he had been born on 19 June 1919, in Racine, Wisconsin. Young in years, he had been endearingly known as 'The Old Man' by all of us in the squadron. Like so many squadron and group commanders in Eighth Air Force units during World War II, he had catapulted to the top as the result of a combination of circumstances. He had been a top-notch pilot who had survived almost fifty night combat missions. Group and Wing Headquarters had recognized his operational and leadership qualities by making him the Operations Officer and promoting him to the rank of Major. And finally,

and this happened all too often during the war, he had become the squadron commander when his predecessor had crashed and was killed. In Lt Col Aber, the 406th had an outstanding leader with infectious energy and inspirational leadership. He was well liked by all his personnel, in spite of the high standards and constant demands for excellence on the part of air crew and ground crew alike.

"I had flown my fifty-first and last combat mission as his navigator on the night of 5 February 1945 when we went to Frankfurt. We had been targeted one of the largest and most heavily defended cities in Germany and had expected to encounter intense anti-aircraft fire and nightfighter activity from the Luftwaffe, but it turned out to be a relatively uneventful flight, for which I was extremely grateful. That was not the case a month later, on the night of 4 March, when Lt Col Aber decided to fly with a 'make-up' crew, personnel who usually flew with a regular crew, but had missed a previously scheduled mission for some reason, and were trying to catch up with their fellow crew members so they could finish their tour together.

"This mission was expected to be a 'milk run,' an easy trip to the Netherlands, dropping leaflets on Amsterdam, Utrecht, and Rotterdam. The flight out of England and over the targets was routine, and the crew could visualize the news leaflets fluttering down to be eagerly picked up the next morning by the Dutch people.

"Only two weeks earlier, on 14 February, the Dutch Prime Minister, Pieter Gerbrandy, had visited Cheddington and, in a highly emotional speech, told the 406th Squadron how much it meant to the Dutch populace to receive the leaflets with their accurate recounting of war events.

Reminders of the presence of RAF and USAAF airmen who "smoked" their names and wartime units on the ceiling of the Eagle pub in Cambridge during the Second World War.

"Shortly after Lt Col Aber had turned the B-17 westward, after the last leaflet bomb had been dropped, and started the slow descent toward the designated entry point into England at Clacton-on-Sea, a series of events came together to produce one of the most ironic endings to an Eighth Air Force bomber mission of the war. In the days preceding the mission, the German Air Force had clevely used Ju 88s at night to make hit-and-run bombing missions against airfields just inside the east coast of England, usually when RAF bombers were returning from their own raids, in order to add further confusion to the situation. After several nights of such activities, the British anti-aircraft batteries along the coastline were understandably tired, frustrated, and 'trigger happy.' Unknown to Lt Col Aber and his crew, which included co-pilot Lt Maurice Harper, and the navigator, Captain Paul Stonerock, who also planned to make this flight his last mission, the Ju 88s had carried out another attack and were heading back to Germany.

"As the B-17 passed through 10,000 feet on the descent, a loud noise was heard and the plane shook violently. The crew didn't know what had happened. They first thought that they had collided with another aircraft. Then the plane was hit again, and all aboard quickly realized that the British anti-aircraft batteries had zeroed in on them instead of on an outgoing Ju 88. With engines on fire and flight controls shot away, Lt Col Aber and Lt Harper struggled to keep the plane in level flight. Finally, Aber, in a strong, unemotional voice, directed the crew to bale out. Miraculously, one by one, the crew was able to leave the bomber. In some cases, their parachutes opened only seconds before they touched down on the marshy land near the cold and unforgiving North Sea. All that is, except Aber and Harper. Time had run out for them before they could leave the plane. The rest of the crew saw a fireball as the stricken aircraft crashed into the ground nearby. The next day when search crews went to the crash site, all they found of this great airman and

outstanding commander was a hand with his ring on it.

"As I prepared to leave Lt Col Aber's grave site to rejoin the others, I found myself saluting and saying a few words of prayer. After we had climbed aboard the bus for the return trip to Luton, I looked back across this beautifully landscaped and very special bit of England, and Thornton Wilder's words came to mind: 'All that we can know about those we have loved and lost is that they would wish us to remember them with a more intensified realization of their reality. What is essential does not die but clarifies. The highest tribute to the dead is not grief but gratitude.' "
—Brian Gunderson, 305th Bomb Group, Eighth USAAF

In its psychological warfare operations in World War II, the U.S. Eighth Army Air Force dropped a total of 1,493,760,000 propaganda leaflets over German-occupied Europe.

YANKEE DOODLE

At the start of the Battle of Britain in July 1940, British Prime Minister Winston Churchill, still smarting from the set-back at Dunkirk, wrote to Lord Beaverbrook, his Minister of aircraft production, "When I look round to see how we can win the war I see that there is only one sure path . . . and that is absolutely devastating, exterminating attack by very heavy bombers from this country upon the Nazi homeland. We must be able to overwhelm them by this means, without which I do not see a way through."

Shortly before seven in the evening of 17 August 1942, all twelve of the 97th Bomb Group B-17Es that had taken off from a base at Grafton Underwood, Northamptonshire, three and a half hours earlier were sighted from the Grafton control tower. They approached the field from the west and in the next few minutes all landed, having returned safely from the U.S. Eighth Army Air Force's first heavy bombing raid of World War II.

Their target that summer afternoon had been the huge Rouen-Sotteville rail marshaling yards near the French coast. Twice in the preceding week the raid had been scrubbed due to what the mission planners decided was unacceptable weather.

The B-17s on the mission that day all had nicknames. They were called *Yankee Doodle*, *Dixie Demo*, *Johnny Reb*, *Big Punk*, *The Big Bitch*, *Heidi Ho*, *Birmingham Blitzkrieg*, *Butcher Shop*, *Prowler*, *Baby Doll*, *The Berlin Sleeper* and *Peggy D*. Colonel Frank Armstrong had led the mission in *Butcher Shop*. Flying in *Yankee Doodle* was Brigadier General Ira

Remains of the old main runway at Lavenham,
home of the 487th Bomb Group in WWII.

Eaker, Commander of Eighth Bomber Command, the new kids on the block, untried and unproven. Ira Eaker had come to England at the head of a small group of U.S. Army Air Force officers to work with the British in arranging for the presence of the first American combat flying units to be based there. He and his staff focused immediately on three needs: To mount a bomber offensive against German-occupied Europe in conjunction with the RAF; to begin fighter operations in conjunction with the RAF—at first in defense of the British Isles and later in the escort of daylight bombers; to organize the logistical support required to meet the first two needs.

He was soon to become embroiled in a heated controversy over the method the USAAF intended to use in its bombing activity. He and Major General Henry "Hap"

Arnold, then head of the U.S. Army Air Forces, were key advocates of daylight bombing, a thing that had been tried by the Royal Air Force and rejected after painfully unsuccessful efforts and their attendant losses.

British doubts about the American daylight bombing approach were publicly expressed on 16 August by Peter Masefield, Air Correspondent of the *Sunday Times*. Masefield welcomed the prospect of the Americans joining the British in the air war against Germany. He struck out at the B-17 and B-24 though, as being, in his opinion, unsuited for bombing over heavily defended enemy territory: "American heavy bombers—the latest Fortresses and Liberators—are fine flying machines, but not suited for bombing in Europe. Their bombs and bomb loads are small, their armor and armament are not up to the standard now found necessary and their speeds

are low." In that the American bombers were certainly not suited (nor designed) for night bombing, Masefield concluded that the best use to be made of them would be Atlantic anti-submarine and shipping patrols. The next day Hap Arnold read the Masefield column and wired Major General Carl Spaatz for the facts as Spaatz knew them. Timing being everything, Spaatz was, on this occasion, in a position to answer Arnold with an actual combat report for the Rouen mission, and a relatively good one at that.

One British newspaper took the position that "it was a great pity the Americans hadn't seen fit to build Lancasters, Britain's finest bomber, and fly them by night instead of clinging to the discredited theory of daylight raids." Prime Minister Winston Churchill agreed, and managed to convince President Roosevelt to halt the daylight bombing. General Eaker wrote: "My most unforgettable meeting with the Prime Minister occurred at the Casablanca Conference. A cable had come to me at my Eighth Air Force headquarters near London, from General H. H. Arnold, Commanding General of U.S. Army Air Forces, directing me to meet him at Casablanca the next day. When I arrived after a night flight and reported to him, I could see at once that he was unusually disturbed and unhappy. There was no vestige of the normal, smiling disposition which had won for him the nickname of 'Hap' while a cadet at West Point. He said, 'Churchill got an agreement from President Roosevelt that your Eighth Air Force will stop daylight bombing and join the RAF in night bombing . . . what do you think of that?' I said, 'General, that is absurd; it represents complete disaster. It will permit the Luftwaffe to escape. The cross-

Channel operation will then fail. Our planes are not equipped for night bombing; our crews are not trained for it. We'll lose more planes landing on that fog-shrouded island in darkness than we lose now over German targets. The million men now standing on the 'Westwall,' anti-aircraft, fire wardens and bomb repair squads—can now go back to work in the factories or make up another sixty divisions for the Russian front. Every time our bombers show on radars, every workman in the Ruhr takes to the shelters. If our leaders are that stupid, count me out. I don't want any part of such nonsense.'

"When I paused for breath, Arnold said, 'I know all that as well as you do. As a matter of fact, I hoped you would react that way. The only chance we have to get that disastrous decision reversed is to convince Churchill of its error. I have heard him

left: The WWII flak tower at Hamburg; above: An 8AF shoulder patch; below: One of the B-17s that flew the first American raid of the European air war, on 17 August 1942.

speak favorably of you. I am going to try to get an appointment for you to see him; stand by and be ready.'

"That evening I was advised that I was to see Mr Churchill at 10:00 a.m. the next day. Shortly after I was admitted to his villa, he came down the stairs, resplendent in his Air Commodore's uniform. I had been told that when he was receiving a naval person, he wore his Navy uniform—the same for the other services—but this was the first time I had seen him in Royal Air Force uniform. This struck me then as a good omen.

"The P.M. said that he understood from General Arnold that I was very unhappy about his suggestion to our President that my Eighth Air Force

above: 8AF bomber crewmen synchronize their watches before a mission; below: The jubilant crew of *Jersey Jinx* on their safe return to England after a bombing raid.

join the RAF Bomber Command in night bombing, abandoning the day-time bomber effort. Without awaiting my response, he continued, 'Young man, I am half American, my mother was a U.S. citizen. The tragic losses of so many of your gallant crews tears my heart. Marshal Harris tells me that his losses average 2 percent while yours are at least double that and sometimes much higher.'

"I replied to Churchill that I had learned during the past year, while serving in Britain, that he always heard both sides of any controversy before making a decision and for that reason I wished to present a brief memorandum, less than a page long (it was well known that he seldom read a 'minute' of greater length, having it 'briefed' instead). This I hoped he would read.

"Mr Churchill motioned me to a seat on a couch beside him and began to read, half aloud, my summary of the reasons why our daylight bombing should continue. At one point, when he came to the line about the advantages of round-the-clock bombing he rolled the words off his tongue as though they were tasty morsels. When he had finished reading the memo, he handed it back and said, 'Young man, you have not convinced me you are right, but you have persuaded me that you should have further opportunity to prove your contention. How fortuitous it would be if we could, as you say, 'bomb the devils round the clock.' When I see your President at lunch today, I shall tell him that I withdraw my suggestion that U.S. bombers join the RAF in night bombing and that I now recommend that our joint effort, day and night bombing, be continued for a time.

"When I reported to General Arnold the result of this meeting, he said, 'Apparently you accomplished the mission I had in mind. Now I suggest you return to England at once and make sure you prove our case for daylight bombing.' "

Churchill did as he had promised Eaker, and thereafter, found many occasions to refer to "bombing round the clock" until it became a standard expression of the time.

General Eaker and his staff were stationed at RAF Bomber Command Headquarters, High Wycombe, Buckinghamshire, so they could rub elbows with and learn something of the procedures and methods then in use by the RAF. The Americans were headquartered in what had been a girl's school before the war years. At war's end the complex would revert to its former role.

Eaker clearly recognized and valued RAF Bomber Command's knowledge and experience and set about to take full advantage of their proximity, even though he disagreed entirely with the British position on American daylight bombing. He then patterned the organization of Eighth Bomber Command on that of RAF Bomber Command to ensure maximum cooperation between the two forces. His assignment to England had come when Major General Carl Spaatz, a top commander under Hap Arnold, was given overall charge of the Army Air Force in Great Britain. It was at the suggestion of Spaatz that the American air combat presence in the UK be constructed around the fledgling Eighth Air Force, only recently activated and as yet lacking a mission. Arnold agreed and then Spaatz ordered Eaker to England to get the show on the road. Arnold and Eaker decided that this was their golden opportunity to prove the doctrine of high-altitude daylight precision bombing.

Eaker faced an early and pressing need for airfield and base facilities for the American air combat units that would be arriving in Britain. For some time before the Pearl Harbor attack and the U.S. entry into the war, British and American military officials had been in conversation about arrangements for such units should the United States come into the war at some point, and such accommodation had already been considered. Thus, when the United States did go to war, the Air Ministry could implement a vital, large-scale airfield construction program almost immediately. The Americans were planning an ultimate strength of some 3,500 aircraft based in Britain by April 1943. These included sixty combat groups composed of seventeen heavy, ten medium, and six light bomber; twelve fighter, seven observation, and eight transport groups. Certain airfields in the English Midlands were already under construction for RAF Bomber Command in 1942 and these were quickly turned over to the Americans. As the American air build-up in Britain increased, their airfield requirement was also reassessed and increased, with the majority of the bases and sites allocated for the use of USAAF units in East Anglia.

Another problem requiring Eaker's urgent attention was that of adequate supply and maintenance capability for his forces in Britain. In addition to the on-going, ever-increasing need of his units for food, clothing, coal, and many other domestic requirements, operationally they needed enormous quantities of aviation and motor fuels, ordnance, spare parts, oil, lubricants and other consumables, as well as the massive inventory of items essential to keep such a dynamic military organization up and running. Here again, the British stepped in to meet the needs of their American cousins, providing both temporary and permanent facilities for depot storage, aircraft repair and maintenance, and technical support.

In line with Eaker's determination that the Eighth Air Force profit from the experience and learn the procedures of the RAF, it was decided that the Americans must adopt the RAF systems for air traffic control and communications. The British were wholly generous in sharing what they knew about the German enemy, and they provided instructional staffing for the USAAF personnel who were to attend training sessions at special units called Combat Crew Replacement and Training Centres. Primary among these was a new RAF base at Bovingdon, Hertfordshire, and its satellite at Cheddington, Buckinghamshire, which were both near Eaker's headquarters, and were promptly leased to the Yanks. It was apparent early on that the American crews had, in the urgency to mobilize, been insufficiently trained for the task they were to meet in the coming bombing campaign. This added to the doubt and polite scepticism, impatience and curiosity focused on them and their daylight offensive by the British. Gunners, especially, were found wanting and required additional training. The British, whose early experience with the B-17 Flying Fortress was unsatisfactory in the extreme, had grave misgivings about the equipment to be used by the Yanks.

It was the English weather, however, that proved the greatest challenge to the U.S. crews who had done most of their flying training in the clear, blue skies of Texas and the American west. They were having to learn to cope with the rapidly changing weather conditions in the UK and flying much of the time in poor visibility. The frequently nasty weather of England and the Continent tended to work against their efforts to fly high-altitude precision raids, complicating Ira Eaker's job considerably.

Getting the first aircraft and crews to the UK was yet another concern of the American general and his staff at High Wycombe. In June the first transport unit to provide logistical support for the Eighth Air Force, the 60th Transport Group, operating C-47s, completed their training and prepared for the move to England. On 18 June the first combat air units of the Eighth were staged to Presque Isle, Maine, to be made ready for their departure east. Their first leg was some 570 miles to Goose Bay, Labrador, and the first fifteen B-17s arrived there in the late afternoon of 26 June, where they were refueled. They left that same evening for Bluie West One, a landing field on southwest Greenland about 775 miles from Goose Bay. At Bluie West One the arriving bombers were unable to land owing to extremely poor visibility and had to elect to either return to Goose Bay or go on to another landing site, Bluie West Eight about 400 miles further along the Greenland coast. One B-17 went on to land safely at BW8, while eleven others returned to Goose Bay. The other three planes became lost and, out of fuel, were eventually forced to crash-land on the Greenland coast. All of the crews survived and were rescued. Additional B-17s, navigating for a large group of P-38 fighters, began the long trip on 19 June and by 27 July, 180 aircraft, B-17s, P-38s, and C-47s, the Eighth's first major ferrying movement of the war, had arrived at Prestwick, Scotland. In the movement, six P-38s and five B-17s were lost, but all of the crews were saved.

Eighth Fighter Command headquarters, under the command of Brigadier General Frank O'D. Hunter, was established at Bushey Hall, near

The cockpit of a B-17 bomber with the throttles and propeller controls visible at center.

Watford in Hertfordshire, quite near its counterpart, RAF Fighter Command headquarters at Bentley Priory. Gradually, the important fighter support for the bombers of the Eighth was taking shape.

By the beginning of August 1942 Generals Spaatz and Eaker believed the Eighth was ready for action at last, and soon committed an admittedly tiny force to the Rouen raid, Mission No 1. Getting to 17 August and the actual launch of that first American heavy bomber raid against a German target, had been a test of patience strained nearly to the breaking point for Eaker. Continuing delays in supply and in the arrival of crews and equipment, the wholly inadequate training his crews had received prior to embarking for the UK relative to the realities of the air war with the German enemy, and the often poor weather, mitigated against his determined effort to bring the new air force into the war.

General Spaatz had decided early in the Eighth's UK tenure that it was more important to bring the first heavy bomber crews and equipment to England as soon as they were organized, equipped, and trained well enough to negotiate the ferry route, than to give them the more thorough training Stateside that they would so desperately need. Tight formation and high-altitude flying was all but completely missing from the repertoire of his first bomber pilots and co-pilot to arrive. Many of the radio operators were unable to either send or receive Morse code. And the previously mentioned deficiencies of most of the arriving gunners were, perhaps, most worrying of all. Those in the top echelon of the Eighth were convinced that the only way the bombers could hit and destroy enemy targets by daylight without suffering prohibitive losses

above: USAAF cooks at work on an 8AF base in WW2 England; below: A Flying Control officer on duty at the 44th Bomb Group's Shipdham base; right: the painted leather A2 flying jacket of Sidney Rapaport.

clockwise from top left: Postwar views of RAF Hemswell and the USAAF bases at Deenethorpe, Podington, Grafton Underwood, Rattlesden, and Bury St Edmunds.

was through being able to defend themselves effectively against the enemy fighters.

Carl Spaatz stood on the roof of the flying control tower at Grafton Underwood with several Eighth Air Force and RAF staff officers and approximately thirty members of the U.S. and British press. They had gathered to watch the take-off of the twelve American bombers of the 97th Bomb Group, the first and only heavy bomb group of the brand new Eighth U.S. Army Air Force. The first raid was vitally important to Spaatz, Eaker, and to Hap Arnold back in Washington—all of whom were betting the whole kitty on the concept of daylight bombing in the manner they intended to practice it. After months of frustrating delays, set-backs, and the scepticism of the British and American publics and nearly everyone else involved in the war against the Germans, their duty and opportunity to get into the fight and show what they could do had finally come.

All twelve B-17s were airborne from Grafton by 3:40 that afternoon, as were six more from the base at Polebrook, Northamptonshire. The Polebrook planes were to act as a diversion for the main force.

"When the mission has gone the ground crews stand about looking lonesome. They have watched every bit of the take-off and now they are left to sweat out the day until the ships come home. It is hard to set down the relation of the ground crew to the air crew, but there is something very close between them. The ground crew will be nervous and anxious until the ships come home. And if the *Mary Ruth* should fail to return they will go into a kind of sullen, wordless mourning. They have been working all night. Now they pile on a tractor to ride back to the hangar to get a cup of coffee in the mess hall. In the barracks it is very quiet; the beds are unmade, their blankets hanging over the sides of the iron bunks. The pin-up girls look a little haggard in their sequin gowns. The family pictures are on the tops of the steel lockers. A clock ticking sounds strident."
—from *Once There Was A War* by John Steinbeck

Ira Eaker was riding in *Yankee Doodle*, the lead ship of the second flight of six bombers, to see for himself how this first mission would go.

The Rouen target was important to the Germans because of its major repair shops and large locomotive depot, as well as the many hundreds of freight cars there and the links it provided to the Channel ports and the west of France. The aiming points for the bombers were the locomotive workshops and the Buddicum rolling stock repair shops.

The RAF, for its part, contributed a great many Spitfires to provide close air support for the B-17s—four squadrons of Mk IXs going with the bombers to the target, and five squadrons of Mk Vs for withdrawal support.

The weather cooperated too with excellent visibility for the attacking force, and all twelve planes dropped their loads of general purpose bombs, 36,900 pounds, from an altitude of 23,000 feet. Official records indicate reasonably accurate bombing with approximately half the bombs falling in the general target area. Results were surprisingly good for a small, inexperienced force, with direct hits on two large trans-shipment sheds in the heart of the marshaling yards, with significant track damage, and the destruction, damaging or derailing of quite a lot of rolling stock. There was one direct hit on the locomotive

A B-17 gunner with his aircraft at Bassingbourn.

workshop. In all, however, the damage caused was—while sizable—not sufficient to seriously impair rail operations there. Clearly a much larger bombing effort would be needed to take out the Sotteville yard.

Neither the attacking or diversionary forces suffered any losses and they incurred only minimal damage. The Germans were barely responsive to the attacking forces with only slight flak damage to two aircraft. The Luftwaffe did respond with an attack by three Me 109 fighters with no damage resulting. There were no injuries to the bomber crews apart from the bombardier and navigator of one plane who were slightly injured when the plexiglas nose of their B-17 shattered in a bird strike on the return flight to England.

In a letter to General Spaatz on 19 August 1942 Ira Eaker observed that the crews on this initial American raid were alert and enthusiastic, but nonchalant to the point of being blasé. They needed more drill in the use of oxygen equipment and, in general, better discipline. The formations needed tightening for improved defense against enemy fighters. Other items requiring considerable immediate attention included the timing of the rendezvous with fighter escort, navigation, bombing training, and gunnery. Pilotage needed a lot of work with the aim of refining formation flying to the point where tight and maneuverable formations could be flown with the shortest possible level bomb run on a target, thus minimizing exposure to enemy flak and fighter opposition. As to the ability of the bombers to defend themselves against enemy fighters, it was too soon to know. Certainly the Rouen raid had not provided any meaningful test of that, and both Spaatz and Eaker determined to tread with utmost caution in committing their bombers to subsequent missions that required much deeper penetration into German-occupied territory.

"For us the war was very new. The word was that the average life expectancy for a tail gunner in combat was thirty seconds. All kinds of rumors were floating around. England was very different from the United States. It had already suffered three years of war, but the people were very friendly and helpful. We had to get used to a different monetary system, and I found out that Brussels sprouts and some of the other food they gave us were not the best things to eat when you were going to fly at high altitude in an unpressurized airplane. I bought a bike and, though I didn't get off the base as much as some of the guys, I really enjoyed myself when I did. I had a 36-hour pass in London and had a cab driver take me for a tour. I liked the scotch, but could never get used to the dark warm beer. England has the most beautiful countryside to fly over. We did a lot of that."
—Ed Leary, 97th Bomb Group (H), Eighth USAAF

On 18 August General Eaker received the following message from Air Marshal Sir Arthur Harris, Air Officer Commanding-in-Chief, RAF Bomber Command: "Congratulations from all ranks of Bomber Command on the highly successful completion of the first all-American raid by the big fellows on German-occupied territory in Europe. Yankee Doodle certainly went to town and can stick yet another well-derved feather in his cap." To paraphrase Mr Churchill, for General Eaker and his staff, it was, perhaps, the end of the beginning.

"A jounalist will say anything to earn a fast buck. I get my information from the horse's mouth, not from the rear end where they do."
—Marshal of the Royal Air Force Sir Arthur Harris

"We walked toward the ship through nacreous pools of oily water on the asphault parking area. Visibility was less than a hundred yards. We couldn't begin to see *Erector Set* and *Finah Than Dinah*, the Forts that were parked on hardstands on either side of ours on the perimeter. It was stations time, a quarter to ten, and we went into *The Body*. The pearly ground fog had lifted; low clouds were running down to the eastward like suds in a rocky river bed. From my seat in the cockpit I could see the cubical control tower in the far distance, and I could even make out some tiny figures—members of the operational staff—on the iron-railed balcony of the tower. Eight or ten Forts were visible, scattered at their hardstands along the perimeter track, dark and squat, imponderable, rooted to the ground by their tail wheels. A big camouflaged RAF gasoline lorry and trailer moved slowly along the main road toward the hangars. Jeeps busy-bodied up and down the perimeter track."
—from *The War Lover* by John Hersey

"Presently he turned off on a side road, propped his bike against a hedge and strode slowly a hundred yards out onto an enormous flat, unobstructed field. When he halted he was standing at the head of a wide dilapidated avenue of concrete, which stretched in front of him with gentle undulations for a mile and a half. A herd of cows nibbling at the tall grass which had grown up through the cracks, helped to camouflage his recollection of the huge runway. He noted the black streaks left by tires, where they had

struck the surface, smoking, and nearby, through the weeds which nearly covered it, he could still see the stains left by puddles of grease and black oil on one of the hardstands evenly spaced around the five-mile circumference of the perimeter track, like teeth on a ring gear. And in the background he could make out a forlorn dark green control tower, surmounted by a tattered gray windsock and behind it two empty hangars, a shoe box of a water tank on high stilts and an ugly cluster of squat Nissen huts."
—from *Twelve O'Clock High* by Beirne Lay Jr and Sy Bartlett

below: The Orderly or Day Room at Deenethorpe, home to the 401st Bomb Group in World War II.

Most USAAF personnel got around their large air bases by bicycle. This is the Ridgewell base of the 381st Bomb Group, Eighth Air Force.

CHAPEL

BOMBERS

Among the best aircraft of the Second World War is the Avro Lancaster bomber, and this example is being serviced at its hardstand on an air station somewhere in wartime England. 7,377 Lancasters were produced. It entered service with the Royal Air Force early in 1942.

The delta-winged Avro Vulcan bomber was the mainstay of the RAF airborne strategic nuclear deterrent through much of the Cold War.

"As they watched it the bomber seemed to swell up very gently with a soft whoomph that was audible far across the sky. It became a ball of burning petrol, oil and pyrotechnic compounds. The yellow datum marker, which should have marked the approach to Krefeld, burned brightly as it fell away, leaving thin trails of sparks. The fireball changed from red to light pink as its rising temperature enabled it to devour new substances from hydraulic fluid and human fat to engine components of manganese, vanadium, and copper. Finally even the airframe burned. Ten tons of magnesium alloy flared with a strange greenish blue light. It lit up the countryside beneath it like a slow flash of lightning and was gone. For a moment a cloud of dust illuminated by the searchlights floated in the sky and then even that disappeared."
—from *Bomber* by Len Deighton

"Night bombing towards the end of 1916 and early 1917 was carried out mainly with Sopwith Strutters in which the rear seat was removed to accommodate a honeycomb bomb rack taking twelve French Le Pecq liquid twenty-pound bombs. The two old twin Anzani-engined Caudron G IVs were also used and they carried an observer or bomb aimer as well as a pilot. One took off down a paraffin flare path usually about two hours before dawn and on return waited until sufficient light enabled one to see the ground clearly before landing. Our usual night targets were the docks and shipping at Ostend, the docks and submarine pens at Bruges, and the Mole and shipping alongside at Zeebrugge. All three were heavily defended by AA and rocket batteries and bristled with searchlights, while more searchlights were spaced along the coast right up

to the Dutch frontier, especially at Westende, Middlekerke, Wenduyne and Blankenberghe.

"A truly wonderful fireworks display attended us on our night stunts, the long chains of vivid jade-green balls which streaked up, invariably reaching one's height before falling away and dying out, were a magnificent sight providing they didn't come too near. They must have been in the nature of a rangefinder as they always seemed to come to, or slightly above one's level, whatever one's height, before fading out, and were immediately followed by HE bursts pretty well on target. We called them 'Flaming Onions' and at first imagined they were connected by wire which would entangle one's propeller, but of course they were not, their regular spacing, like a glorious jade-green necklace, being due to some sort of machine mortar from which they were fired. I never heard of their doing any damage but occasionally one fell on a wing, being quickly swept off by the airspeed and slipstream, the fabric only showing a slight scorching, but I wouldn't have welcomed one in the cockpit. The advantage of coastal targets was that one could creep up the coast two or three miles out to sea without being heard, then turn in when approximately level with the objective, so giving the defenses very little warning of one's approach. If one was heard the signal went up from Nieuport and was repeated all the way up the coast, on came the searchlights and the guns were ready for you."
—from *Bomber Pilot 1916-1918* by C. P. O. Bartlett

During the winter of 1916, the Germans decided that, as their airship raids over London had become impossible to sustain, they should

launch a campaign of bombing attacks by airplane against the British. Their new strategic battle squadron 3, *Englandgeschwader*, was assigned the long-range attacks on British war industry, coast ports, transport, and communications. The squadron was equipped with Gotha G-series bombers powered by two 260 hp Mercedes six-cylinder in-line engines. For the time, the Gotha operated in relative safety from attack by British fighters, as it bombed from an altitude of 16,000 feet and was then able to climb even higher for its return trip to base. On 13 June 1917, in a bold daylight attack on the heart of the British capital, a force of fourteen Gothas dropped a total of seventy-two bombs on the area of Liverpool Street Station in London, killing 162 people and causing a profound psychological reaction among the populace and a heated debate on the organization of the home defense. All of the attacking force returned safely to their base at Gontrode in Belgium. By October, however, the British defenses got the better of the Gothas, with much-improved anti-aircraft and fighter opposition, and the Germans switched to night bombing. This offensive included a few significant incendiary raids, the beginning of a planned campaign of fire raids which was called off shortly before negotiations to end World War I began. The psychological effect on Britons by the Gotha offensives remained after the end of the war. Fearful memories of being bombed from the air were to be long-lasting.

It fell upon its victims while emitting a terrifying shriek. An icon of the Nazi Blitzkrieg, it typified the "lightning strike" of the hard-charging German forces at the beginning of World War II. All across Poland, Czechoslovakia, the Low Countries and France, the siren scream of the Ju 87 Stuka announced the imminent arrival of Hitler's legions. The dive-bombing of the Stuka was as much psychological warfare as anything else.

The Stuka's command of the skies was relatively short-lived, however. The Hurricanes and Spitfires of the Royal Air Force saw to that rather quickly and without much fuss. It was no match for the Merlin-engined fighters and fell to them in great numbers throughout the summer and fall of 1940. While it was still to perform with some distinction against Allied shipping in the Mediterranean and their convoys sailing the arctic route to Russia, in the Balkans and against Crete, it was no longer the threat it had once been.

The name Stuka came from the German term *Sturzkampfflugzeug*, referring to dive-bombers. The Germans were fascinated with the concept and potential of aerial dive-bombing as early as the late 1920s, and in the Ju 87 they produced a rugged, if somewhat ugly and slow two-man machine, capable of terrifying the folks below in the target area while doing damage as well.

The plane was significantly improved through the development and production of several later marks, making it formidable to Germany's opponents right up to the summer of 1940 when reality struck in the form of RAF Fighter Command and the heyday of the Stuka was over.

The Bristol Blenheim was a pioneering effort in the British aircraft industry; the first all-metal, stressed-skin, cantilever monoplane bomber. It gave the Royal Air Force just the edge it needed, and brought an end to the older, prevailing philosophy about bomber aircraft design. It was a bomber of the 1930s capable of outpacing most fighters of the day.

The Blenheim had its detractors, and was certainly not one of aviation's greatest achievements, but in its time it met a need of the RAF and, in a sense, kept them in the game until the bigger, better, more capable bomber types came on stream.

Powered by two Bristol Mercury XV air-cooled radial engines rated at 995 hp each, the Mk IV Blenheim was the best of the breed. It cruised at 259 mph at 15,000 feet with a normal cruising speed of 198 mph and it carried a normal bomb load of 1,000 pounds.

The Blenheim was widely used and performed commendably, and while it was not particularly outstanding among all the bomber aircraft of the war, it did represent an important transition for RAF Bomber Command.

The Vickers Wellington carried the brunt of RAF Bomber Command's night bombing offensive against German-occupied Europe in World War II until the coming of the new heavy bombers. Known affectionately as the Wimpy, after the character J. Wellington Wimpy in the *Popeye* comic strip, it served effectively throughout the war. Much of its success was due to its geodesic construction, a revolutionary "basket weave" structure employed by the design engineer Barnes Wallis, who also designed the "bouncing bombs" used in the Dam Busters attack of May 1943. This construction technique resulted in an amazing combination of high strength and low weight, and an airplane able to take terrific battle damage and still bring its crew home safely.

The Wellington B Mk X had two Bristol Hercules VI radial engines rated at 1,585 hp for take-off, a cruising speed of 180 mph and a service ceiling of 24,000 feet. Its range, with a 4,500-pound bomb load was 1,325 miles.

While a solid performer, the Wellington also demonstrated conclusively to the British Air Staff the futility of daylight bombing raids without fighter escort when the enemy had obvious air superiority. At one point, two raids cost the RAF twenty-one Wellingtons of a total force of thirty-six despatched. From that day the daylight bombing campaign of the RAF was abandoned.

They sounded odd . . . out of sync, the Daimler Benz DB 601 (and later the Junkers Jumo) engines of the Heinkel He 111s that visited London and other English cities on so many nights during the great Blitzes of 1940-41, and after in World War II. The He 111 had good flying characteristics and was presented to the German public initially in early 1936 in the form of a ten-passenger commercial airliner. It was clear to aviation experts, however, that this was a mean machine intended for a far more aggressive role than that being conducted by Deutsche Lufthansa.

This relatively light and fast medium bomber cruised at 224 mph at 16,400 feet and had a service ceiling of 25,500 feet, but a range, with a maximum bomb load, of only 760 miles.

The 111 broke its maiden in the skies over Spain with the bomber element of the German Air Force's Condor Legion in 1936 and, though lightly armed with only three 7.9mm machine-guns, was quite effective and suffered only negligible losses in the Spanish Civil War. Daylight bombing, however, always a tricky prospect for any air force, proved too much for the Heinkel when it ran into the Spitfires and Hurricanes of the RAF

A Consolidated B-24J Liberator bomber in wartime England..

in the Battle of Britain. It was under-gunned and not really fast enough to put up much of a struggle against the excellence of the British fighters and their extraordinarily courageous pilots who had the added incentive of defending their island against Nazi invasion. The Germans scrambled to improve the armament of the 111 but, by the final phase of the Battle, were forced to withdraw the bomber from day raids and put it on the night shift.

In the mid-morning of 3 February 1940, a Heinkel He 111 had the dubious distinction of being the first German warplane to fall on English soil in World War II. The bomber was under the command of pilot Hermann Wilms and carried a crew of four, all

Unteroffiziere: Peter Leushake, Johann Meyer, and Karl Missy. Their airplane, No 3232, was operating with 2nd Gruppe, KG 26 "lion" Geschwader from Schleswig-Jagel, a base north of Hamburg. Their assignment that frigid winter morning was to attack an enemy convoy off the northeast coast of England. Shortly after 9:00 a.m., Blue Section of No 43 Squadron, RAF, got the call at Acklington and in a few minutes Flight Lieutenant Peter Townsend and Sergeants "Tiger" Folkes and Jim Hallowes were climb-ing to intercept the hapless Heinkels. Their Hurricanes joined with the German planes of the Schleswig flight and Wilms' bomber was badly shot up by Townsend. It crash-landed near Whitby.

The front-line heavy bomber of the Japanese Army Air Force for most of World War II was the Mitsubishi Type 97 Ki.21-11b, known to the Allies as the Sally. Dating from 1937, it was a twin-engined aircraft with a 236 mph cruising speed at 16,400 feet and a top speed of 297 mph at 13,000 feet. It had a 1,350-mile range with a maximum bomb load of 2,200 pounds. Its power was provided by two Mitsubishi Ha.101 Type 100 radial engines rated at 1,490 hp each. The Ki.21 as operated by a four-man crew: a pilot, co-pilot/navigator, radio oper-ator/gunner, and a bombardier/gunner.

Initial combat operations for the Ki.21 came in August 1938 when the first units to receive the aircraft, the 60th and 61st Sentai, began flying it in

The much-maligned Martin B-26 Marauder medium bomber (Martin Murderer, One-a-day-in Tampa Bay, etc.) ultimately proved to be a good airplane with a fine safety record.

Manchuria against the Chinese, where it showed that it was not up to the task at hand. It was being flown to its objectives without escort, and, with insufficient defensive armament, could not adequately defend itself and suffered alarmingly high losses in this, its first trial by fire.

Subsequent models of the bomber, produced with features such as improved fuel tanks, increased armament and enlarged flaps, replaced the older, inferior model in early 1941, giving a new, but unwarranted sense of confidence and security to the crews who flew it. This confidence was soon dispelled when they encountered fighter opposition from the P-40s of General Claire Chennault's American Volunteer

Group, the Flying Tigers, and RAF Hurricanes. In an engagement with the AVG and the RAF on 20 December 1941 over Kunming, the Japanese lost twenty of their attacking force of sixty bombers.

After the fall of Singapore in mid-February 1942, Japanese units flying the latest version of the Sally were assigned to hit British and Canadian garrisons at Hong Kong, which they did very well, albeit with no enemy fighter opposition.

With the increasing presence of U.S. and British high performance fighters in the western Pacific, Sally losses rose sharply and its days in the region were numbered. The Sally was thought to be a comparatively easy target by Allied fighter pilots, with its

inadequate defensive armament. The bomber fared no better in the China-Burma-India theatre of the war where, despite operating with significant fighter protection, its losses continued to climb. A pattern began in which the Sally was withdrawn from front-line units until, finally, its role was reduced to transport and suicide attack.

Widow-Maker, Flying Torpedo, Flying Prostitute, Martin Murderer, and One-A-Day-In-Tampa Bay—were all references to the B-26 Marauder medium bomber. It had a reputation among American pilots learning to handle it. U.S. Government investigators convened on four separate occasions to consider discontinuing its development. The unusually small wing area

and the resultant high wing-loading led to the Marauder's bad name. Ultimately, though, it rose above it all and, by 1944, the U.S. Ninth Air Force was operating Marauders in the European theatre with a lower operational loss rate than that of any other American aircraft type.

With a 1,100-mile range at maximum cruising speed, a 283 mph top speed at maximum weight, and a service ceiling of 19,800 feet, the Martin bomber was not the most impressive of performers, but it got the job done. It began to make a name for itself beginning with the run-up to D-Day when it was the first USAAF aircraft in the European theatre to operate at night. Its ability to hit and destroy bridges and other targets requiring a high degree of precision was exceptional. The B-26 flew more than 29,000 sorties in its first year of combat in Europe, dropping 46,430 tons of bombs and incurring a relatively tiny loss rate for the effort. 5,157 Marauders were made at Martin by the end of the war and, despite the views of its early detractors, it was in fact a good and reliable airplane, if one that demanded pilots of a high standard.

Among the most interesting and successful of all bombing aircraft is the De Havilland Mosquito, whose designers believed that the airplane could accomplish its mission and defend itself primarily by relying on its great speed to outrun enemy fighter opposition. They were correct, as if more proof were needed of the adage that "an airplane that looks right will fly right," the Mosquito was as graceful and elegant of line as she was swift, powerful, and a joy to fly. Her secrets were: a small, highly practical airframe, a wonderful aerodynamic aesthetic, an amazingly high power-to-weight ratio, and energy from two superb and reliable Rolls-Royce Merlin engines.

The De Havilland design team was working on a high-speed bomber concept as early as October 1938. When

Brand new Boeing B-17G aircraft on an air depot field in England awaiting delivery to the bomb groups of the Eighth Air Force; right: The Boeing B-29 Superfortress, successor to the B-17 and the backbone of the American campaign in the Pacific against Japan.

war broke out in September 1939, the British Air Ministry began to show serious interest in the idea of a bomber capable of "fighter" speeds. It asked De Havilland if they could come up with a design for such an aircraft, that could carry a 1,000-pound bomb load and have a range of 1,500 miles. The manufacturer agreed to have a go and was given latitude to take a revolutionary approach to the problem. The Air Ministry was thinking "unarmed" high-speed bomber, but the airplane maker had other ideas and proceeded to design an aircraft with provision for guns or cameras, as well as bomb-carrying capability, with an eye to making their new bird a model of versatility as well as one of supreme performance. It would, they thought, be as competent in the photo reconnaissance or fighter roles as it would in the bomber role. Not only would it be the fastest bomber in the world, and brilliant in its other capacities, it would be made of WOOD. The designers incorporated the timely advantages of a new process for fabricating the plane from wood laminates, and when it was finished, the "wooden wonder" as the Mosquito was often referred to, was indeed a 400 mph airplane that cruised at well over 300 mph, climbed to 15,000 feet in less than eight minutes, had a service ceiling of 37,000 feet and a range (with a 4,000-pound bomb load) of 1,370 miles at 245 mph. As a bomber, the Mossie normally went to its target at an economical cruising speed of 300 mph at about 22,000 feet or down around sea level at a similar speed.

The airplane was extremely successful in a wide range of activities, not least being the vital Pathfinder role later in the war. The outstanding performance and legendary combat record of the Mosquito assure its place among the great planes of all time.

The North American B-25 Mitchell provided a great psychological boost to the American people, inspiring

The Vickers Wellington medium bomber
employed geodesic design developed by the
famous design engineer Barnes Wallis.

them and raising their spirits at a point in the Second World War that was desperately needed. In April 1942, Colonel Jimmy Doolittle led a small force of sixteen B-25s from the deck of the carrier *Hornet* to bomb Tokyo, Kobe, Yokohama, and Nagoya, Japan, in the first U.S. retaliation for the Japanese attack on Pearl Harbor the previous December 7th. The raid caused little significant damage, but showed the enemy that it was definitely vulnerable to American air strikes. Named for the U.S. Army bombing pioneer, Billy Mitchell, it was an excellent and highly efficient performer, able to deliver a 3,200-pound bomb load over a range of 1,275 miles at 200 mph. It served in most WWII operational theatres.

The Douglas A-1 Skyraider came into service in 1946, too late for World War II but in time for the Korean conflict. Many consider it the most unique, sophisticated and utilitarian single piston-engine combat plane in history. Capable of carrying a load of bombs heavier than its own empty weight, the Skyraider was used extensively in Korea, and in Vietnam by the U.S. Air Force, the U.S. Navy and Marines, and by the South Vietnamese Air Force. Known in that war as Sandy or Spad, the A-1 was produced in a quantity of 3,180 by 1957 when its assembly line closed. The big plane had a top speed of 318 mph and an operational range of 3,000 miles and was armed with four 20mm wing-mounted cannon. Its engine power came from a Wright R-3350 2,700 hp radial engine. Capability, versatility, and endurance summed up the virtues of the impressive Douglas bomber.

The Short Stirling of WWII might have been a much better bomber had it not been for the short-sighted approach of those Air Ministry types who specified it in the mid-1930s. They insisted on a 100-foot wingspan to fit the opening of the then-standard RAF hangar doors. That requirement doomed the plane to a second-rate career, operating lower and slower with less ability to climb and to survive flak damage than its superior heavy-weight cousins, the Halifax and Lancaster.

Indicative of the Stirling's shortcomings was the position it had to accept when flying on large-scale raids in company with Lancasters and Halifaxes. Those other heavies were going to the target at 18,000 to 20,000 feet, while the fully-loaded Stirlings were unable to climb much higher than 12,000. As the war went on, the Stirling was ultimately relegated to lesser roles including raids on fringe targets, supply drops to partisans in enemy-occupied Europe, mine-laying, transport, and glider-towing. In these roles it performed admirably.

In 1940, British Ministry of Aircraft Production was keen to convert the Avro and Vickers production lines from the assembly of the less than impressive twin-engine Manchester bomber to assembly of additional Handley-Page Halifax heavy bombers. But Avro chief designer Roy Chadwick argued forcefully that his new Manchester III four-engine bomber was not only superior to the Halifax; it could be made on the existing Manchester production line without the delays inherent in converting to the Halifax manufacture. He won the argument and, by 1945, some fifty squadrons of the resulting Lancaster heavy bomber were operational.

The Lancaster was the backbone of the famous "thousand bomber raids" and, in August 1942, the elité new 8

Eighth Air Force heavy bomber nose art examples.

Group Pathfinder Force was launched with Lancasters of No 83 Squadron. Using the navigational aid "Gee," the Pathfinders went to the targets ahead of the main bomber force and marked the aiming points using flares and incendiaries to ease the task of the bombers bringing the high explosives.

Most Lancasters were powered by four 1,460 hp Rolls-Royce or Packard-built Merlin XX engines. They were operated by a crew of seven and weighed as much as 72,000 pounds all-up with the maximum bomb load. As such they had a maximum speed of 287 mph and a cruising speed of 210 mph at 12,000 feet and a range of 1,660 miles. Their .303 machine-guns were ultimately replaced with the more potent .50 calibre Browning machine-guns. A total of 7,377 Lancasters were built.

At the end of the war Marshal of the Royal Air Force Sir Arthur Harris wrote to the Avro Production Group: "As the user of the Lancaster during the last 3 years of bitter, unrelenting warfare, I would say this to those who placed that shining sword in our hands; without your genius and your effort we would not have prevailed—the Lancaster was the greatest single factor in winning the war."

The Boeing B-17 was made for high-altitude daylight precision bombing and, in most respects, performed superbly. The B-17 made a powerful impression on the German war effort. It also contributed greatly to the defeat of the German Air Force both in the air and on the ground. Of the models produced, the G was the most effective, and 4,035 Gs were built by mid-1945, with Boeing, Douglas, and Vega all producing them. At the peak of its utilization, nearly 4,600 B-17s of various marks were in the active USAAF inventory.

The maximum bomb-carrying capacity of both the principal American heavy bombers of WWII, the B-17 and B-24, was considerably less than that of the British Lancaster. Both of the American bombers were designed with crew protection and defensive firepower as primary considerations. Both required a crew of ten men and were fitted with substantial armament and armor. They were mounted with as many as thirteen .50 calibre machine-guns and their ammunition. All of this extra weight resulted in a hefty bomb-load penalty. However, the Americans believed strongly in the concept of daylight precision bombing. They felt that they could hurt the enemy more through the surgical placement of fewer bombs on key industrial, supply, and resource targets than the RAF could through its campaign of nighttime area bombing.

Which service was right? Both were, to the extent that the Allied strategic bombing "round-the-clock" campaign helped to bring about the defeat of Germany in the war.

As the American General Curtis LeMay, a brilliant combat leader in the U.S. strategic bombing campaigns against both Germany and Japan, put it: "The Air Force kind of grew up with the B-17. It was as tough an airplane as was ever built. It was a good, honest plane to fly—a pilot's airplane. It did everything we asked it to do and did it well."

Probably it is fair to say of the B-17 and Lancaster crews that each thought their airplane was the finest, safest, most reliable bomber then flying. Certainly, few of them would have traded places with their British or American counterparts. Most would probably agree that the Flying Fortress and the Lancaster are the most admired . . . and the classic bomber aircraft of all time.

Designed for a 1936 Air Ministry requirement,
the Short Stirling was the first RAF four-engine
bomber of the Second World War.

She was like the less attractive sister of the beauty queen—the chunky, slab-sided B-24 was the product of General Hap Arnold's request of the Consolidated Aircraft Company to design a new bomber that would have better performance than the B-17. It was January 1939; war clouds loomed and Arnold wanted a bomber with a maximum speed of 300 mph, a ceiling of 35,000 feet, and a range of 3,000 miles. The B-24 Liberator lacked the grace and glamor of the B-17 Flying Fortress, but she performed brilliantly on more operational war fronts for a longer period and with greater versatility than her sister ship.

The B-24 did slightly out-perform the B-17. She had a maximum speed of 300 mph at 30,000 feet and a range of 1,700 miles with a 5,000-pound bomb load at 25,000 feet. Her power came from four 1,200 hp Pratt and Whitney Twin Wasp radial engines.

Of all the famous missions flown by B-24s, probably the most controversial and horrendous was the Ploesti oilfield raid of 1 August 1943. 177 Liberators were sent that day on a low-level attack against the Astra Romana, Columbia Aquila, Steaue Romana, and Romana Americana oil complexes. One hundred and sixty-three made it to the target and delivered their bombs. The bombing did a lot of damage, but the attacking force paid dearly with the loss of fifty-four bombers and 144 crewmen.

By the end of the war, 18,188 Liberators had been built. They served with the U.S. Army Air Forces, the Royal Air Force, the U.S. Navy, the Royal Australian Air Force, the South African Air Force, and later with the Indian Air Force.

Like the Liberator, the Handley-Page Halifax bomber was less lovely than

The primary partner of the Avro Lancaster in the strategic bombing campaign against Nazi Germany in WWII, the Handley Page Halifax performed with disctinction throughout the conflict.

its RAF counterpart, the Lancaster, but more versatile and a powerful, effective workhorse, as a bomber, a maritime reconnaissance aircraft, a freighter, a glider tug, an air ambulance, and a personal transport. The Halifax shared the major responsibility for RAF Bomber Command's night-bombing offensive against German targets across Europe. Some 40 percent of the heavy bombers built in the UK during the war were Halifaxes. They operated with distinction against Germany, throughout Europe and in the Far East and the Middle East, as well as serving in the airborne operations over Normandy, Arnhem, and the Rhine crossing. 6,176 Halifaxes were produced through 1946.

The successor to the B-17 Flying Fortress was the Boeing B-29 Superfortress, a bomber with a top speed of 357 mph at 30,000 feet, a cruising speed of 220 mph at 25,000 feet, and a range with a 10,000-pound bomb load of 3,250 miles. The B-29 operated mainly in the Pacific theatre with most of them being based initially in the Marianas Islands. They also operated from bases in China and India.

Referred to as "Mister B" by the Japanese, the B-29s began their bombing campaign against targets on the home islands of Japan in November 1944 with raids on the Nakajima Aircraft factories at Musashino near Tokyo.

On 20 January 1945, General Curtis LeMay took charge of the 20th Bomber Command and immediately began a program of reorganization and redirection of its resources. He went with his B-29s on some of the missions to Japan, mainly conventional high-altitude precision daylight strikes. But he ordered a few experimental "fire raids" using incendiary ordnance instead of high explosives. These raids were inspired by his experiences with the Eighth Air Force and the firestorm attacks on Hamburg. The results of the Japanese fire raids led to new targeting priorities for his Superforts: aircraft engine factories, cities, and aircraft assembly plants. The city targets were to be attacked with incendiaries and approximately sixty Japanese cities were earmarked for such attention.

left and below: The elegant and impressive De Havilland Mosquito.

LeMay knew of the problems faced by his crews in the high-altitude raids on Japan: jet-stream winds of extreme velocity, frequent heavy cloud cover over the targets, inconsistent engine performance and reliability issues ("three turning, one burning" was a common reference to the B-29s at the time), inability to carry the required bomb load, strong and determined, fighter opposition, and heavy exposure to enemy flak. He directed that the bombers would henceforth fly the incendiary fire raids at low level by night. He believed the engines would run cooler, use less fuel and would last longer. He had them fly in a bomber stream rather than a formation, to save more fuel. There was little genuine threat from Japanese night

fighters, thus reducing the need for defensive firepower on the B-29s. He had all guns but the tail turret stripped out of the bombers, eliminating excess turrets, guns, ammunition, and gunners; the weight saving translating into additional bomb tonnage carried.

Along with all the other changes, LeMay had Pathfinder B-29s fly out ahead of the main force to set massive fires on which the rest of the bombers would drop their loads. The first of his great fire raids took place on 9 March 1945. It was the single most drestructive air raid in history, including Dresden, Hamburg, and both atomic attacks. Twenty-five percent of all the buildings in Tokyo were destroyed. One hundred and fifty thousand inhabitants were killed,

injured, or missing. One million citizens were made homeless.

In that time many structures in Japan were made of cedar, bamboo, and paper, materials that burned well, and in the course of many fire attacks made by the B-29s, most of the country's cities and towns were turned to ash. The fire raids continued into August 1945 with increasing ferocity.

In June, the first B-29s to occupy the giant new base at North Field, on the island of Tinian arrived. On 6 and 9 August, two of the new atomic bombs were dropped by B-29s of the 509th Composite Group on Hiroshima and Nagasaki respectively, leading to the unconditional surrender of Japan to the Allies on 14 August. The Convair B-36 Peacemaker was

LA GLACERIE

MUNICH
JULY 16
AUGSBURG

HAMBURG
JUNE 18

POSE
NOV

ANTWERP
JUNE 22
ST. MARTIN-BERNAY
JUNE 23

HAMBURG
JUNE 25
VILLACOUBLAY
JUNE 26
ST. NAZAIRE
JUNE 28
TRICQUEVILLE
JUNE 29
LEMANS
JULY 4
VILLACOUBLAY
JULY 10
AMIENS-GLISY
JULY 14

HANOVER
JULY 17
HEROYA
JULY 24
HAMBURG
JULY 25
HAMBURG
JULY 26
ALTENBAUNA
JULY 28
KIEL
JULY 29
KASSEL
JULY 30

TRIUMPHANT
WE FLY

381ST
BOMB GROUP

WESEL
NOV. 7
KNABEN
NOV. 16
BREMEN
NOV. 26
SOLINGEN
NOV. 30
LEVERKUSN
DEC. 1
PARIS
DEC. 5
EMDEN
DEC. 11
BREMEN
DEC. 13
BREMEN
DEC. 16
BREMEN
DEC. 20
OSNABRUC
DEC. 22
COCOVE
DEC. 24
LUDWIGSH
DEC. 30
COGNAC
DEC. 31
KIEL
JAN. 4
TOURS

Coffee in the Officers' Club at
the 381st Bomb Group base,
Ridgewell in Essex.

aptly nicknamed. For the ten years in which she roamed the world's skies, peace reigned, for the most part. Big in every respect—47 feet high, 162 feet long, with a wingspan of 230 feet, she dwarfed the size of a modern 747 jumbo jet airliner. Able to cruise at 230 mph with a service ceiling of 45,700 feet, the B-36 had a top speed of 435 mph. When full of fuel, bombs, ammunition, and her sixteen-man crew, she weighed more than 205 tons and could range 10,000 miles, staying aloft for more than two days while carrying forty-three tons of conventional or nuclear bombs. She was armed with sixteen 20mm cannon and driven by the power of six enormous Pratt and Whitney R-4360 pusher-type piston engines mounted on the trailing edge of her wing with each producing 3,800 hp, and four General Electric J47 jet engines of 5,200 pounds thrust each in twin wing-mounted pods.

Such was the enormity of the noise and vibration she generated that, when approaching at low altitude in her landing pattern over a city, she announced her presence as much as a full minute before coming into view. The earth literally shook when a B-36 was in the neighborhood. In San Diego where more than a hundred of the big planes were modified during the 1950s, engineering test flights were conducted frequently. Windows rattled and cars waiting at a traffic light at an intersection near the end of the Lindbergh Field runway were often "nudged" where they sat if one of the bombers was having its engines run up prior to take-off.

More than 380 B-36s were built by Convair at Fort Worth, Texas, by August 1954 and the end of production. The B-36 never saw combat—a tribute to her role as a peace keeper. They were the V-force, Britain's

bomber delivery system for her Cold War nuclear capability. The Vickers Valiant, the Handley-Page Victor, and the Avro Vulcan formed the sharp end of a powerful deterrent force that served effectively into the early 1970s.

Avro chief designer Roy Chadwick's superb delta-wing Vulcan bomber began RAF service in 1956. Operated by a five-man crew, the Olympus-powered planes were based on ten UK airfields from the late 1950s and were assigned a readiness state called Quick Reaction Alert (QRA) during periods of international crisis. Positioned near base main runways, the Vulcans were required to be airborne in five minutes or less. They often carried air-launched nuclear weapons on their high-altitude missions. Gradually their role changed, and the companion Valiants and Victors experienced serious operational faults and set-backs. By the late 1960s Britain decided to switch its nuclear deterrent responsibility to the Royal Navy's Polaris missile-equipped nuclear submarines. The V-bombers were phased out of service early in the 1980s and replaced in the air by the then-new Panavia Tornado multi-role force.

It took the gigantic resources of the Boeing Airplane Company to conceive, design, organize, sub-contract and manufacture the plane that was the mainstay of America's strategic bombing force for most of the period since the end of World War II. Originally planned to carry four B-28 or B-61 thermonuclear gravity bombs in internal weapons bays, the B-52 Stratofortress first flew in April 1952, to replace the aging B-36 intercontinental bomber.

Beginning front-line service in 1955, the B-52's capability was linked to the then-revolutionary Pratt and Whitney

J57 jet engine, eight of which were needed to drive the huge plane. The J57 developed its great power (10,000 pounds thrust) through very high compression achieved by the use of two compressors in tandem, each turned by separate turbines. Later in the development of the bomber, it was re-engined with still more powerful, cleaner, and more economical turbofans.

Remembered chiefly for their bombing role in the Vietnam War, the big black-painted B-52s delivered 84,000-pound bomb loads on jungle guerrila targets and were said to be the American weapon most feared by the North Vietnamese. The B-52 is the longest-lived combat aircraft design ever produced.

In the 1980s, the U.S. Air Force wanted a bomber able to operate entirely on its own with virtual impunity against all conceivable air defenses, the airplane that would become the B-2 Spirit stealth bomber.

The bat-like wing configuration, the ability to operate on very short notice with no forward basing support, minimal detectability, enviable intercontinental range, and the wildly amazing price tag believed to exceed one billion dollars a copy, position the B-2 among the most outrageous man-made creations of all time. Originally, B-2 production was planned for 132 planes, but many factors, including the collapse of the Soviet Union, whose extensive radar network it was intended to evade, and the staggering unit cost of the advanced bomber, combined to reduce the final quantity to just twenty-one aircraft. The radically reduced order resulted in a lean, mean operational force more than capable in the view of its advocates, of delivering on its original broad promise.

The design criteria calling for ultra-low radar observability as well

A Stuart Reid painting, Bombing of the Wadi Fara, 20 September 1918; far right: Employee badge of a Pratt & Whitney aero engine plant worker in the Second World War years.

as exceptional aerodynamics, for a uniquely stealthy package led to one of history's better-kept secrets. Throughout the 1980s, the black project was the subject of many rumors. The facts of its existence, capabilities and special design, however, remained secret until the Air Force decided to show it to the press and public at a November 1988 factory roll-out before the flight-test phase of development.

The Spirit can deliver a variety of conventional and nuclear weapons, including 500-pound to 2,200-pound general purpose bombs, sea mines, nuclear gravity bombs, and other ordnance. Fully loaded it weighs 336,500 pounds. With a range of approximately 6,000 miles, it can take off and land on any field capable of accommodating a medium-sized airliner. The B-2 operates with a fly-by-wire control system giving it fairly conventional handling and flying qualities. This radical airplane is made up largely of carbon-fibre-epoxy composite materials.

The B-2s are based at Whiteman Air Force Base in Missouri and are operated there by the 509th Bomb Wing, descended from the WWII 509th Composite Group whose B-29s took the first atomic bombs to Hiroshima and Nagasaki. The B-2 is meant to lead the attack in the first night of raids in any future conflict. It is dedicated to hit the best-defended, most vital and significant enemy sites. It can strike such targets from its U.S. base while operating independently and virtually on its own terms.

While not strictly a bomber, the incredibly versatile F/A-18 Hornet family of multi-role aircraft has for several years been the principal strike aircraft of the U.S. Navy. The Boeing McDonnell Douglas airplane first flew in 1978 and entered service in 1980.

The Hornet is probably the most capable fighter-bomber in the history of the American Navy. In the Iraq and Bosnian conflicts the Hornet showed its worth in both the air-to-air and air-to-ground missions. It is a twin-engined, supersonic, all-weather, carrier capable combat jet with a top speed of 1,190 mph at 40,000 feet and can carry a wide variety of bombs and missiles. It is light-weight and relatively low-cost and is fairly small and easily accommodated in the limited space of an aircraft carrier. With a relatively small fuel capacity, its operation generally involves aerial refueling.

The Hornet was designed primarily as a naval plane to operate from carriers, but in the inventories of the Canadian, Spanish, and Australian air arms, it is operated from land bases. It is a highly automated aircraft whose computers significantly reduce the workload of the pilot, freeing him or her to concentrate on fighting

the enemy and flying the mission. Its electronic offensive and defensive systems make it an extremely potent adversary. The Hornet has a gun, the M61 20mm cannon, an electric Gatling gun with a 540-round magazine, in addition to the ability to carry a combination of very capable weapons including the AIM-9M all-angle heat-seeking anti-aircraft missile, the AGM-88 anti-radar missile, and the 1,000-pound laser-guided bomb.

Pilots and maintenance personnel share respect for the F/A-18's reliability and ease of maintenance, despite the complexity of its systems. In the Gulf War and over Bosnia, the Hornet force had an amazing availability rate of better than 90 percent, reaching a peak of 95 percent in the Gulf. No other naval attack aircraft has inspired such admiration and high regard from those who fly it.

ORDNANCE

From its beginning in World War I, the true bomber was designed to carry and deliver bombs in level flight against specific targets at medium to long range. Combatants who were utilizing airships for this purpose soon discovered their vulnerability to both ground fire and air attack by the scout planes of the day. They quickly shifted to the use of two-seat craft like the BE 2e, operated from the summer of 1916 by the Royal Flying Corps. It arrived in time for the Battle of the Somme, but left much to be desired as a bomber. Cruising at little more than sixty miles per hour at only a few thousand feet of altitude, this flimsy craft was also prey to ground fire and its marginal performance was seriously reduced through having to carry the added weight of bombs. When sent to attack a target, and carrying a maximum bomb load, the observer had to be left back at the base.

Probably the earliest recorded concept of aerial bombing comes from the Hindu epic poem, the *Mahabharata of Krishna-Dwaipayana-Vyasa*. In it is a description of the enemies of Krishna inducing demons to construct a winged chariot to be driven through the sky until it stood over Dwarakha, home of the followers of Krishna. From it missiles would be thrown down upon the city, destroying everything on which they fell.

In 1670 the Italian Jesuit Francesco Lana de Terzi designed an "aerial ship" which was to be borne aloft by four copper globes from which the air had been evacuated. He is said to have allowed, though, that "God might prevent its construction since such a device might descend on an enemy's fleet, kill their men and burn their ships by artificial fireworks and fireballs. And this they may do not only to ships but to great buildings, castles and cities, with such severity that they which cast these things down from a height out of gun-shot, cannot on the other side be offended by those from below."

It was in 1793 that aeronautic inventor Joseph-Michel de Montgolfier proposed that his balloon might be used to drop two large bombs on the port of Toulon, France, which was then rebelling against the Republican government. It didn't happen. But in 1849, Austrians laying siege to Venice became the first combatants to drop bombs on their enemy. In fact, while the Germans, French, and British dithered over the concept of aerial bombardment by balloon, the Austrians had already established several balloon battalions using the balloons of Montgolfier, which were capable of lifting thirty-three pounds of bombs and staying aloft for more than half an hour. The Austrians utilized trial balloons for testing the strength and direction of the wind before successfully flinging some of their bombs on Venice, whose residents' morale suffered more than their property.

above left: The Flying Control tower at RAF Bovingdon; right: The remains of the bomb dump at Grafton Underwood, wartime home of the 384th Bomb Group.

below: A B-17G of the 388th Bomb Group at Knettishall, England; left: An engine of the B-17 Sally B at Duxford, Cambridgeshire.

Eighth Air Force gunners preparing their weapons for installation at their positions in this B-17 bomber.

Among the earliest proponents of aerial bombing from balloons was Henry Tracey Coxwell who, in the mid-1800s wrote: "I have no doubt that it would be possible to drop, with tolerable nicety, a host of aerial vessels charged with agents calculated to produce stupefaction, if not fatal effects. If by this method our warriors could secure prisoners instead of increasing carnage, humanity would rejoice at so desirable a consumation by such ingenious means." Balloons then, however, had certain drawbacks. They could only carry a relatively light bomb load, were at the mercy of the winds and were difficult to maneuver and their ordnance could not be delivered with accuracy. They were, in fact, really only a terror weapon for their time. This changed to some extent with the coming of the steerable rigid airships like the great Zeppelins at the beginning of the twentieth century. By 1910 Zeppelins had become capable of carrying a substantial bomb load over a considerable distance and were quite maneuverable.

In 1903 the brothers Orville and Wilbur Wright demonstrated their heavier-than-air flying machine at Kittyhawk in North Carolina, and in 1911 a Wright biplane was tested as a potential bombing aircraft by the U.S. Army. In that year the first actual use of airplanes to drop bombs took place in North Africa when an Italian expeditionary force utilized six Blériot aircraft to drop a total of four ten-kilogram hand grenade "bombs" on Turkish positions.

In Britain during 1912, the Royal Flying Corps was formed and soon began to develop offensive plans for aerial warfare, including the attacking of troop concentrations, supply centers, and ammunition dumps, as well as facilities for communications. The naval wing of the RFC split off from the parent organization in July 1914 and became the Royal Naval Air Service, which was then headed by the First Lord of the Admiralty, Winston S. Churchill. He made it the mission of the RNAS to seek and destroy the enemy, and took the lead in developing bombing and aerial torpedo operations, relying mainly on aircraft from private companies like Sopwith and Shorts rather than Government-sponsored planes from the Royal Aircraft Establishment, Farnborough. Prior to this, in 1913, Churchill had written about the German airships: "The Zeppelin should be attacked . . . by an aeroplane descending on it obliquely from above and discharging a series of bombs or fireballs, at rapid intervals, so that a string of them more than a hundred yards in length, would be drawn like a whip-lash across the gas bag."

From the start of World War I the idea of aerial bombing was still suspect in most quarters and few military men believed that aircraft at that stage could even be useful in a reconnaissance role, much less as bombers. The only possible threat they could perceive was that of being bombed by the Zeppelins, and even that was offset to an extent by the difficulties facing the airship crews in crossing and navigating the great distance to England and locating worthwhile targets. Among the warring nations there was, in fact, little if any real priority given then to the development of bomber aircraft. The British War Office, for example, was interested in only three types of aircraft: a light single-seat scout; a two-seat reconnaissance machine; and a heavier two-seat fighter. While employed in a token bombing role through the occasional lobbing of grenades or "bomblets," all of these aircraft were relatively underpowered and incapable of lifting more than a tiny bomb load. Thus, when the war came the Royal Flying Corps was operating aircraft with no real aerial bombing capability.

Initially, airmen of the various warring nations tried out the aerial bombing concept by dropping grenades. Some filled and dropped gasoline canisters and, in an interesting approach to anti-personnel bombardment, the French tried the dropping of fléchettes (steel darts) on the German cavalry units.

In the first true bombing attack of the war, the Germans sent the Zeppelin Z.VI to drop thirteen bombs on a fort defending Liege. The fort was untouched but nine civilians were killed in the raid. Ground fire damaged the airship which crashed on its return to Cologne. Various nuisance raids by individual scout aircraft of both sides followed and, within a month of the war's opening shot, it was the Royal Naval Air Service that conducted the war's first real bombing offensive. RNAS Sopwith biplanes based in Antwerp were modified to carry crude bomb racks and on 22 September 1914, four of the planes took off to attack the Zeppelin sheds at Cologne and Düsseldorf. Navigation and weather problems caused the raid to fail, but another strike by the Sopwiths two weeks later yielded significant results when one of the pilots located the main Düsseldorf Zeppelin shed. He dropped two twenty-pound bombs on the shed and managed to set aflame the new Z.IX Zeppelin inside. The airship was destroyed as were three additional Zeppelins during this period. Then, in November, three specially-equipped Avro 504s flew from a field near the

French frontier to hit the Zeppelin works at Friedrichshafen. Through clever planning and execution, the Avros surprised the Germans and damaged a Zeppelin then under construction. They further damaged the airship works and the local gasworks was destroyed as well.

Now the miniscule bombing capability of existing aircraft, and the extreme vulnerability of the airships, led visionary planners of several nations to conclude that development of dedicated bomber aircraft was important, even essential. They further realized that they had to differentiate between bomber aircraft to be developed for tactical purposes and those meant for strategic attack. Tactical requirements were evident by the end of 1914 when both sides in the conflict were firmly dug in and stalled from the Channel coast all across France. Targets such as ammunition and supply storage, communications centers and troop concentrations were ripe for attack and were hit by the reconnaissance planes of the day operating in a dual capacity as bombers. Between early March and late June of 1915, some 141 tactical bombing raids were launched by the Allies, mostly on German-occupied rail junctions, but only a few of these attacks were successful.

The Kaiser had ordered German airship raids on British military targets such as arsenals in January 1915. The attacks were to be flown by night as they had lost the Zeppelin Z.VI and two other airships to ground fire in the early days of the war. Their airships did, however, tend to drift off course, and with the blackout in England, they frequently bombed undefended villages in East Anglia rather than the military targets they had been sent to hit. Often the airship commanders didn't know where their bombs had fallen and were unable to differentiate between military targets and civilian sites. On 19 January 1915 King's Lynn and Yarmouth, both in the county of Norfolk, received bombs from two Zeppelins. Six people were killed when the airships dropped their loads of 110-pound high explosive bombs and 6.5-pound incendiaries. The British reaction was one of shock and outrage. By the summer months the relative inaccuracy of the raids had led to the Kaiser ending his ban on the bombing of British cities and concerted German airship attacks on London and the Tyneside areas began. More than fifty Zeppelin raids hit London. Across Britain reprisal raids were demanded and a program was initiated to radically improve anti-aircraft defenses. By the end of 1915, more than 700 Britons had been killed or injured in the Zeppelin raids. These raids continued into the summer of 1918, but with far less effect.

The best of the early British bombers was the Handley-Page 0/400 which, in 1917, equipped the first RFC strategic bombing unit. While only eighty of these aircraft were produced, it was an excellent bomber for the time. Powered by two 250 hp Rolls-Royce V engines and capable of 100 mph, the 0/400 biplane had a range of 745 miles and carried a four-man crew armed with either four or five movable Lewis guns. It carried a 1,984-pound bomb load.

Into the spring of 1917, the British and Germans traded raids and reprisals until, in May, a new and more sinister series of bombing attacks was begun by the Germans—the year-long Gotha offensive. The Gotha was a large, twin-Mercedes-powered heavy bomber made by the Gothaer Waggonfabrikwerk. It carried a crew of three, up to four machine-guns, and a 1,300-pound bomb load. It was capable of eighty-seven mph and had a ceiling of 21,300 feet and a range of 520 miles. Daylight Gotha raids on London and British port cities continued with devastating effect until September when British anti-aircraft guns got the better of them, and the Gothas were switched to night attacks. In that same month a new and formidable four-engined German bomber, the "Giant," made its debut. With a crew of nine, it had virtually the same wingspan as the Boeing B-29 Superfortress of WWII. Together with the Gothas, the Giants dropped nearly 100 tons of bombs in twenty-seven raids, killing about 800 Britons, mostly civilians, and injuring nearly 2,000 more. Again, British defenses improved significantly and the effectiveness of this major bombing campaign dropped off markedly.

Probably the most important result of this bombing offensive was the 1917 report by General Jan Christiaan Smuts, who had been authorized by the British Cabinet to investigate the effects of the German raids and British defense capabilities. His far-sighted recommendations included a radical overhaul of the British home defenses; a doubling of the strength of the air forces; the creation and swift development of a large strategic bombing force to bring the air war to the German homeland, and the immediate creation of an independent air service separate from both the Army and the Navy. The report also stated: "The day may not be far off, when aerial operations with their devastation of enemy lands and destruction of industrial and populous centers on a vast scale may become the principal operations of war, to which the older forms of military and naval operations may become secondary and subservient." It was only at the end of the war in late 1918, that the Inter-Allied Strategic Bombing Force, composed of British, French, U.S. and Italian squadrons, was formed. More importantly, in April of that year, as a direct result of the Smuts report, the Royal Air Force was created.

During World War I, considerable advances were made in the development of aerial bombs. Great strides were made in design to improve their stability and predictability in flight, their fusing mechanisms and their destructive capacity.

In 1913 the British bomb-design pioneer F. Martin Hale, developed a bomb for the RNAS, a twenty-pound high explosive type representing one of the first departures from older bomb shapes in an attempt to improve the weapon's stability in flight. The Hale, and the German Carbonit series of high explosive bombs, were somewhat pear-shaped and had tail fins. Less accurate than the Hale, the Carbonits had a steel-tipped nose for improved penetration. They were made in a range of sizes from 4.5 kg to 50 kg.

An aerial bomb had to be transportable in safety; the bomber crew

had to be able to jettison their bombs safely if necessary, and the bombs had to arm themselves as they were dropped, and detonate on impact. Thus, there was a major emphasis on bomb-fusing mechanism design in the war years.

Three types of explosive were required in the aerial bombs of World War I. Amatol, a relatively insensitive type, was used as a main bursting charge until later in the war when it was largely replaced by TNT. An exploder was needed to detonate the bursting charge and an explosive called Tetryl was commonly used for

Armorers at work in the bomb dump of an 8AF bomber station in WW2 England.

this purpose. A fulmonate of mercury detonator was used to set off the exploder and required great care in handling as it was highly sensitive. Before the bomb was loaded into the aircraft, the detonator and exploder were fitted into it. On impact with the ground or the target, a striker pin hit the detonator causing the exploder to ignite and this then caused the bursting charge to explode.

A small propeller was used to arm the fusing mechanism of the Hale and Carbonit bombs. The tail-mounted propeller would unwind a spindle in the bomb when it was dropped, ultimately letting the striker contact the detonator on impact. The propeller had a guard clip attached to prevent premature arming, and was removed before the bomb was released.

In time, bomb racks and release mechanisms were devised. Next to come along were bomb types with nose-fuses and nose-mounted arming propellers such as the twenty-pound Cooper, which created an instantaneous explosion when the bomb impacted with the ground, scattering deadly fragments over a large area. Made with a light case, this bomb, along with the French flechette dart canister, were among the first anti-personnel bombs to be developed. Tail-fused bombs, on the other hand, had a delayed action, from 1/20th of a second to up to fifteen seconds, and would bury themselves into the ground before exploding. Many bombs of British manufacture were designed to carry two fuses, one in the nose and the other in the tail, as a fail-safe solution to the all-too-common problem of fuse mechanism failure.

Standardization of British bomb types came in near the end of the war, with four basic types then in use. Weights ranged from the old twenty-

Armorers fusing bombs to be loaded in this Consolidated B-24 Liberator bomber.

pound heavy-case Cooper, to the 3,360-pound bomb that was developed to be carried by the Handley-Page V/1500 bomber.

Finally, the first true forerunner of the bombs of World War II was the German PuW. It had an aerodynamic torpedo-like shape and a high-grade steel casing, as well as fin design quite similar to that of WWII bombs, which caused the bomb to rotate as it fell, arming the fuses by centrifugal force. The PuW could be carried and dropped from a horizontal position in the bomb racks as well as in internal bomb bays, thus reducing drag and improving the performance of the aircraft.

The incendiary bomb was a concept developed primarily by the Germans during World War I. Earlier British incendiaries utilized a black powder or petrol filler. They were largely ineffective and were replaced late in the war by a phosphorus version. The French were also active in the development of this type of weapon, but it was the Germans who pursued the refinement of the incendiary. Their early efforts were filled with an inflammable mix of kerosene, petrol, and liquid tar, requiring last-minute insertion into the bombs before flight. A later variation using tar, thermite, and benzol produced a 3,000-degree C fire. In 1918 the Germans created an incendiary with a magnesium body that was itself the main burning material. It was intended fundamentally as an anti-personnel weapon.

Throughout the war it was mainly the British and the Germans who made strides in bomber and bomb design and development. They both sought to perfect a combination of long-range heavy bomber aircraft and stable, accurate, and effective bombs capable of generating terror and significant destruction on each other's cities.

Between World Wars I and II, some highly significant bombers were developed. This was the period when aircraft construction techniques gradually changed from conventional wood and fabric biplanes to stressed-alloy monoplanes. Large bomber types were multi-engined, many of them four-engined for greater safety and reliability.

In the 1930s, the reborn German Air Staff was headed by General Max Wever, a staunch advocate of the strategic bombing concept. Wever planned and was building a sizable strategic bomber force for Germany when, in 1936, he died in an accident and was replaced by General Albert Kesselring, who later was to command the Luftwaffe units in the Battle of Britain and in North Africa. Kesselring favored a purely tactical role for the German bomber, and immediately scrapped Wever's strategic force program. Had it been allowed to continue to fruition, the course of World War II might have been quite different.

After 1937, the science of bomb development began to escalate. Britain pioneered a new range of weaponry in both armor-piercing and demolition bombs for fragmentation, blast or mining effect, and the RAF concentrated on a new program including an improved class of pyrotechnic devices, flares, flame and smoke floats, as well as aerial mines and combustible magnesium incendiaries. In the early days of World War II, the principal "ordnance" being delivered by the RAF on enemy targets was incendiaries and leaflets. By the end of the first two years of the war, the British were employing more 250-pound and 500-pound general purpose bombs in their strikes that any other bomb types. Their sizes were the most practical for

the capabilities of all the then-standard RAF bomber aircraft.

German bombs available at the start of the Second World War ranged from fifty-pound to 1,100-pound types and were similar in fundamentals to those of the British, but a high incidence of failure soon led to the development and implementation of a new and more reliable electrically-fired fuse device. By spring 1940, the Germans were concentrating heavily on their parachute mine designs and it was these weapons which became the mainstay in attacks on British cities. Both the Germans and British went on to design and develop ranges of more sophisticated mines including magnetic, acoustic, and influence types.

There followed the development of the radio-activated proximity fuse which allowed a bomb to be detonated at a prescribed altitude above the ground. The RAF then began experimenting with the so-called "light-case" concept in bomb design. Having discovered in practice during the first year of World War II that streamlining the shape and design characteristics of its bombs in order to minimize drag and prevent tumbling was, in fact, unnecessary, British scientists went to work on a new type of bomb. It was to be a 4,000-pounder containing an explosive compound called RDX which offered both ease of manufacture and relative safety in handling it. The new LC bomb was actually a welded drum of thin gauge steel and the empty casing was filled with the molten RDX material. The highly powerful blast bomb that resulted was known by the Allies as the "blockbuster" and by the crews of RAF Bomber Command as the "cookie."

There was no more efficient and effective heavy bomber in World War II than the Avro Lancaster with its unobstucted bomb bay and its impressive load-carrying capability. As early as 1942 RAF Bomber Command was using its Lancasters to deliver both the 4,000-pound cookies and an 8,000-pound version of the same bomb, which was really two cookies bolted together for twice the effect. The immense bomb bay of the Lanc could accommodate even greater weapons, such as the triple-cookie unit known as the "tallboy," for use against special targets such as the 42,000-ton German battleship *Tirpitz*. The *Tirpitz* was sunk by Tallboy bombs of 617 Squadron off Tromso Harbor in northern Norway on 12 November 1944, with the loss of more than 1,400 German crew. The British had been determined to sink the *Tirpitz* since her commissioning in 1941 and had pursued her doggedly. The development of the Tallboy provided the RAF with the means for eliminating the great German warship.

To meet a requirement for a bomb of even more destructive force than Tallboy, the RAF turned to the innovative Vickers Aircraft Chief Engineer and designer Barnes Wallis, whose geodesic construction approach for the Wellington bomber had contributed hugely to the effectiveness of that aircraft. Wallis had also been asked to design a bomb for use by a new special-task squadron, No 617, against the Mohne, Eder, and Sorpe dams of Germany's industrial Ruhr Valley. His solution to the problem of how to breach these enormous structures came in the form of a large, drum-shaped device to be carried partially extended from the bomb bay of the Lancaster. Before release, the "dam buster" bomb was made to rotate on its mount at a high rate of speed by an motor within the fuselage of the Lanc. Wallis calculated that, to function properly, the spinning

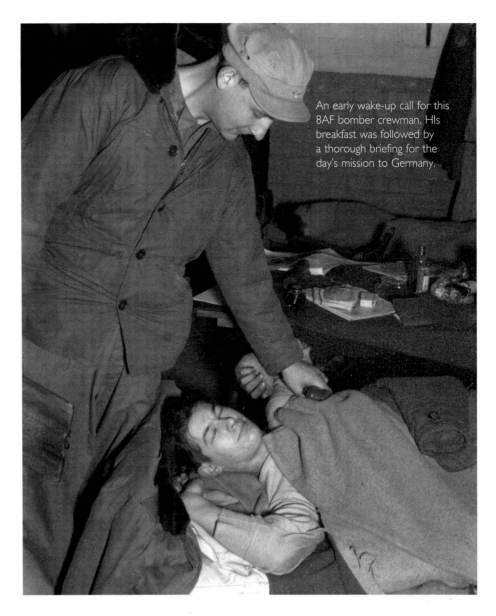

An early wake-up call for this 8AF bomber crewman. HIs breakfast was followed by a thorough briefing for the day's mission to Germany.

bomb must be released at a height of exactly sixty feet above the water of the reservoir behind such a dam. In theory, the spinning device would then bounce along the surface of the water to contact the wall of the dam and then sink towards the bottom and be detonated at a precise depth by a hydrostatic fuse. After much rehearsal it was felt that the squadron and the weapon, now called Upkeep, were ready, and the raid was carried out on the night of 16-17 May 1943

by a small force of bombers which managed to reach the target area and breach two of the three dams. Wing Commander Guy Gibson led the attack and for his effort was awarded the Victoria Cross, Britain's highest military distinction. Later in the war, Gibson was killed while flying as a Pathfinder for bombers attacking the Ruhr.

Now Wallis was asked to find a way of damaging targets such as the seemingly impenetrable German sub-

below: Life in a Nissen hut;. right Pancakes for the customers of the combat mess; below: American bombs for delivery to German targets in occupied Europe.

above: Target selection at 8AF HQ, Pinetree,
High Wycombe; top right: Entering the briefing
for a mission; below: Delivering bombs to a
B-17 Flying Fortress somewhere in England.

left: An 8AF armorer attends to fuse warning tags on the bombs in his aircraft before a mission; below: The Flying Control tower at Molesworth, home of the 303rd Bomb Gourp, Eighth Air Force.

marine pens along the Biscay coast of France. These massive reinforced concrete structures, with walls and roofs many feet thick, had proven utterly bomb-resistant in attacks by both the RAF and the American Eighth Air Force. In fact, the RAF's Sir Arthur "Bomber" Harris believed that the effort expended attacking the sub pens was futile and that his force was better utilized in attacks

on the shipyards where the U-boats were being built. Harris targeted the submarine construction facilities with considerable effect even though he felt that the requirement for such attacks diverted his force from its primary assignment, the all-out assault on German cities.

Wallis, meanwhile, thought that a possible solution for attacking the sub pens lay in a notion he had for

what he called an "earthquake" bomb. It was to be a conventional high explosive device, but with a weight of 22,000 pounds. Streamlined, the bomb had canted tail fins to make it spin as it fell, and was made with a heavy case. Wallis intended that the bomb be dropped against great, solid structures like the pens. He expected it to go deep underground on impact and then be detonated, causing an

earth tremor that would literally shake down the target structure. It worked well when employed against a target such as the enormous railway viaduct at Bielefeld, but as visitors to France's Brittany coast will see, the great sub pens of Brest, Saint Nazaire, Lorient, La Pallice and Bordeaux remain today, largely, unaffected by all Allied attempts to destroy them.

Other bombing weapons and techniques resulting from this wartime development period included the Royal Navy Disney rocket bomb, a 4,500-pound hard-case bomb with a rocket in the tail, though to be useful against hardened targets like the sub pens. The rocket was ignited by a barometric fuse after the weapon had fallen freely from release altitude to 5,000 feet. The rocket accelerated the bomb to a velocity of 2,400 feet a second. The U.S. Eighth Air Force made limited use of the bomb in the spring of 1945 with arguable results. Another development of the time was the fire weapon, Napalm, a jellied petroleum mixture taking its name from the combination of naptha and palm oil. The mix was carried mainly in 108-gallon U.S. fighter fuel drop tanks with small igniter units. The Napalm "bombs" were first used

against German strong points on the French coast in 1945.

Yet another amazing bombing technique was the Aphrodite Project, in which an American bomber, usually a war-weary B-17, was completely filled with the high explosive Torpex, 20,000 pounds of it, and was flown to a point on the English coast. There the pilot baled out and the aircraft continued to its target under radio direction guidance from a ground station. The intended targets were the German V-weapon sites in the Pas de Calais. One such sortie cost the life of the pilot, U.S. Navy Lieutenant Joseph Kennedy, Jr., son of the former U.S. Ambassador to Britain and elder brother of the post-war President John F. Kennedy. Kennedy, and another crewman were killed when their B-24 Liberator drone prematurely

above: Richard E. Bynum, pilot of this 388th Bomb Group B-17 at Knettishall.

exploded near Blythburgh, Suffolk, on 12 August 1944. A similar radio-guided "aircraft drone bomb" program of the Germans called *Mistel* involved a variety of fighter and bomber combinations in which the fighter was mounted on top of the bomber, which was guided toward its target by the fighter pilot who then released the "bomber-bomb" which was supposed to continue to its target under radio-control. The effect of this effort was minimal.

Probably nothing contributed more to the success of the Eighth and other American air forces' bombers than the Norden bombsight. As famous as the Andrews Sisters, Lucky Strike Green, and Kilroy, the ultra-secret Norden was the standard high and medium-altitude bomb sight of the U.S. bomber forces throughout the war. The device was, for the time, quite sophisticated. Its development was begun in 1928 by the Dutch-born inventor Carl L. Norden. Utilizing ground speed, drift, trail, and bomb ballistics information fed into it by the bombardier, the instrument was able to compute a precise release point for the bomb load. The bombardier used a telescopic element on the Norden unit to establish and compensate for deflection and synchronize the sight. For the final moments of the bomb run, he "flew" the airplane through the Automatic Flight Control Equipment (AFCE) of the sight package, which was linked to the autopilot of the bomber. Thus he was able to make flight adjustments through the marvelous bombsight. It was the accuracy of the Norden sight that, in large part, gave the Americans confidence to persist with their daylight bombing philosophy in World War II.

The other principal aid to bombing accuracy in that war was radar. A range of radio navigation and radar systems was developed and deployed to bring improvements in accuracy of placement and in target marking by the Pathfinder aircraft. The British H2S and Oboe systems were key elements in the bombing campaigns of Bomber Command. The H2S was a radar set mounted in RAF bombers which provided a terrain image that enabled the aircraft to bomb more effectively at night and through heavy cloud cover. It was used for the first time in RAF attacks on Hamburg in July 1943. The Oboe system was a means by which the British bombers could be directed to their targets at night through the use of two radio beams being transmitted from England. The beams intersected over the bomber's target and the aircraft's pilot simply flew along one beam until he crossed the other beam, indicating he had reached the bomb release point over his target.

With the final weeks of the war came the advent of the most significant and terrifying weapon yet devised. The bombs called atomic were the products of scientists of many nations and many disciplines. The story of these weapons is told in another chapter of this book, and it is perhaps enough to note now that the concept behind the first atom bombs revolved around a staggering release of energy which caused the surrounding air to be heated to an extremely high temperature, coupled with the emmission of high levels of radiation on a variety of wave lengths.

The first two atom bombs were known by their makers as Fat Man and Little Boy. Little Boy, the weapon delivered over Hiroshima, Japan, on 6 August 1945 by the B-29 *Enola Gay*, which was piloted by Colonel Paul W. Tibbets, was a "gun-type" device. Within its casing lay a shaped element of Uranium U-235 which, when the bomb reached detonation altitude over its target, was "fired" into another U-235 shape, resulting in a nuclear explosion. The blast, heat, and radiation release of Little Boy killed more than 80,000 people in Hiroshima. The second atom bomb, Fat Man, killed 40,000 more Japanese at Nagasaki three days after the Hiroshima raid. The immensely powerful and destructive weapons which helped to bring World War II to an end were but relative firecrackers when compared to the force and fury of the nuclear and thermonuclear weapons to follow in the post-war years. Ultimately, several nations were to join the nuclear club, and the world arms race was on in earnest.

In the years since the end of that war, the world's nuclear arsenals have grown to the point where the estimated casualties in a major nuclear confrontation range from a few hundred million to upwards of 25 percent of the earth's population. The United States alone is believed to have the nuclear capability to obliterate all human life several times over. But in the time since the end of the war, the United States and other world powers have continued the development of conventional bomb-type weapons and have produced them in the hundreds of millions. They range from demolition and high explosive to incendiary, fire and chemical types, to depth charges and aerial mines, fragmentation, cluster, unguided aerial rockets and laser-guided "smart" bombs. In the Gulf War, the range of Paveway laser-guided bombs included high and low speed, penetrator and glide bomb types in 500-, 1,000-, and 2,000-pound weights. In the precision-guided bombing system a target designator-supplied infra-red or daylight image appears on a screen

The Norden bombsight used in the bombers of the 8AF in WW2 combined an analog computer and linkage to the airplane's autopilot, and was extremely accurate.

The B-24 Liberator bomber *Exterminator* of the 330th Bomb Squadron, 93rd Bomb Group, 8AF, based at Hardwick, England.

in the attacking aircraft cockpit. The pilot or the weapons systems officer then aligns the cross hairs on the target impact point and locks the impact point into the system. Now the infrared sensor and its laser stay locked on the target IP. The laser-guided bomb or bombs are released in the vicinity of the target and, just seconds before impact, a pre-coded energy beam is fired by the designator at the targeting impact point. A seeker in the nose of the weapon picks up reflected laser energy which aims the missile at the precise impact point, "flying it" by means of movable fins on the weapon.

Typically in the Gulf, four RAF Tornado bombers utilized three 1,000-pound British LGBs each in a successful attack on an Iraqi bridge, whereas destroying a hardened aircraft shelter usually required only a single aircraft carrying two of the smart weapons. Tornado GR.Mk 1s flew more than 1,600 sorties in the Gulf War, dropping more than 4,200 conventional free-fall bombs and more than 950 LGBs, Coalition aircraft using mainly LGBs destroyed approximately 350 of Iraq's 594 hardened aircraft shelters in the war. Additional airfield targets included fuel and ammunition storage facilities, command bunkers and runways. F-117A stealth fighter/bombers starred in their ultra-precise delivery of laser-guided weapons on Iraqi command and control facilities, bridges and other difficult targets, many in Baghdad itself.

In the late 1970s one estimate of the combined destructive power of just the conventional bombs arsenal of the United States at that time was a capability to destroy 10 percent of the Earth's inhabitable surface and up to 35 percent of its population. Weapons development continues

world-wide at a pace at least as frenetic as that of the debate over the ethics and effectivity of bombing. The characteristics of the weapons are limited only by the imaginations of the designers and those who cause them to be developed. Aerial bombardment has been with us through most of the twentieth century and the concept and practice continues in its many forms into the new century.

In 1999 Lieutenant Commander Horace Taylor died. He was 90 and had won the George Cross for his actions as a wartime bomb and mine disposal expert in Britain. In his preparations before dealing with a weapon, Taylor always dug what he called a "funk hole," "not very deep, but fairly wide, as I should be coming over the top at some speed. My colleagues used to think that my funk holes were too close to the job, but I reckoned they were better too close than just out of reach." In one incident "a bomb went off on me as I was working and blew me right through two houses. I came down four streets away. When the thing exploded I forgot to lose consciousness. I was so excited. I knew exactly what had gone wrong, and all I wanted to do was to tell my boss what had happened for the sake of the rest of the crew." All of Taylor's clothes had been blown off by the explosion and he had been temporarily blinded by the dust, but he managed to telephone his superior before being taken to hospital at Leamington Spa . . . in a ladies ward.

Ground personnel and other airmen of this American heavy bomber group awaiting the return of their airplanes from the day's mission. This was referred to as "sweating them in."

DANGERS

If the crewmen of Eighth Bomber Command and RAF Bomber Command were a little paranoid in World War II, who could blame them? It would have seemed to them that practically everything was stacked against their survival. Any insurance actuary would have projected a very low probability for their completing their tours of duty. If the flak didn't get you, the fighters would; and if not the fighters, the cold, anoxia, mechanical failure, outrageous weather, or battle fatigue. Even ordinary everyday fear could nail you.

Now, he will spend a few sick years in institutes, and do what things the rules consider wise. And take whatever pity they may dole. Tonight he noticed how the women's eyes passed from him to the strong men that were whole. How cold and late it is! Why don't they come and put him into bed? Why don't they come?
—from *Disabled* by Wilfred Owen

FLAK, n. German, *Flieger Abwehr Kanone*; anti-aircraft cannon.

"I could hear him yelling, 'I've been hit. I've been hit.' He was standing in the middle of the floor. He had his hands between his legs . . . he was jumping up and down and yelling, 'I've been hit.' "
—Larry Bird, 493rd Bomb Group (H), Eighth USAAF

"Most of the time when you are over enemy territory you have a funny feeling, particularly when you can see flak. You know that it can hurt you, but you look out there and it's fascinating because it comes up like a little arm-

less dwarf. There's a round puff here and then there's usually two strings that come out of the bottom like legs, and this thing will appear out of nothing. You don't see any shell; you don't hear anything. You just see this little puff of smoke and then shortly after, it might sound like somebody is throwing gravel all over the airplane. You're fascinated by it. You know it can hurt you very badly, but you're fascinated by it . . . you watch it. It's kind of like watching a snake."
—W.W. Ford, 92nd Bomb Group (H), Eighth USAAF

"It wasn't always the long trips that were the worst. Sometimes we got more flak near the English coast than we did over the target. That was the Royal Navy. It didn't matter what we did—shoot off the colors of the day and everything—the Navy always fired at us."
—Leonard Thompson, No 550 Squadron, RAF

"The flak was unpleasant, although one always felt we were unlikely to get a direct hit. On the run into the target it became more accurate, mainly because we had to fly straight and level for a few minutes for the bombsight to settle down and the bomb aimer to ensure that the cross hairs were on the target when he released the bombs. With a hundred or so aircraft making virtually the same run, the anti-aircraft gunners had an opportunity to get some steady shooting in."
—John Curtiss, Nos 578 and 158 Squadrons, RAF

". . . Kept telling myself, just the way I told the men, that it was going to be a lot better to fly straight instead of zigging. We'd get through the area where they could shoot at us more

Among the most common wounds suffered by the airmen of the Eighth USAAF was flak, pieces of exploding anti-aircraft shells that pierced the thin aluminum skin of their aircraft.

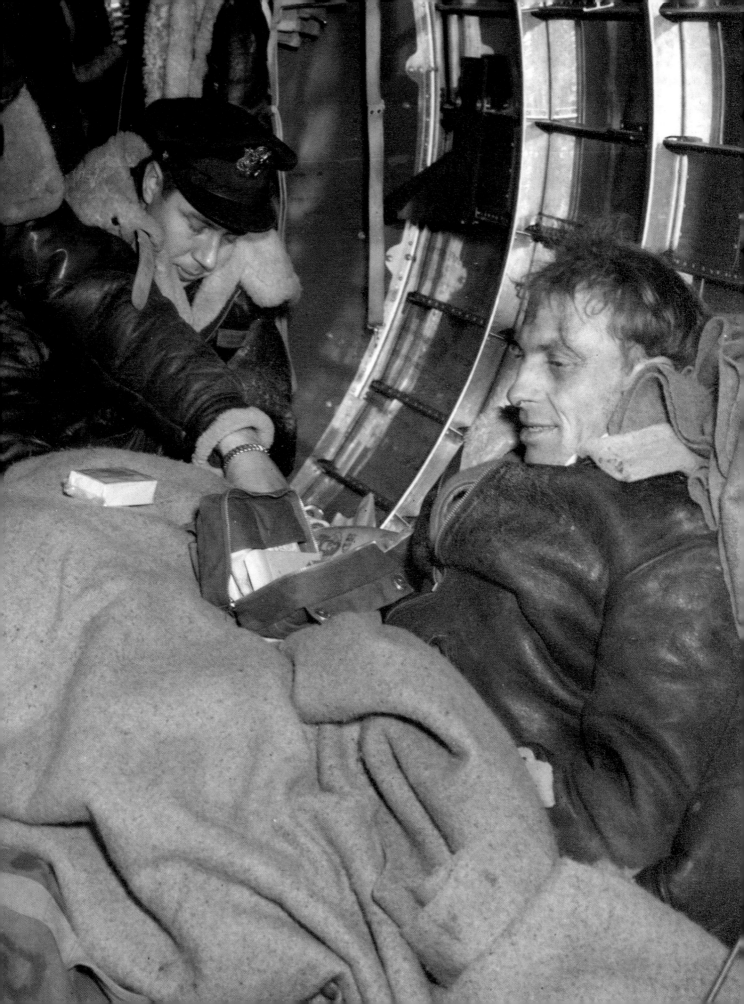

rapidly, and the enemy would necessarily fire fewer rounds. All in all, we'd have a better chance of getting off with whole hides—people and airplanes alike."
—from *Mission With LeMay* by General Curtis E. LeMay and MacKinlay Kantor

"Flak was ever-present, a fact of life, a thing to be endured. We encountered flak on all but a half dozen missions. We learned to live with it, but we never became used to it."
—Robert F. Cooper, 385th Bomb Group (H), Eighth USAAF

"The noise is the soft flak. You can't hear it hit the airplane. I remember vividly on a raid . . . it wasn't Schweinfurt. It wasn't that rough on our crew, but it was terrible. We lost about half a dozen planes, and one of them was right in front of me in the formation, and it just absolutely exploded, just a big ball of debris and we could feel that debris hit our airplane, and that was a very unpleasant sensation."
—David Parry, 390th Bomb Group, Eighth USAAF

above: Ambulance personnel on an 8AF base in WW2 England; below: A wounded gunner is helped from his B-17 bomber to a waiting ambulance on the airfield.

"Flak is flak is flak, right? Wrong! Depending upon your mental state, the same flak that on one given mission might only make your mouth dry and your breathing labored could cause near panic. Take for example, our mission of 23 March 1945 to the marshaling yards at Gladbach, Germany. On that day each nearby burst of flak convinced me that the next one would tear our plane out from under us.

"Each time the Fort bucked and rocked as the pilots juggled the throttles and wheels, trying to maintain combat formation, I expected to hear the propellers of another Fort ripping

through our wing or tail surface, sending us scurrying to an escape hatch—a not uncommon occurrence on bomb runs.

"On reaching the Initial Point, our pilot ordered me to begin throwing chaff. On this clear day it was a useless effort, but at least it gave me something to do. I swivelled my seat around, grabbed the foot-long triangular cardboard package of aluminum foil strips and heaved it out of the chaff chute. With my two-piece flak vest tied snugly above each hip and my steel helmet pulled down over my goggles I waited the recommended twenty-second interval and heaved out another batch of chaff. At 25,000 feet with unlimited visibility our squadron began its unwavering run into the target while the enemy flak batteries began tracking our progress. With the ever-closer flak bursts causing our plane to bob and bounce I thought, 'To hell with the twenty-second interval' and started chucking out chaff at the chute as quickly as I could.

"Suddenly, a near burst sent pieces of shrapnel tearing through our airplane's thin skin. I was seeing bright blue and was terrified. The countdown began and, at 'bombs away,' the Fort lurched abruptly upward as it shed its three-ton bomb load. The pilot poured on the power and banked us quickly out of harm's way, and I started to breathe again."
—David C. Lustig, 384th Bomb Group (H), Eighth USAAF

"We put a pressure bandage on Ralph's leg wound, but the temperature at our altitude really did more to stop the bleeding and the blood started to freeze around the wound. I took the morphine out of the first aid kit. The syrette looked like a small tube of toothpaste with a needle on the end. I warmed it up under my heated suit

and aimed the needle at the muscle a few inches from the anterior hole in his thigh. At first I pushed kind of easy, but the darned thing didn't go in, so I shoved hard and it slid into his thigh. Then I squeezed the contents into him and in a few minutes Ralph drifted off to sleep."
—Roger Armstrong, 91st Bomb Group (H), Eighth USAAF

ARMOR, n. A defensive covering, such as chain mail, worn to protect the body against weapons.

Like the medieval knights, the airmen who flew in bombers during World War II were well motivated to protect themselves in any way they could from occupational hazards. They feared flak more than enemy fighters, and many had rather crude items of personal armor made for them by obliging, sympathetic ground personnel.

Late in 1942, at the behest of the Chief Surgeon of the Eighth Air Force, Brigadier General Malcolm Grow, the Wilkinson Sword Company designed and produced a bullet-proof vest composed of overlapping magnesium steel plates. The plate network was covered in heavy canvas and was called a "flak vest" or "flak suit." It was designed to be worn over the parachute harness. It could be removed in a hurry by the use of a pull cord, and it weighed twenty pounds. Production of this personal body armor began in October 1942 and was first worn on an Eighth Bomber Command mission by crews of the 91st Bomb Group (H) on 12 December. Eventually it was determined that, of the personnel wounded by flak shrapnel fragments while wearing the flak vest, two-thirds escaped significant injury.

ANOXIA, n. A pathological deficiency of oxygen.

Many bomber crewmen experienced severe problems from an insufficient supply of oxygen during their missions in World War II. A number of fatalities resulted from faulty or inadequate oxygen equipment in the early days of the British and U.S. bombing offensives in the European Theatre of Operations.

"I knew nothing about the guns, but anything else was supposed to be my department. Oxygen, everything. One night we were over Mont Blanc, on our way to Munich throught the back door. We'd gone over Italy and were coming back over the Alps when Jeff, our pilot, started going a bit weird. Woozy . . . drunk almost. It was lack of oxygen. That's one of the signs. So, I whipped off his pipe. We had portable oxygen bottles strewn about and I put one on him and turned it on full. It took quite some time before it had any effect. He was still woozy and we were going to yank him out of his seat. I could fly the thing. I'd had some instruction and I'd flown it on air tests, as the flight engineer was supposed to fly it in case of an emergency. All I could have done was fly it straight and level so everybody could bale out. Then Jeff came round and said, 'What the hell are you doing?' I said, 'You suffered from lack of oxygen, Jeff. Are you all right now?' I shook his disconnected oxygen tube and ice had collected in it."
—Jack Clift, No 463 Squadron, RAF

Fire, n. A rapid, persistent chemical change that releases heat and light and is accompanied by flame, especially the exothermic oxidation of a combustible substance.

Probably the airman's greatest fear is fire. More than any of his other worries—oxygen starvation, extreme

Flak so thick you could get out and walk on it, was how the aircrews of the Eighth tended to describe this fearsome hazard; below: A wounded gunner is lifted from the waist window of his bomber on its return to England after a raid.

cold, fatigue, frostbite, enemy fighters, and flak—it was the horror of a fire in the aircraft that disturbed the sleep of bomber crewmen and went with them every time they flew.

"On 25 January 1945, we flew on a fighter affiliation training sortie with a Spitfire. After completing the training we started our recovery to base when the port inner engine caught fire. We were unable to put the fire out or to feather the prop. The oil pipeline to the feathering motor had cracked, spraying oil onto the hot engine.

"The fire quickly spread to the whole wing and the aircraft became very difficult to control. Our pilot ordered us to abandon the aircraft. In the Halifax the navigator's seat was over the forward escape hatch so that I was quickly able to fold the seat, put on my parachute, jettison the hatch and jump out.

"We were very low, about 1,500 feet, but the canopy deployed quickly and almost before I had time to look around and see the aircraft plunge into the ground I had landed in a ploughed field.

"A farmer arrived on the scene promptly and took me to his nearby farmhouse where I was able to phone the base, which was only a few miles away. When I arrived back at base I found to my great distress that only the wireless operator had survived and that my pilot and four of the crew had been killed. The bomb aimer was a stand-in as ours had laryngitis. He should have been second out, but he was a young Canadian sergeant who froze. The wireless operator sensibly decided to go next."
—John Curtiss, Nos 578 and 158 Squadrons, RAF

"I was flying a B-52 night training mission out of Bergstrom Air Force Base, Austin, Texas. After the usual lengthy pre-flight, the crew boarded the airplane. We stowed our equipment and strapped ourselves in our ejection seats. We ran the checklists and, with all eight engines running, completed the taxi checklist and received clearance into the number one position for take-off. I aligned the bomber with the runway heading and set the brakes. I set the power, released the brakes and we started to roll.

"The co-pilot adjusted the engine pressure ratios evenly, and all engine instruments checked OK. A hundred things were going through my mind . . . acceleration, engine output, exhaust gas temperatures, what to do in case of an emergency, and many more. I was watching the runway marker boards as they flashed by—12,000 feet of runway with a 2,000-foot over-run marker at 180 knots of airspeed as the airplane got light and began to fly. I climbed to 1,000 feet and started my flaps-up profile, trying not to lose too much altitude. I climbed out to 37,000 feet on an easterly heading and then started a long navigation leg toward Albany, New York. We completed the take-off and climb checklist and settled down for the long, twelve-hour flight.

"At about the four-hour mark I had to go downstairs to relieve myself. There was a fireplug urinal that you could stand at, and while doing this I decided to flip on the bomb bay lights and look in there. I was shocked to see a three-inch stream of jet fuel running on top of the alternator bay to the deck underneath, which had a four-inch lip. The fuel was pouring over the edge onto the tires in the wheel well and down onto the bomb bay. As I snapped up, I studied the situation. I went over to where the navigator was sitting and told him what was happening. His eyes got as big as saucers and he said something about baling out. I said, 'No, but plot me a course that will take me back to Bergstrom, avoiding any populated areas.' I went back up the ladder to my seat and told Tom, my co-pilot, about the situation in the bomb bay and asked him about the fuel state. He said that about 10,000 gallons or 60,000 pounds were missing. I didn't know then that the Marmon clamp, which held the three-inch fuel lines together at the top of the fuselage, had come apart and no amount of valve closing or cross-feeding would stop the flow of fuel.

"The alternator deck was located just below the four alternators which supplied electrical AC power to the aircraft, and was now full of JP5 fuel. The alternators were evidently vapor-proof as they did not create sparks that might have ignited the fuel fumes.

"Tom brought up the question of our ejecting, and I said, 'No, not yet.' I banked the airplane five degrees and headed back to Texas. I then called the SAC Command Post and told them about our problem. I said that I was not transferring fuel across the airplane and that I had more than 10,000 gallons of JP5 running out into the alternator bay. They asked about my intentions and I said I would continue the flight back to Bergstrom. They asked if we intended to eject, and they left that to my discretion.

"We arrived back in the Bergstrom area where it was still dark. We had returned there at 44,000 feet to conserve fuel, and we were still losing fuel at the same rate and had now lost some 20,000 gallons, We had a major leak.

"As the sky became lighter, I called our base. They knew what was going on as they had been monitoring the SAC Command frequency. I set us up in a holding pattern in the Bergstrom area and asked the radar operator to go take a look in the bomb bay. He said I would have to give him a direct order to do so, and I decided to go myself. I went back downstairs and saw to my dismay that the fuel was still pouring out of the three-inch pipe at the same rate. I then returned to my seat, strapped in with oxygen mask on and the bale-out bottle knob in a handy position, and advised everyone to get ready for a quick ejection. Some of the crew said that they wanted to eject, but I told them that there was nothing electrical that wasn't vapor-protected, and that it was safe. They reluctantly agreed. I then ordered the radar operator to open the bomb bay doors. At Bergstrom they had a telephoto camera aimed at us and we were in good range as we had now descended to 6,000 feet, the minimum bale-out altitude. The bomb doors opened and all 20,000 gallons of fuel seemed to evaporate in an instant, but some of it covered the airplane. The engine exhaust then ignited it and there was a big flash, but we flew out of the flash in one piece.

"All of the fuel that had accumulated in the bomb bay was now gone, but there was a fuel stream coming out through the bomb bay doors, which could certainly be lethal. We were now very low on fuel, having flown some seven hours, and we needed to land soon. I had Tom lower the flaps and they worked fine, as the flap motors were sealed. Next came the landing gear. We had steel-impregnated tires, which meant that we could land on ice, snow, or a wet runway and have a good co-efficient of friction for stopping the plane. But all of the four forward tires were saturated with jet fuel and I expected them to lay a trough

of fire when we touched down. I lowered the gear and again nothing happened, except for more streaming fuel. I flew the downwind leg to the north, turned base and final and approached the end of the runway at 145 knots indicated. We touched down at the 1,000-foot marker. It was a smooth landing, but as soon as we touched, a streak of flame erupted from the tires and they began to burn the fuel that had soaked into them.

"I braked hard and had Tom pull the drag chute; we stopped in 7,000 feet. I immediately cut the eight engines and rang the bell to evacuate the airplane. I was out of my harness and behind Tom as we jumped down the ladder and out of the bottom of the plane, where the fire was burning real well. We ran ahead of the airplane and off the left wing to our crew assembly point in case of a crash-landing.

"The crash crew arrived with their foam and hoses. They had to go into the bomb bay to squirt foam up into the alternator deck. It took them thirty minutes to get the fire under control and put out all of the smouldering tires. A crew bus picked us up and took us to the maintenance debriefing room. All the 'wheels' were there wanting to know what had happened. After cleaning up the foam, the maintenance inspectors looked at the Marmon clamps and saw what had happened. They wired SAC headquarters and Boeing in Seattle. All B-52s were promptly grounded until they had been inspected. A permanent fix was made and all of the clamps were changed. For us it had been a rather hair-raising experience."
—Joseph Anastasia, B-52 pilot, U.S. Air Force

FATIGUE, n. Physical or mental weariness resulting from exertion.

"We would make runs in formation, on fictitious targets in England, get back to base, and make some instrument approaches and landings for hours—just touch the wheels down, give it the gun, go around, and come back for another. All the time there was something to do—work on your radio operator's speed, your engineer's know-how, there was always training to do. We carried a very high fatigue factor at that time. If I had five minutes in a chow line I could go to sleep standing up."
—Lawrence Drew, B-17 pilot, 384th Bomb Group (H), Eighth USAAF

"I remember that period of forty hours in which I flew three ops. On 14 October 1944, Harmer, our pilot, was grounded with a cold. Flying Officer Lewis needed a bomb aimer, so I went along with him to Duisburg in daylight. I had just gone to bed when I was dragged out to go to Duisburg again with Lewis. Take-off at 00.39 on 15 October. It was a bad trip. We could see the target burning 100 miles away, from our morning attack. There were nightfighters around and we were nearly coned by searchlights over the target. I began to appreciate the talents of my own crew. So, I got back home, ate my bacon and eggs with sleepy eyes, and suddenly found that I was scheduled for another trip, with Harmer and my own crew, at 1800. I napped for a couple of hours in the mess, checked my bomb load, perspex, guns, circuits—check, check, check—dozed through the ops briefing, and took off for Wilhelmshaven. On the way home I could hardly keep my eyes open, but I was with my own crew so it didn't really matter. At the interrogation, the squadron commander suddenly realized that I had been out on the last three. He was impressed. I was not—

all I wanted was a bed. One more, to Essen, and my tour was over. Thirty-nine trips."
—Ken Roberts, No 158 Squadron, RAF

"The people playing poker in our Nissen hut had the lights on, and they would play all night. An officer said, 'C'mon fellas, have a heart—some

guys have got to fly tomorrow.' They just said something back to him and went right on playing. So, he took a .45 from the head of his bed, walked down the line and shot all those lights out. We had it dark in there after that, for the rest of the night anyway.
—Lawrence Drew, B-17 pilot, 384th Bomb Group (H), Eighth USAAF

left: Administering a transusion under the wing of an 8AF bomber; here: Examining flak damage in the skin of an RAF heavy bomber.

The result of a collision at Thorpe Abbotts, the base of the 100th Bomb Group, on 27 December 1943. The gropup suffered appalling operational losses and became known in the Eighth Air Force as the "Bloody 100th."

WEATHER, n. The state of the atmosphere at a given time and place, with respect to variables such as temperature, moisture, wind velocity, and barometric pressure. Adverse or destructive conditions such as high winds or heavy rain.

December 1940. The crews of RAF Bomber Command were operating in the worst European weather in living memory. The Hampdens, Wellingtons, and Whitleys they flew in were being subjected to ice that formed on their wings, in their turrets and hydraulic systems, instruments and radio equipment, causing catastrophic malfunctions. Perspex windscreens were opaqued, bringing cockpit visibility down to zero. Airmen whose jobs required them to remove their leather gauntlets and lining gloves to attend to some essential task, risked severe frostbite. If they were unfortunate enough to touch bare skin to any

metal surface in the aircraft while at the sub-zero temperatures of high altitude, their flesh would freeze instantly to that metal.

Flying missions at high altitude in the big, heavy Liberators, Lancasters, Fortresses, and Halifaxes meant prolonged exposure to extreme cold and the hazards it could bring. Frostbite was a very real concern for the men who flew in the bombers of World War II. For the unfortunate airmen who experienced this injury, exposure to the bitter -20 to -50° F cold at operational altitudes could and did bring about the destruction of the skin and underlying tissues of the nose, ears, fingers, and toes. To combat this natural enemy, specially-designed flying clothing had to be worn. Often, it failed to provide the necessary levels of protection, and led to additional problems for already overburdened aircrew. The General Electric F-1

"blue bunny suit" first utilized by the B-17 and B-24 gunners of the Eighth Air Force in the winter of 1942-43 had an inherent flaw. Its wiring tended to short out and the suit then failed. It happened so often that the majority of those using the suit elected to wear additional heavy fleece-lined leather flying clothing over the electric suit. In addition, gunners wore electrically-heated gloves and boots.

They were also provided with electric muffs for use on hands and feet should the gloves or boots fail. Instead of trusting the reliability of the various electrically-heated garments, many airmen chose to wear a suit of thick pile sheepskin that included a B-6 jacket and A-5 trousers. This outfit was worn over heavy woolen underwear, usually long johns, two pairs of wool socks, sometime a pair of felt, electrically-heated moccasins, a shearling-lined helmet and standard A-6 boots. Pilots had the problem of

The sad end of a Liberator.

keeping their hands warm while being unable to properly feel the cockpit controls through the heavy or heated flying gloves issued at the time. Many wore a thin silk glove under a relatively thin USAAF-issue A-10 goatskin winter flying glove, providing reasonable warmth and allowing enough sensitivity. With cockpit heating, pilots and co-pilots were often comfortable wearing their A-2 leather flying jackets.

As the war progressed, so too did the efficiency of garments developed for the Allied bomber air crews, and the overly bulky, cumbersome and awkward togs of the war's middle years gave way to ones of greater comfort and reliability.

"It was fairly cold in the Nissen hut and we never did have enough coal to heat it well. People were forever tossing CO_2 cartridges into our stove. You'd be backed up to it on a cold day, when all of a sudden it would just

blow up and hot coals would fly all over the place and scare everybody."
—Lawrence Drew, pilot, 384th Bomb Group (H), Eighth USAAF

"No bomber went off without a rear gunner. I went up in a Wellington, just an air test with a squadron leader up in Scotland near Lossiemouth, and I think he forgot about me. He said we were not going far. He just wanted to air-test it and he went up about 10,000 feet. I hadn't got any gear on at all. Mae West and parachute. No flying gloves. Nothing. Ended up nearly frostbitten on my fingers and hands. To this day they get white when its cold. Hands are always cold in there. It was dreadfully cold in the tail of the Halifax. You had no heating. You had an electric suit. Sometimes they worked all right. Sometimes. But if you got a duff one, you wouldn't know it until you plugged in. I had four

guns, .303 Brownings, and we had a removable slide in the turret, so we were completely open there, along with two panels at the side which we removed as well. At night, when you are looking out, the least little speck on that turret, after four hours of looking, that speck is a German fighter. You keep coming back to it and you convince yourself it's a fighter. So you remove the panels to see better. Of course, you have your goggles up on your forehead. We never had them on over our eyes. You could see better without them. But, oh, the cold. I had both my eyes operated on while I was in the Air Force, for cysts from the cold."
—Fred Allen, No 158 Squadron, RAF

"The weather reports were real inaccurate, so if they said you should break out of the clouds at 1,500 feet, it might actually be 18,000 feet—and I

recall one time when it was."
—Ray Wild, pilot, 92nd Bomb Group (H), Eighth USAAF

FEAR, n. A feeling of agitation and anxiety caused by the presence or imminence of danger.

"There is an old saying which goes something like this: 'Cowards die many deaths, but a brave man dies but one.' If this saying be true, then I am not only a coward myself, I am fighting the war with a lot of other cowards. A story in the Eighth Air Force tells about a group commander who read an advertisement in a magazine which asked the question, 'Who's afraid of the new Focke-Wulf?' This group commander cut out the ad, signed his name to it and pinned it on the group bulletin board. After all of the pilots in the group had confessed their fear by signing, the page was mailed back to the U.S. advertiser.

"We are all afraid and only liars or fools fail to admit it. There are a variety of possible deaths which face a member of a bomber crew and each man is free to choose his own pet fear. A tire could blow out or an engine could fail on take-off. The oxygen system or electric heating system might fail at high altitude. There is the fear of explosion or mid-air collision while flying formation. In addition to these there is the ever-present possibility of being shot down by enemy fighters or anti-aircraft fire.

"In dealing with the enemy, there is a certain feeling of helplessness about the bomber business which I find to be very distasteful. Imagine, for a moment, that you are required to carry two five-gallon cans of gasoline down a dark alley. These cans weigh over thirty pounds each so your hands are full and you can't run very fast. As you pass a certain corner in this alley, you know

that a number of thugs are waiting to club you as you pass. However, there is a policeman patrolling this beat (your fighter escort) and if he happens to be at the dangerous corners at the time you arrive, then everything will be OK, unless, of course, there are more thugs than the policeman can handle. Some of the thugs don't attack with clubs, but stand back (out of sight) and throw firecrackers at your cans of gasoline.

"The bomber pilot can't fight back, but must just sit there and take it. I believe this explains why there is such a difference between the bomber and fighter boys. The man in this latter group can match his skill against the enemy. He carries a club of his own with which to fight back. I do not find the light-hearted, devil-may-care spirit on the bomber station which has been so often described in stories about pilots in the last war. Our men go about their grim business with sober determination. When we are alerted for a mission, the bar closes early and everyone goes to bed. To be sure, at our monthly parties, if there is no mission the next day, the boys get pretty drunk. I do not discourage this as I feel it gives them a much-needed chance to blow off some steam.

"When a new crew arrives on the station I try to have a talk with the men during the first twenty-four hours after arrival. One of the points stressed is that we are all afraid. I tell them that the worst part of a mission is just before the take-off. If they can 'sweat it out' through this period, they will get through the rest all right. The flight surgeons are particularly helpful in spotting men who are showing signs of anxiety. If a crew goes through a particularly rough mission and is badly shot up, we try to send them to the 'flak house' (rest home) for a week. In fact, all crews are sent to the flak house for a rest at some time during their combat

tour. Although I never find time to get to one of these rest homes myself, I am told that they are well run and very successful.

"Winston Churchill's personal physician, Lord Moran, wrote a book about courage in combat. I like his definition of courage: 'a moral quality . . . not a chance gift of nature like an aptitude for games. It is a cold choice between two alternatives, the fixed resolve not to quit; an act of renunciation which must be made not once but many times by the power of the will . . . Some men were able to see more clearly that there was no decent alternative to sticking it out and to see this not in a hot moment of impulse but steadily through many months of trial. They understood on what terms life was worthwhile.' "
—from the World War II letters of Major General John M. Bennett, Jr, a commander of the 100th Bomb Group (H), Eighth USAAF, to his father.

HAZARD, n. A chance of being injured or harmed; danger.

"I arrived at No 19 Operational Training Unit, RAF Kinloss in Scotland around 10 November 1940 and was greeted with the news that nineteen aircrew had been killed during training in the previous week, which was rather daunting. The morning after our arrival, I was asked to escort a coffin to the railway station. There was only one casualty on our course—a trainee who went under the wing of a Whitley bomber to pick up a practice bomb that had fallen off. He was struck by a propeller and suffered brain damage. Generally, training was more or less incident-free."
—Alfred S. Tarry, No 51 Squadron, RAF

Severe flak damage to the cockpit of this B-24 Liberator.

FIGHTERS

Lieutenant Colonel Beirne Lay, Jr, who after the war co-authored *Twelve O'Clock High!*, among the finest books and films about the Second World War, was co-pilot of an Eighth Air Force B-17 on the Regensburg raid of 17 August 1943. The target was the Messerschmitt factory where Me 109 fighters were being assembled, a target of prime importance both to those who planned the missions of the Eighth, and to the young men who had to fly them. "The fear was unpleasant, but it was bearable. I knew that I was going to die, and so were a lot of others . . .

"A few minutes later we absorbed the first wave of a hailstorm of individual fighter attacks that were to engulf us clear to the target in such a blizzard of bullets and shells that a chronological account is difficult. It was 10:41 a.m. over Eupen, that I looked out the window after a minute's lull, and saw two whole squadrons, twelve Me 109s and eleven Fw 190s climbing parallel to us as though they were on a steep escalator. The first squadron had reached our level and was pulling ahead to turn into us. The second was not far behind. Several thousand feet below us were many more fighters, their noses cocked up in a maximum climb. Over the interphone came reports of an equal number of enemy aircraft deploying on the other side of the formation.

"For the first time I noticed an Me 110 sitting out of range on our level out to the right. He was to stay with us all the way to the target, apparently radioing our position and weak spots to fresh Staffeln waiting farther down the road.

"At the sight of all these fighters,

I had the distinct feeling of being trapped—that the Hun had been tipped off or at least had guessed our destination and was set for us. We were already through the German fighter belt. Obviously, they had moved a lot of squadrons back in a fluid defense in depth, and they must have been saving up some outfits for the inner defense that we didn't know about. The life expectancy of our group seemed definitely limited, since it had already appeared that the fighters, instead of wasting fuel trying to overhaul the preceding groups, were glad to take a cut at us.

"Swinging their yellow noses around in a wide U-turn, the twelve-ship squadron of Me 109s came in from twelve to two o'clock in pairs. The main event was on. I fought an impulse to close my eyes, and overcame it.

"A shining silver rectangle of metal sailed past over our right wing. I recognized it as a main exit door. Seconds later a black lump came hurtling through the formation, barely missing several propellers. It was a man, clasping his knees to his head, revolving like a diver in a triple somersault, shooting by us so close that I saw a piece of paper blow out of his leather jacket. He was evidently making a delayed jump, for I didn't see his parachute open.

"A B-17 turned gradually out of the formation to the right, maintaining altitude. In a split second it completely vanished in a brilliant explosion, from which the only remains were four balls of fire, the fuel tanks, which were quickly consumed as they fell earthward.

"I saw blue, red, yellow, and aluminum-colored fighters. Their tactics were running fairly true to form, with frontal attacks hitting the low squadron and rear attackers going for the

lead and high squadrons. Some of the Jerries shot at us with rockets, and an attempt at air-to-air bombing was made with little black time-fuse sticks, dropped from above, which exploded in small grey puffs off to one side of the formation. Several of the Fws did some nice deflection shooting on side attacks from 500 yards at the high group, then raked the low group on the breakaway at closer range with their noses cocked in a side-slip, to keep the formation in their sights longer in the turn. External fuel tanks were visible under the bellies or wings of at least two squadrons, shedding uncomfortable light on the mystery of their ability to tail us so far from their bases.

"The manner of the assaults indicated that the pilots knew where we were going and were inspired with a fanatical determination to stop us before we got there. Many pressed attacks home to 250 yards or less, or bolted through the formation wide open, firing long bursts, often presenting point-blank targets on the breakaway. Some committed the fatal error of pulling up instead of going down and out. More experienced pilots came in on frontal attacks with a noticeably slower rate of closure, apparently throttled back, obtaining greater accuracy. But no tactics could halt the close-knit juggernauts of our Fortresses, nor save the single-seaters from paying a terrible price.

"Our airplane was endangered by various debris. Emergency hatches, exit doors, prematurely opened parachutes, bodies, and assorted fragments of B-17s and Hun fighters breezed past us in the slipstream.

"I watched two fighters explode not far beneath, disappear in sheets of orange flame; B-17s dropping out in every stage of distress, from engines on fire to controls shot away; friendly

German fighter ace Adolf Galland flew 705 combat missions on the Western Front and in the Defense of the Reich. He was credited with 104 aerial victories, all in action against the Western Allies.

left: Bombing up on a hardstand adjacent to a farm on the airfield property. Airmen on the bases of the Eighth often bought "real" eggs from their farm neighbors, rather than eat the powdered eggs served in the mess; right: The control tower at RAF Tangmere where some of the escort fighters were based.

and enemy parachutes floating down, and, on the green carpet far below us, funeral pyres of smoke from fallen fighters, marking our trail.

"I took the controls for a while. The first thing I saw when Murphy resumed flying was a B-17 turning slowly out to the right, its cockpit a mass of flames. The co-pilot crawled out of his window, held on with one hand, reached back for his parachute, buckled it on, let go and was whisked back into the horizontal stabilizer of

the tail. I believe the impact killed him. His parachute didn't open.

"I looked forward and almost ducked as I watched the tail gunner of a B-17 ahead of us take a bead right on our windshield and cut loose with a stream of tracers that missed us by a few feet as he fired on a fighter attacking us from six o'clock low. I almost ducked again when our own top-turret gunner's twin muzzles pounded away a foot above my head in the full forward position, giving a

realistic imitation of cannon shells exploding in the cockpit, while I gave a better imitation of a man jumping six inches out of his seat.

"Still no let-up. The fighters queued up like a bread line and let us have it. Each second of time had a cannon shell in it. The strain of being a clay duck in the wrong end of that shooting gallery became almost intolerable. Our plane, *Piccadilly Lily,* shook steadily with the fire of its .50s and the air inside was wispy with smoke. I checked the engine

instruments for the thousandth time. Normal. No injured crew members yet.

"Near the Initial Point, at 11:50, one hour and a half after the first of at least 200 individual fighter attacks, the pressure eased off, although hostiles were still in the vicinity. Almost idly I watched a crippled B-17 pull over to the kerb and drop its wheels and open its bomb bay, jettisoning its bombs. Three Me 109s circled it closely, but held their fire while the crew baled out. I remembered now

that a little while back I had seen other Hun fighters hold their fire, even when being shot at by a B-17 from which the crew were baling out. But I doubt if sportsmanship had anything to do with it. They hoped to get a B-17 down fairly intact.

"And then our weary, battered column, short twenty-four bombers, but still holding the close formation that had brought the remainder through by sheer air discipline and gunnery, turned in to the target. I

knew that our bombardiers were grim as death while they synchronized their sights on the Me 109 shops lying below us in a curve of the winding blue Danube, close to the outskirts of Regensburg. Our B-17 gave a slight lift and a red light went out on the instrument panel. Our bombs were away. We turned from the target toward the snow-capped Alps. I looked back and saw a beautiful sight—a rectangular pillar of smoke rising from the Me 109 plant. Only one burst was over and into the town. I could see that we had smeared the objective."

"When a Fortress goes down it doesn't suddenly go into a violent manoeuvre. Everything seems to happen very slowly. The first thing you notice is a thin trail of smoke, usually from one of the engines. The ship then slowly turns out of the formation and starts losing altitude. At this point he's a dead duck for enemy fighters because he doesn't have the supporting firepower of the rest of the ships. Now its course may follow any number of general patterns of behavior. The fire in one ship increases as the gasoline tanks in the wing begin to burn. Parachutes begin to blossom out as the crew abandons ship. As the wing becomes enveloped in flame, there is an explosion and there's practically nothing left but four orange balls of fire. These are the main gas tanks.

"Another ship burns hardly at all but goes into an ever-tightening turn until it spins. As it goes down twisting, the tail come off and you may see three or four 'chutes as the gunner are thrown out. Because of centrifugal force the pilot and co-pilot don't usually get out. This ship slowly disintegrates as increasing speed tears it apart."
—from the World War II letters of Major General John M. Bennett, Jr, a commander of the 100th Bomb Group (H), Eighth USAAF, to his father.

The favorite mount of Feldwebel Oscar Boesch of IV Gruppe, 3JG, German Air Force, was the Fw 190-A8. In it he downed eight four-engined heavy bombers and ten Allied fighters. "On 8 May 1944, I was diving and firing at a B-24 formation when I ran out of ammunition midway through my firing pass. I decided to ram a B-24 and aimed at one of the bomber's ailerons. However, the turbulence was so severe that I missed.

above: John Godfrey, wingman of Don Gentile, both of them great aces of the 4th Fighter Group.

I found myself out in front of some B-24s in a vertical dive. My Fw was being shredded by many impacting shells. At 26,000 feet I baled out and was lucky to get out because my aircraft was in a dive at full throttle, going more than 800 kph. I was also lucky because I did not hit the tail of my aircraft. Being machine-gunned in our 'chutes was always our concern when baling out, and I fell 25,000 feet before opening my 'chute at 1,000 feet above Goslar."

No 433 Squadron, RCAF pilot Ray Mountford was flying a Halifax bomber near Bonn, Germany, on the way back to England after attacking a target at Bochum in 1944. A German nightfighter rose to meet the bomber, flying straight up into Ray's starboard inner engine and starting an uncontrollable fire. The crew's only option was to abandon the aircraft as quickly as they could. Ray gave the order and stayed at the controls of the crippled Halifax to keep the plane level while

above left: Horst Petzschler and above right: Werner Mölders, distinguished Luftwaffe fighter pilots.

of them out of the formation, and all seven of us students fired from all directions, trying to shoot it down. We opened fire from a thousand yards away and, naturally, had no success. You had to go in closer to score hits. All of the other B-17s flew home to England. The one that had been hit flew south and crashed near Orléans. We counted ten parachutes. All the crew baled out between Paris and Orléans. When we flew home and reported to Colonel Leppla, our school commander, he wanted to put us all in jail for our behavior. 'Next time,' he told us, 'they will come with escort. You missed your great chance.' We did. The next time they did come with escort and we 'felt' it."

Gordon Wright, a bomb aimer on Stirlings at RAF Mildenhall, was shot down while on an op to Kassel in west-central Germany on 3 October 1943. On the way to the target that evening, Wright made his way back to relieve the wireless operator of the task of throwing out bundles of "window," the thin strips of silver foil paper dropped by Allied bombers to confuse German radar images. He began the job there on the floor of the Stirling just in front of the main spar.

After only a few minutes of ejecting the window, Wright heard the rear gunner tell the pilot. "Go port." The gunner had spotted a German fighter closing quickly on their bomber and the pilot immediately began the diving maneuver to port. Just as he did so, the rear gunner began firing at the fighter and at almost the same instant the German opened fire on the Stirling, raking the big bomber with hits from tail to cockpit.

Though seriously wounded in the right hip, the wireless operator came forward at this point. The navigator had left his table to confer with the

his crew baled out. When at last he released his grip on the control column he was thrown violently out of the nearby hatch, hitting his head on the way out and lapsing into unconsciousness. Freefalling, he revived just in time to pull the D-ring and deploy his parachute. After a hard landing he made a kind of tent arrangement of his parachute and paused to collect his thoughts and have a cigarette. It was midnight and he found that he had lost his flying boots and his socks in the descent. He then noticed a light in a house near the field where he had fallen, and walked to the house in his bare feet. He knocked and a lady answered the door. He told her he was an "Englander" and she invited him into her home. There was a man in the house, and a teenage girl who could speak some English. The woman treated him kindly, bathing his feet. She then gave him a pair of slippers and showed him a photo of her son, a German airman who had been lost over England. Shortly thereafter, the man left the house and soon the Gestapo arrived with drawn guns. Ray spent the rest of the war in Stalag Luft III at Sagan, Silesia.

Horst Petzschler, of JG3 and JG51, flew 297 combat sorties in Me 109s and Fw 190s and was credited with twenty-six confirmed victories, including twenty-two Russian, one B-17, one B-24, and two P-51s. In his combat career he was shot down thirteen times, survived eleven crash-landings and two bale-outs. Every time he was shot down it was by flak, except once, on 28 May 1944, when a Mustang brought him down near Magdeburg.

"We students had barely flown four hours on the new Fw 190-A2 type fighter, with as yet no air-to-air shooting practice. We took off to do a job we had not yet been trained to do. Over the city of Paris we intercepted the shiny, silver B-17s at about 24,000 feet. Our instructor shot one

pilot about their position. He then returned to his table to try and recover his maps which were being blown around in the fuselage due to a large hole that had been blasted just above his position. Had he been sitting there during the fighter attack, he would almost certainly have been killed instantly. Now the dazed and injured wireless operator reached the navigator and asked him what they were going to do. Gordon Wright joined them by stepping carefully over the body of the flight engineer, who had been killed in the attack. The pilot, who was struggling to keep the crippled bomber stabilized, then gave the order, "Abandon aircraft."

Wright responded quickly, grabbing the pilot's parachute from behind his seat and fastening it onto his skipper. He then followed the wireless operator to the front exit in the nose, followed by the navigator. When he reached the escape hatch he found it had slammed shut again. Now the Stirling, in its death throes, was entering a slow spiral, pinning the navigator alternately to the floor or the ceiling and frustrating his attempts to leave the plane. Finally, he managed to open the hatch again and, after contacting the pilot, baled out. With the Stirling now down to less than 3,000 feet, the pilot was able to switch on the "George" autopilot, leave his seat and make his way forward to the escape hatch, only to find that it had once again slammed shut. The big bomber

left: The cockpit of a North American P-51 Mustang escort fighter, this example is under restoration in England; below: A fuel filler cap from a B-17 bomber, found near the remains of a hardstand on the former Grafton Underwood airfield site.

continued to spiral downward, the center section of the right wing now burning furiously, and the 6,000-pound load of incendiaries remained in the bomb bay. With the disabled hydraulic system, the crew had been unable to get rid of the bomb load as the bomb doors could not be opened.

The Stirling fell through a height of 1,500 feet when the pilot at last got to the escape hatch and somehow re-opened it. He left the aircraft with no time to spare.

"On beginning my third operational tour in 1944, I took command of No 138 (Special Duties) Squadron at Tempsford. Our task was to drop agents and supplies to Resistance groups in enemy-occupied countries of Europe. We usually operated during the moon period to have the best chance of locating the dropping zones. While these conditions assisted navigation, they also helped enemy fighters. We flew as low as possible to avoid detection. I recall one occasion

on a sortie to Belgium when we were attacked by an Me 110. He came in fast, unseen by my rear gunner, and overshot. My upper gunner spotted him first off our starboard wing silhouetted against a full moon We were higher than usual because of the terrain. I immediately descended, taking evasive action at the same time while the gunner opened fire. The enemy fighter dived and got below us where he could use his upward-firing cannons. My bomb aimer took up posi-

tion in the nose of the Halifax from where he opened fire while I continued to take evasive action. I kept decreasing height until my navigator warned me that we were lower than some of the hills ahead. The enemy pilot must have realized the danger as well, and with a parting burst broke away—probably like us—unscathed. We carried on to our dropping zones but found no reception. We later learned that there were enemy forces in the area and the Resistance had to abandon the DZ. On the return journey, we saw two of our aircraft shot down in flames near the place where we had been attacked. We learned subsequently that a Luftwaffe nightfighter training school was in operation near our route. Our attacker must have been a trainee as nightfighter attacks were usually more conclusive. We had been lucky."
—Wilfred Burnett, Nos 76, 49, 408, 138 and 148 Squadrons, RAF

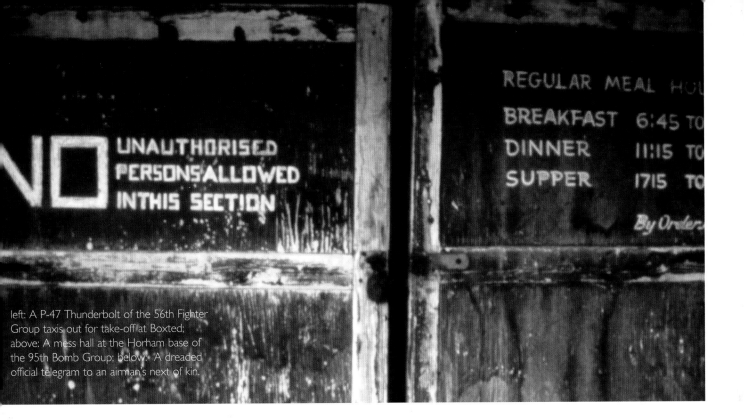

left: A P-47 Thunderbolt of the 56th Fighter Group taxis out for take-off at Boxted; above: A mess hall at the Horham base of the 95th Bomb Group; below: A dreaded official telegram to an airman's next of kin.

REGULAR MEAL HOU

BREAKFAST 6:45 TO
DINNER 11:15 TO
SUPPER 1715 TO

By Order

NO UNAUTHORISED PERSONS ALLOWED IN THIS SECTION

STANDARD TIME INDICATED
CEIVED AT
Grand Central Air Terminal
Glendale, Calif.

Postal Telegraph
Mackay Radio   All America Cables
                      Canadian Pacific Telegraphs

THIS IS A FULL RATE TELEGRAM, CABLE-GRAM OR RADIOGRAM UNLESS OTHERWISE INDICATED BY SYMBOL IN THE PREAMBLE OR IN THE ADDRESS OF THE MESSAGE. SYMBOLS DESIGNATING SERVICE SELECTED ARE OUTLINED IN THE COMPANYS TARIFFS ON HAND AT EACH OFFICE AND ON FILE WITH REGULATOR AUTHORITIES.

AUG 25 PM 4 54

S-NB361   N-WC318

LA348W (TWO) 40GOVT= PXXWMU WASHINGTON DC 25 538P=

MRS MYRTIS P TYLER=

916 MANNING ST (BURBANK CALIF)=

I REGRET TO INFORM YOU REPORT RECEIVED STATES YOUR SO

TECHNICAL SERGEANT ALBERT P TYLER MISSING IN ACTION IN

EUROPEAN AREA SINCE SIXTEEN AUGUST IF FURTHER DETAILS OR OTHER

INFORMATION OF HIS STATUS ARE RECEIVED YOU WILL BE PROMPTLY

NOTIFIED=

      JL10 THE ADJUTANT GENERAL=

FOR VICTORY
BUY
UNITED STATES
WAR
SAVINGS
BONDS
STAMPS

LANCASTER

Sir Arthur Harris took over RAF Bomber Command in February 1942 and soon directed: "It has been decided that the primary objective of your operations should now be focused on the morale of the enemy civil population and in particular, of the industrial workers."

Many of her crews owe their lives to the strength and power of the Avro Lancaster bomber. One such crew was that of my late friend and former co-author, Lancaster pilot Squadron Leader Jack Currie, DFC. From his fine book *Lancaster Target*: "Hamburg had taken a terrible pounding while we were enjoying our first leave from Wickenby at the end of July. We returned in time to help deliver the final blow on Monday, 2 August. We started DV190 Baker Two's engines at 11:30 p.m., and took off twenty minutes later. We circled base on the climb and emerged into a clear sky at about 9,000 feet, setting course for Mablethorpe twenty-five minutes after midnight. An hour and ten minutes later we were roughly thirty miles west of Heligoland and in trouble. One port engine was giving no power, the airspeed indicator had iced up and the 19,000 feet of altitude that we had struggled to attain were steadily slipping away. Paths became more difficult to find between the towering thunderclouds that had built up over the North Sea, and whenever the turbulent masses closed about us Baker Two took on more ice and fell another couple of hundred feet.

"Johnny Walker left the cabin and crawled aft. The Command's new

A still from the 1955 movie *The Dam Busters* which told the story of the May 1943 attack by RAF Lancaster bombers on the great dams of the Ruhr Valley, Germany.

Air crewmen on an RAF heavy bomber station in wartime England, awaiting transport to their aircraft for a raid.

tactic to confuse the enemy was the use of 'window,' thin strips of metal foil, and Walker's chilly task was to drop them through the flare chute in the dark and shaking fuselage. Fairbairn left his radio compartment to assist, remarking as he went, with his usual regard for accuracy, that ice on the aerials had increased their diameter from 3/16 of an inch to 1 1/2 inches, and was still growing.

"We plunged on southeast for thirty minutes, as hail beat harshly on the canopy and mauve light flickered about the aerials and front guns. Vivid stabs of lightning opened sudden gorges in the sky, then swirling vapour wrapped us round again. I felt the ice begin to grip the aircraft, now losing height more rapidly. I spoke to the navigator. 'Where are we, Jimmy?' 'Should be about twenty miles south of the target, but I haven't had a fix for some time. Can you see any flares?' 'Can't see anything but cumulo-nimbus.'

"The bombs fell into the storm from 14,000 feet. Baker Two leaped at their release and settled into a slow and lurching climb. At 18,000 feet we broke into a shaft of clear air as lightning played among the anvil-headed clouds. Then the guns found us, and the aircraft shook and rattled as the shells burst close. As I turned to miss them, the cloud enveloped us again, and now its icy grip became like iron. Within seconds the thirty-ton bomber was a toy for the storm to play with, the wheel locked, immobile as a rock. Baker Two was out of my control.

"I could see nothing through the window, nothing but a blue, infernal glow. I heard no engines, only roaring wind and savage thunderclaps. For the first time in the air, I felt impotence and, with that, a sudden prick of panic. There was nothing I could do—and yet surely I must do something. I held the wheel, watched the instruments,

An RAF Lancaster heavy bomber and its ground service crew.

and waited for a clue to action. The instruments belied each other: no air-speed, but climbing fast.

"I felt the stall. The harness straps were pressing hard on my shoulders, my legs were light, loose objects fell about the cabin. Was I hanging in my harness upside-down, or was the aircraft falling faster than my weight? I tried to reject the evidence of the whirling gyro-controlled instruments and to believe the others, which showed nose down, a spin to port, and mounting speed. The ASI had left its ice-bound stop, and was swinging round the dial a second time.

"Pilot to crew, prepare to abandon aircraft—prepare to abandon.'

"I tried to judge the rate of our descent, and chose 8,000 feet as the height where I must tell the crew to jump. They had to get the hatches open, and push themselves into the roaring slipstream, and still leave time for me to follow, before we fell too low to give the silken canopies time to open.

"I don't know whether Baker Two or I recovered from the spin, but now there was only the tearing rush of wind, and the steady movement clockwise of the ASI. The needle made a second circuit of the dial, and verged upon the limit of its travel at 400 miles per hour. If the pitot head were free of ice, so might be the elevators; I pulled back on the wheel with all my strength, as the altimeter read 10,000 feet. At 9,000 feet the wheel jerked violently in my hands, still I pulled slowly felt my weight increase, and press into the seat, as the diving angle decreased. Briefly, we emerged below the cloud base, and shot up into it again as I struggled with the wheel.

"At last, I found a level attitude at 8,000 feet, and brought the ASI

back into the realm of reason. But there was something badly wrong: the wheel, although answering my back and forward pressures to climb or dive, wagged loosely left and right without response from either aileron to bank or turn. I wondered if the control cables had snapped—that might have been the violent tremor of the wheel. I pushed the rudders alternately, and Baker Two yawed gently in reply.

" 'OK, I've got some control now. Let's have an intercom check—rear gunner?'
No reply from Charlie Lanham.
'Mid-upper?'
'Mid-upper OK, Skipper.'
'Wireless operator?'
'Wireless operator strength nine.'
'Any idea what's happened to Johnny?'
'Last time I saw him, we were both floating up and down the fuselage like a brace of pheasants on the glorious twelfth.'
'OK, Charlie, go back and see if you can find him. And check the rear gunner too.'
'Wireless op going off intercom.'

"Fairbairn's microphone clicked off, and I continued with the roll call.
'Navigator?'
'Navigator loud and clear.'
'Bomb aimer?'
'Bomb aimer OK, Skip.'
Cassidy could hardly wait for the bomb aimer to reply before he called.
'What course are you on?' I spun the compass dial.
'210 magnetic.'
'You're heading straight for Bremen. Turn on to 330.'
'330. I'll try.'
'Mid-upper to Skipper. A bloody great piece of your starboard wing is miss-ing—did you know? Jesus, the port wing's the same.'
'Thanks, George.'

"So, that was it. Both ailerons had been torn off in that screaming, spin-ning dive. I pushed the starboard rud-der, and Baker Two veered right for a few degrees, wings level, and then swung back as I released the pressure on the rudder. I tried again, held the pressure on, and pulled the wheel back slightly. A slow, slithering turn developed. Halfway round, I remem-bered the rotary potential of the engines—the port outer, free of ice, was running smoothly. Playing with the throttle, I let the Merlin bring the port wing up, and Baker Two settled into a steady, balanced turn.

"A familiar 'puff-puff' in my ear-phones indicated that Fairbairn was checking his microphone before ven-turing an utterance.

" 'Wireless op here, Jack. I can't find any sign of Johnny, I'm afraid. The main door's open—he might have fallen out. Or jumped. There's a ter-rible mess down here—"window" all over the place. The rear gunner's in his turret.'

"Myring chimed in from the nose compartment. I'll have a look for the engineer, Skip. I want to go to the Elsan anyway.
'Go ahead, Larry. Better get back to your set, Charlie. Pilot to rear gunner.'
'Rear gunner, Jack.'
'Where were you?'
'I got out to find my 'chute. I sat down on the doorstep while you were bringing her down . . .'

"I liked that; she was bringing me down. Lanham continued: 'The whole kite was covered in St Elmo's Fire—ice all over the wings—really a mar-vellous sight.'
'I'm glad you enjoyed it. Did you see anything of the engineer?'
'You can't see anything in the fuselage. There's window and stuff everywhere. Shall I . . .'

"Protheroe interrupted.
'Mid-upper to Skipper.'
'Go ahead, George.'
'I thought the rear gunner ought to know—I shan't be able to fire my guns. The interrupter gear's gone unserviceable. I think something broke off in the spin. Shall I get out and look for Johnny?'
'No. Leave that to Larry. Stay in the turret and keep your eyes peeled.'
'Wireless op here, Jack. I've been checking the external aerials, and there aren't any. I guess they blew off.'
'Bad luck.'

"I flew on, holding Baker Two just below the cloud base, at 8,000 feet. When Myring called from the fuselage, he was panting, and I could hear the sound of the slipstream behind his voice.
'I've found the engineer, Skip. Buried in bloody window. He's out cold—I think he's banged his nut.'

'Is he on oxygen?'
'Yep. That's why I don't want to take his helmet off to look at his head. I'm going to put him on the rest bed. I'll be off intercom for a few minutes.'
'Right.'

"We crossed the coast near Bremerhaven at ten minutes to three. Ten minutes later, a searchlight waved towards us from the right, groped closer, and swept the starboard wing. Two more lights from straight below

joined the first, and crept along its beam to find us. The flashing stars of flak began to twinkle round us, and I played what evasive games I could with engines, rudders, and elevators. I looked for clouds, but they had disappeared. I spoke to Jimmy.
'We're in some defenses, nav.'
'Ah, good—oh, Jack, that'll be Heligoland. I've been waiting for a fix. Let me know when it's right underneath, will you?'
'Oh, sure.'

"But now, miraculously, the flak dwindled and the last two searchlight beams climbed higher up the ladder of the first. I looked up, and there on the port beam, 5,000 feet above us, cruised another Lancaster, majestic, straight and level. The searchlights settled on her, the twinkling flak shells clustered, but she passed on oblivious.
'Mid-upper here, Skipper. What d'you think of that bugger at ten o'clock high? They must all be asleep.'

"I was glad when another drift of cloud hid the sacrifice from my view. The feeling came that Baker Two

and we were leading charmed lives that August night, and it was with a degree of confident abandon that, five minutes later, I threw her into steep corkscrew turns to evade a prowling fighter.

"At 3:30 we turned west-south-west, with 400 miles to go for Mablethorpe. I began to consider how I might make a landing. I had heard no precedent for a Lancaster landing without aileron control, but in my present mood I couldn't think it impracticable, not that night. Larry shattered my euphoria when he returned from nursing Johnny. Crouching beside me, his eyes squinting with alarm, he growled: 'Cripes, Jack, we're bloody short of petrol. These tanks are damn near empty— we'll never make the coast.
'They should be half full. How's Johnny?'
'He's conscious, but I reckon he's got concussion.'
'Pilot to engineer. I need you here to check the fuel. Go and give him a hand, will you, Larry?'

"Walker reached the cabin, white-faced and pale-lipped, but with enough sense to get the true readings from the fuel gauges. Charlie Lanham cackled from the rear turret, 'Duff gen, Myring! Larry crept down into the nose, muttering. Walker was slumped against the starboard cabin window, fumbling at the intercom switch on his mask. I leaned over to turn it off for him, and looked into his eyes. They seemed unfocused, and his face was drained of blood. I told him to go back to the rest bed. But he didn't move, and the wireless operator had to take him aft. When Fairbairn reported that he had made the engineer comfortable, and checked that he was breathing oxygen, Lanham's voice came through my headphones: 'Pilot from rear gunner. Do you reckon we're clear of fighters?'

'I don't know. I should think so. Why?'
'I'll come up and take Johnny's place. Give you a hand.'

"It crossed my mind that he might be feeling lonely in the cold extremity of Baker Two's tail end, or that he had decided that I could use some close moral support. Either way, it would be good to have him by my side.

'OK, rear gunner, you're clear to leave the turret.'

"Lanham appeared in the cabin a few minutes later, and perched on the engineer's bench seat. Crawling up the fuselage in his heavy suit had brought him out in a sweat. He wiped the back of his gauntlet across his face, then folded his arms and stared ahead into the darkness. His gravely alert expression was exactly suited to the situation, but it made me want to make him laugh. I nudged him with my elbow, and waggled the useless control wheel loosely with my fingertips. I spun it round from left to right, and back again, grinning at Lanham. He looked worried for a moment, staring at the wheel and back at me, then I saw the gleam of his teeth as he laughed. There wasn't really much to laugh about, but the atmosphere was getting too serious, it needed some of the gravity taken out of it. Lanham settled himself more comfortably, and passed me a pellet of chewing gum. He stayed beside me for an hour or so while Baker Two flew on westward, sometimes side-slipping a little when I picked up a wandering wing too harshly with the rudders, but on the whole making good her course.

"High above the Lincolnshire coast I brought the speed back, put the wheels down, and tried a rate-one ninety degree turn to port. I couldn't get any flap down—presumably another system had fractured

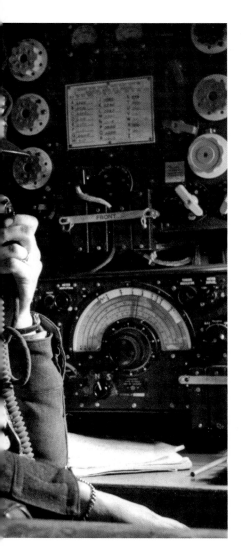

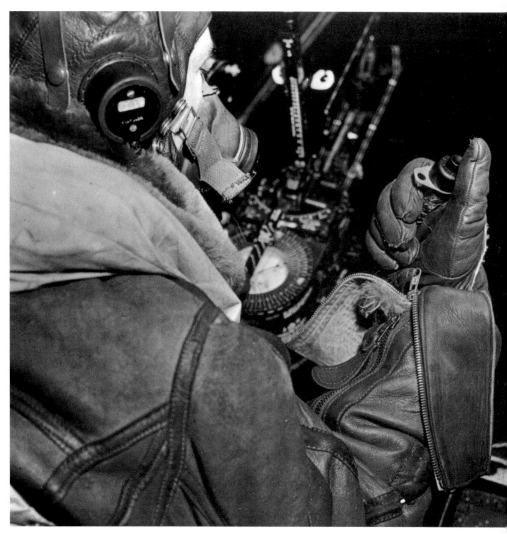

there—and that meant I must make a long downwind leg, a shallow approach and add ten mph to the landing speed. I practiced it at 4,000 feet, and brought Baker Two to the point of the stall. The rudder control was good, but I couldn't manipulate the throttles fast enough to keep the wings level. It would have to be a very straight approach.
'Pilot to crew. The landing may be a bit difficult. You'd better bale out.'

"There was silence for a few seconds, then Lanham called.
'What are you going to do, Jack?'
'I'm going to put her down at base.

But I might make a balls of it.'
'You won't. This is your lucky night. I'm staying on board.'

"I warned them again, but nobody would go. We reached Wickenby five minutes later than the time on our flight plan, and the circuit was clear. I flew parallel with the runway, flashing dash—dot—dot—dot dot—dot—dash—dash—dash on the downward identification light. A green Very cartridge puffed up from the caravan. I made an accurate approach, but half a mile from touchdown I began to doubt the wisdom of my decision to land her. The way the wings were

dipping, left to right and back to the left, was much worse than it seemed at 4,000 feet. However, there was a rhythm in their rolling movement, and, picking the instant in mid-roll when the wings were level, I banged the main wheels down on the runway and held them there. Baker Two pulled up, squealing, in the last few feet of concrete. It was twenty-seven minutes past five.

"The muscles of my legs were tired from the unusual exercise of kicking Baker Two's rudders for three hours, and it was some time before I could stand without support. The crew were less boisterous than usual, oddly gentle as they helped me to get into the crew bus, and had Walker taken to the sick-bay. When we reached the briefing room, the Station Commander strolled towards me as I took a mug of cocoa from the padre's serving hatch.

'Not one of your better landings, Currie.'

'No, sir. If I'd known you were watching I'd have tried harder.'

'He smiled and started to turn away, but Myring stopped him.'

'The Skipper was in difficulties, sir. He did bloody well to get it down at all.'

'Oh? What difficulties were you in, Currie?'

'I hadn't any aileron control, sir, and no flaps.'

'Why didn't you have aileron control?'

"Mentally, I cursed Larry's intervention. I had hoped to report the incident in my own time to the debriefing officer, with a cigarette to smoke and my feet under the table, and let it go through the normal channels. Now here was the Station Commander staring at me imperiously, one eyebrow raised. The Squadron Commander was at his elbow, and other officers were edging closer. I hadn't had time to sip my cocoa.

'I'm afraid they broke off, sir.'

'Broke off. Are you serious, Currie?'

'Yes, sir. We got in a spin, in some cumulo-nimbus near the target.'

'I see.'

"He looked at me quizzically for a moment, then beckoned to the Squadron Commander and walked out to his car. I turned to the crew.

'I don't think he believed me.'

'He'll get a shock when he sees the kite, then.'

"That was the first of several inspections to be undergone by Baker Two, as expert and lay exam-iners looked at her damaged surface areas, sprung rivets and gaping wings. Meanwhile, I called at the sick-bay to see the damaged Walker, who gave a pallid smile of recognition. The MO said he had concussion, confirming Myring's diagnosis, and that he would be moved to hospital in a few hours' time. I trudged back to the hut.

"I felt slightly aggrieved when I was required to report to the Station Commander a few hours later, while the rest of the crew slumbered on. Woody gave me a chair in his office, and he sat at his desk making notes while I told him what had happened to Baker Two. When I had finished, he looked up with a smile.

'Well, I think it was a magnificent show. Has it shaken you up a bit?'

'No, I don't think so, sir. We're all fine, except for the engineer. He's gone into Rauceby.'

'Would you like to take few days leave?'

"I considered the kindly suggestion. We had returned from our last leave on Friday night, and this was Tuesday. The state of our finances varied from poor to very poor. Even Fairbairn's fabulous wealth could be measured in terms of shillings, and I decided that more time off would only be an embarrassment.

'No, thank you, sir. I think we'd better get on with the tour.' His smile became a grin.

'Had enough leave for a while, hm?'

'That's right, sir.'

"I was pleasantly surprised by the reactions of my colleagues on the squadron, some humorous, all generous. It was good to realize that each could emerge from his own embattled world to remark and applaud another's fortune. But, putting personal thoughts aside, the raid had not been a success. Nature, more terrible and more effective than all man-made defenses, had thrown her arms around the city and its ravaged streets and protected it from further horrors. Twenty-five of us had taken off from Wickenby; four thought that they had bombed the target, eight had bombed on ETA, not altogether certain where they were, six had been unable to reach Hamburg and had bombed some other town, three had jettisoned the bomb load in the sea, three had given up the sortie, and one did not return."

Robert M. Owen is the official historian of 617 Squadron Association. "On the night of 16-17 May 1943, a force of Lancasters of Bomber Command executed what has been described as the greatest feat of arms ever carried out by the Royal Air Force. Under the leadership of Wing Commander Guy Gibson, nineteen crews of No 617 Squadron, a specially formed unit of experienced crews, attacked the major dams of western Germany using a unique 'bouncing bomb' designed by engineering genius Barnes Wallis.

"After flying in bright moonlight at treetop height to the targets, the attack was pressed home from precisely sixty feet with tremendous fortitude and skill in the face of formidable resistance. The Mohne and Eder dams were breached, and a third, the Sorpe, damaged. There was a high price to pay. Eight of the Lancasters failed to return, fifty-three men died and three miraculously escaped from their doomed aircraft to survive as prisoners of war. In the flooded valleys, 1,294 people were drowned.

"The intention was to deprive the Ruhr Valley of vital water supplies required for industrial production, while the floods would cause additional destruction and disruption throughout the region. The success of the operation, illustrated by photographs of the breached dams and flooded countryside, was publicized immediately throughout the Allied countries. Leaflets were dropped over occupied countries demonstrating the effeciveness of Bomber Command. The purpose of this exploitation was to magnify the effects of the attack to boost morale, a factor which has been used by some post-war revisionists to question the cost and value of the operation. Nevertheless, the cumulative effects, which extended far beyond those of the physical damage caused, refute those who seek to question its values and effectiveness.

" 'Operation Chastise' as it was known, demonstrated graphically the courage, airmanship and technical ability of Bomber Command. A small force of aircraft could penetrate into the very heart of Germany and inflict a disproportionate amount of damage on the enemy. Crews were now able to navigate accurately at night to locate and successfully attack a small target despite strong defenses and the additional hazards of flying at extremely low level. The aircraft could be controlled by their leader, using radio to allow tactical flexibility and more effective use of resources—a technique which would be developed into the role of Master Bomber.

"The effects cannot be counted only in the loss of industrial output: agricultural land and livestock for vital food production were severly affected, communications distrupted and property damaged. In order to repair the dams before the winter rains, to maintain essential services and carry out other restoration, the Germans were forced to divert thousands of workers, and equipment, from other tasks vital to the war effort, including the construction of the Atlantic Wall

defenses. Fearing repeat attacks, vast numbers of weapons were withheld from the Eastern Front, along with their crews, to defend other dams and similar targets against an enemy who, in the event, did not come.

"The psychological effect of these realizations upon the German leadership, civil and military morale, should not be underestimated. Added to this, the destruction of the dams, previously considered to be such substantial targets as to be almost invulnerable, suggested to the Germans that there could be few places secure from the might of the RAF.

"Thirty-four of the surviving members of No 617 Squadron were awarded decorations for their part in the operation, their leader receiving the Victoria Cross. Reinforced with other experienced crews, the

squadron was retained as a specialist bombing unit. They and their successors, under the inspired leadership of Leonard Cheshire, James 'Willie' Tait, and Johnny Fauquier, would build on the reputation established by the Squadron's initial operation. Pioneering new techniques leading to greater precision and lower casualties, they used new, larger weapons such as the 12,000-pound Tallboy and 22,000-pound Grand Slam (again developed by the fertile mind of Barnes Wallis) denying the enemy the use of large V-weapon sites, U-boat pens, the battleship *Tirpitz* and rail communications vital for ammunition and troop movements. As the catalyst for such developments, the Dams Raid also should be recognized. Such is the true legacy of this one operation."

right: A World War I recruiting poster showing a British bomber in flight over the desert.

The iconic A2 leather flying jacket of the U.S. Army Air Forces lasted just over a decade as standard military issue. but its impact and significance has lasted through the years of the Second World War and continues to the present. Many American veterans of that long ago air war treasured their decorated A2s and brought them home at war's end. Over the years the jackets have become collectable and highly desirable souvenirs of what, for most of those men, was the one great adventure of their lives. Here are but a few examples of the rich and graphic contribution of the jacket to history.

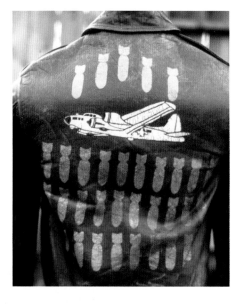

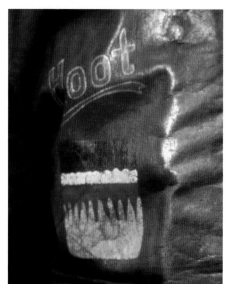

FAT MAN AND LITTLE BOY

"The war situation has developed, not necessarily to Japan's advantage."
—Emperor Hirohito announcing the Japanese surrender after the dropping of the two atomic bombs in August 1945.

The following document was published on 26 July 1945, by the governments of the United States, Great Britain, and China.

1.   We, the President of the United States, the President of the National Government of the Republic of China, and the Prime Minister of Great Britain, representing the hundreds of millions of our countrymen, have conferred and agree that Japan shall be given an opportunity to end the war.

2.   The prodigious land, sea, and air forces of the United States, the British Empire, and China, many times reinforced by their armies and air fleets from the West, are poised to strike the final blows upon Japan. This military power is sustained and inspired by the determination of all the Allied nations to prosecute the war against Japan until she ceases to resist.

3.   The result of the futile and senseless German resistance to the might of the aroused free peoples of the world stands forth in awful clarity as an example to the people of Japan. The might that now converges on Japan is immeasurably greater than that which, when applied to the resisting Nazis, necessarily laid waste the lands, industry, and the method of life of the whole German people. The full application of our military power,

backed by our resolve, will mean the inevitable and complete destruction of the Japanese forces, and just as inevitably the utter devastation of the Japanese homeland.

4.   The time has come for Japan to decide whether she will continue to be controlled by those self-willed militaristic advisers, whose unintelligent calculations have brought the Empire of Japan to the threshold of annihilation, or whether she will follow the path of reason.

5.   The following are our terms. We shall not deviate from them. There are no alternatives. We shall brook no delay.

6.   There must be eliminated for all time the authority and influence of those who have deceived and misled the people of Japan into embarking on world conquest, for we insist that a new order of peace, security, and justice will be impossible until irresponsible militarism is driven from the world.

7.   Until such a new order is established and until there is convincing proof that Japan's war-making power is destroyed, points in Japanese territory will be occupied to secure the achievement of the basic objectives we are here setting forth.

8.   The terms of the Cairo declaration shall be carried out, and Japanese sovereignty shall be limited to the islands of Honshu, Hokkaido, Kyushu, Shikoku, and such minor islands as we determine.

9.   The Japanese military forces after being completely disarmed shall be permitted to return to their homes, with the opportunity of leading peaceful and productive lives.

10.   We do not intend that the Japanese shall be enslaved as a race nor destroyed as a nation, but stern justice will be meted out to all war criminals, including those who have visited cruel-

ties upon our prisoners. The Japanese Government shall remove all obstacles to the revival and strengthening of democratic tendencies among the Japanese people. Freedom of speech, of religion, and of thought, as well as respect for fundamental human rights, shall be established.

11.   Japan shall be permitted to maintain such industries as will sustain her economy and all the exaction of just reparations in kind, but not those industries which would enable her to re-arm for war. To this end access to, as distinguished from control of, raw materials shall be permitted. Eventual Japanese participation in world trade relations shall be permitted.

12.   The occupying forces of the Allies shall be withdrawn from Japan as soon as these objectives have been accomplished, and there has been established, in accordance with the freely expressed will of the Japanese people, a peacefully inclined and responsible Government.

13.   We call upon the Government of Japan to proclaim now the unconditional surrender of all the Japanese armed forces, and to provide proper and adequate assurances of their good faith in such action. The alternative for Japan is complete and utter destruction.

The military men ruling Japan of 1945 rejected the Allied terms of surrender and U.S. President Harry S. Truman ordered the U.S. Army Air Force to proceed with plans for the delivery of two atomic bombs. One would go to Hiroshima and the other to Nagasaki.

"With cheerful semblance and sweet majesty, that every wretch, pining and pale before, beholding him, plucks comfort from his looks. A largess universal, like the sun, his liberal eye doth give to every one, thawing cold fear.

"All the News
That's Fit to Print"

The New York Times.

Copyright, 1945, by The New York Times Company.

LATE CITY EDITION
Partly cloudy, less humid today.
Cloudy and warm tomorrow.
Temperatures Yesterday—Max. 72; Min. 66

OL. XCIV..No. 31,972.

NEW YORK, TUESDAY, AUGUST 7, 1945.

THREE CENTS NEW YORK CITY

FIRST ATOMIC BOMB DROPPED ON JAPAN;
MISSILE IS EQUAL TO 20,000 TONS OF TNT;
TRUMAN WARNS FOE OF A 'RAIN OF RUIN'

W. JOHNSON, BLICAN DEAN HE SENATE, DIES

nist Helped Prevent Entry into League—ssed World Charter

RNIA EX-GOVERNOR

Vice President With re Roosevelt in '12 Washington Since '17

INGTON, Aug. 6.—Senator Warren Johnson of the, a lifelong isolationist d prevent this country's to the League of Nations that all "foreign entangle-through a second World d in his sleep this morn-Bethesda Naval Hospital, after, ill but consistent ired his vote against ratis-of the United Nations.

Death was caused by a of a cerebral artery, ma was with him when

word reached the Capital ming of the oldest member Senate in point of serv-Senator Kenneth McKel-President pro tempore, the

---

Jet Plane Explosion Kills Major Bong, Top U.S. Ace

Flier Who Downed 40 Japanese Craft, Sent Home to Be 'Safe,' Was Flying New 'Shooting Star' as a Test Pilot

By The United Press.

BURBANK, Calif., Aug. 6—Richard Bong, America's greatest air ace, died today in the flaming wreckage of a jet propelled fighter plane which crashed while he was testing it.

Only 34 years old, he wore twenty-six decorations including the nation's highest award, the Congressional Medal of Honor. He had survived countless air battles and shot down forty Japanese planes without a scratch.

KYUSHU CITY RAZED

Kenney's Planes Blast Tarumizu in Record Blow From Okinawa

ROCKET SITE IS SEEN

125 B-29's Hit Japan's Toyokawa Naval Arsenal in Demolition Strike

By FRANK L. KLUCKHOHN
By Wireless to The New York Times.

MANILA, Tuesday, Aug. 7—More than 400 fighters and bombers, speeding at chimney-top level for two hours Sunday over Tarumizu in southern Kyushu in the largest single attack launched by Gen. George C. Kenney's Far East Air Force to date, leveled that city's munitions factories and aircraft and munitions storage depots and waterfront installations.

REPORT BY BRITAIN

'By God's Mercy' We Beat Nazis to Bomb, Churchill Says

ROOSEVELT AID CITED

Raiders Wrecked Norse Laboratory in Race for Key to Victory

The text of Mr. Churchill's statement is on Page 5.

By CLIFTON DANIEL
By Wireless to The New York Times.

LONDON, Aug. 6—The hitherto secret details of the grisly race between Germany and the Allies to find a weapon so destructive that it would insure absolute victory—a race not only between scientists but also between under-cover agents—were recounted in London tonight after it had been disclosed that the first atomic bomb had been dropped on Japan.

Steel Tower 'Vaporized' In Trial of Mighty Bomb

Scientists Awe-Struck as Blinding Flash Lighted New Mexico Desert and Great Cloud Bore 40,000 Feet Into Sky

By LEWIS WOOD
Special to The New York Times.

WASHINGTON, Aug. 6—A blinding flash many times as brilliant as the midday sun and a massive, multi-colored cloud boiling up 40,000 feet into the air accompanied the first test firing of an atomic bomb on July 16, three weeks ago today. Set in the remote desertlands of New Mexico, the experiment was seen against a wild background where rain poured in torrents, and lightning pierced the sky up to the zero hour of the explosion at 5:30 A. M.

NEW AGE USHERED

Day of Atomic Energy Hailed by President, Revealing Weapon

HIROSHIMA IS TARGET

'Impenetrable' Cloud of Dust Hides City After Single Bomb Strikes

Truman, Stimson statements on atomic bomb, Page 4.

By SIDNEY SHALETT
Special to The New York Times.

WASHINGTON, Aug. 6—The White House and War Department announced today that an atomic bomb, possessing more power than 20,000 tons of TNT, a destructive force equal to the load of 2,000 B-29's and more than 2,000 times the blast power of what previously was the world's most devastating bomb, had been dropped on Japan.

MORRIS IS ACCUSED OF 'TAKING A WALK'

Fusion Official 'Sad to Part Company'—McGoldrick Sees Only Tammany Aided

---

CHINESE WIN MORE OF 'INVASION COAST'

Smash Into Port 121 Miles Southwest of Canton—Big Area Open for Landing

By The Associated Press.

CHUNGKING, China, Aug. 6—Chinese troops have broken into the South China port of Yeungkong and cleared a fifty-mile stretch of the Chinese "invasion coast" west of Hong Kong, Generalissimo Chiang Kai-shek's headquarters said today.

ATOM BOMBS MADE IN 3 HIDDEN 'CITIES'

Secrecy on Weapon So Great That Not Even Workers Knew of Their Product

By JAY WALZ
Special to The New York Times.

WASHINGTON, Aug. 6—The War Department revealed today how three "hidden cities" with a total population of 100,000 inhabitants sprang into being as a result of the $2,000,000,000 atomic bomb project, how they did their work without knowing what it was all about, and how they kept the biggest secret of the war.

TRAINS CANCELED IN STRICKEN AREA

Traffic Around Hiroshima Is Disrupted — Japanese Still Sift Havoc by Split Atoms

By The United Press.

WASHINGTON, Aug. 6—The Osaka radio, without referring to the atomic bomb dropped on Hiroshima, hinted tonight at the terrific damage it met have caused by announcing that train service in the Hiroshima and other areas had been canceled.

War News Summarized

TUESDAY, AUGUST 7, 1945

One bomb hit Japan on Sunday night, but it struck with the force of 20,000 tons of TNT. Where it landed had been the city of Hiroshima; what is there now has not yet been learned.

The attack, dramatically announced by President Truman sixteen hours after the missile had struck, was with an atomic bomb, a "harnessing of the basic power of the universe," he said. "The force from which the sun draws its power has been loosed against those who brought war to the Far East. And the end is not yet."

Turks Talk War if Russia Presses; Prefer Vain Battle to Surrender

By SAM POPE BREWER
By Wireless to The New York Times.

ANKARA, Turkey, Aug. 6—Russo-Turkish relations weigh heavy on Turkish minds these days. All leading editors commented today on various aspects of the Russian claims against Turkey.

Reich Exile Emerges as Heroine In Denial to Nazis of Atom's Secret

Special to The New York Times.

WASHINGTON, Aug. 6—How Germany twice narrowly missed the secret of harnessing atomic energy by splitting uranium atoms and releasing the most powerful destructive force on earth was recalled today in War Department reports on the atomic bomb.

Robert Oppenheimer and General Leslie Groves.

Then, mean and gentle all, behold as may unworthiness define, a little touch of Harry in the night. And so our scene must to the battle fly."
—from *Henry V*, act four, prologue, by William Shakespeare

It was in the afternoon of 17 July 1945 that U.S. Secretary of War, Henry Stimson, brought a paper to Prime Minister Winston Churchill, which bore the phrase, "Babies satisfactorily born." Stimson explained to Churchill that it was confirmation of a successful American effort to detonate an experimental atomic weapon at the Trinity Site north of Alamagordo, New Mexico. A day later Stimson returned with a detailed briefing for the Prime Minister. He explained that the weapon or its equivalent, had been exploded on the top of a 100-foot pylon in the desert. All civilian scientists and all military personnel had been moved a distance of ten miles from the blast location and were positioned behind concrete shields. What they witnessed was a massive, rapidly expanding fireball and a great column of flame and smoke rising from the center of what had become in an instant a one-mile circle of absolute devastation. Churchill concluded that here, at last, was at least the possibility of a speedy end to World War II.

In the immediate aftermath of Stimson's visit, Churchill and President Truman conferred on the Allies' conduct of the war's final phase. In their most horrific vision of events to come, the two leaders anticipated a continuing, desperate resistance by the Japanese. Until the advent of the atomic bomb, they had foreseen no viable alternative to a great assault on the Japanese homeland. It would require a gigantic, relentless progression of bombing attacks coupled with an invasion by millions of American and British personnel. Upwards of 1.5 million Allied casualties were expected in what would almost certainly be history's biggest and bloodiest battle.

According to Winston Churchill, the decision whether or not to use the atomic bomb to compel the Japanese surrender, was never an issue in his discussions with the President. They were agreed. "To avert a vast, indefinite butchery, to bring the war to an end, to give peace to the world, to lay healing hands upon its tortured peoples by a manifestation of overwhelming power at the cost of a few explosions, seemed, after all our toils and perils, a miracle of deliverance." Indeed, the leaders saw in the new weapon a way to actually save many lives, of friend and foe alike, and they talked of the terrible responsibilities they bore for the unlimited letting of American and British blood should the planned assault have to be carried out.

It was at this point that the decision was taken to send Japan the ultimatum calling for an immediate unconditional surrender of her armed forces.

"Boys, if you ever pray, pray for me now. I don't know whether you fellas ever had a load of hay fall on you, but when they told me yesterday what had happened, I felt like the moon, the stars, and all the planets had fallen on me."
—Harry S. Truman, the day after the death of President Franklin D. Roosevelt

"It is a profound and necessary truth that the deep things in science are not found because they are useful; they are found because it was possible to find them."
—J. Robert Oppenheimer, Director

of the Los Alamos Laboratory, New Mexico, in the Manhattan Project to design and develop the first atomic bomb.

Robert Oppenheimer was born on 22 April 1904. His father had come to America from Hanau, Germany in 1898 and had prospered importing lining fabrics for men's suits. The family lived in New York City. Young Robert had become interested in science and geology while on a visit with his grandfather in Hanau. There he was helped and encouraged to begin a collection of minerals. He pursued his scientific interests with fervour and, at the age of twelve, was invited to lecture to the New York Mineralogical Club.

In 1922 he entered Harvard University, majoring in chemistry and taking all the additional courses he could manage. Six feet tall and slight of build, he would never in his life weigh more than 125 pounds. He graduated summa cum laude in three years. "Harvard was the most exciting time I've ever had in my life. I really had a chance to learn. I loved it. I almost came alive."

After Harvard, he spent a year working in New Mexico, and from there he went to England, to Cambridge where, for perhaps the first time in his scientific education, he encountered his own limitations. For him, chemistry had become a brick wall. He was struggling with the work one day when he met the Danish physicist Niels Bohr. It was this meeting which caused him to change course and follow Bohr's example.

Offered positions at Harvard, the California Institute of Technology, and the University of California at Berkeley, Oppenheimer accepted the Berkeley and Caltech jobs and shared his time between them. His

journey through the realm of theoretical physics would ultimately lead to his selection to direct the activities of the new lab where the American effort to design and develop an atomic bomb was to be undertaken. He was nominated by U.S. Army General Leslie Groves, director of the Manhattan Project, established to produce the atomic bomb for the United States. Groves had met Oppenheimer at Berkeley during an inspection tour in October 1942 and was impressed by the scientist's interest in developing a fast-neutron laboratory. Groves had become convinced of the necessity for a central lab which would be entirely dedicated to the development of the bomb. Then he learned of Oppenheimer's background (a former fiancée, wife, brother and sister-in-law who had all been members of the Communist Party at one time) and was disturbed by it. He had not yet taken over the control of Manhattan Project security from Army counter-intelligence, which refused to clear Oppenheimer for the role proposed by Groves. Then the Military Policy Committee balked at Groves' choice of Oppenheimer, who had other problems, including never having directed a large organization, not being distinguished by the award of the Nobel Prize, and being proposed for the role of directing a lab devoted primarily to engineering and experiment, when he was, after all, a theorist. Still, Groves wanted him for the job, believing him to be a genius and the best man available. The general asked each member of the committee to propose someone who would be a better choice than Oppenheimer. A few weeks passed and it was clear that no better choice would emerge. Groves then took Oppenheimer to Washington to meet Vannevar Bush, head of the Office of

A Japanese phosphorus bomb explodes beneath B-29s attacking an air depot north of Nagoya.

Scientific Research and Development. Bush approved Groves' choice of Oppenheimer for the post and they set out to find a site for the new bomb-design lab that Oppenheimer would run.

Groves wanted a site with room for at least 265 people, that was at least 200 miles from an international border, and west of the Mississippi River. It had to have some existing facilities and the terrain had to lend itself to adequate fencing and guarded security. The site finally chosen was the Los Alamos Ranch School for boys in New Mexico.

With a site selected, Robert Oppenheimer began a search for the scientists he would need to populate his new lab. He recalled: "The prospect of coming to Los Alamos aroused great misgivings. It was to be a military post; men were asked to sign up more or less for the duration; restrictions on travel and on the freedom of families to move about would be severe. The notion of disappearing into the New Mexico desert for an indeterminate period and under quasi-military auspices disturbed a good many scientists, and the families of many more. But there was another side to it. Almost everyone realized that this was a great undertaking. Almost everyone knew that if it were completed successfully and rapidly enough, it might determine the outcome of the war. Almost everyone knew that it was an unparalleled opportunity to bring to bear the basic knowledge and art of science for the benefit of his country. Almost everyone knew that this job, if it were achieved, would be a part of history. This sense of excitement, of devotion and patriotism in the end prevailed. Most of those with whom I talked came to Los Alamos."

There was, however, significant resistance from many in the scientific community to the prospect of joining the Army in order to be a part of this great, potentially war-winning project. Oppenheimer took the view that "although the execution of the security and secrecy measures should be in the hands of the military . . . the decision as to what measures should be applied must be in the hands of the Laboratory. I believe it is the only way to assure the co-operation and the unimpaired morale of the scientists."

A compromise was reached when General Groves agreed to allow the Laboratory to have civilian administration and a civilian staff until the time of the large-scale trials of the weapon, when anyone wishing to continue with the project would have to accept a commission. The Army would administer the surrounding community, and the Laboratory would be Oppenheimer's responsibility. He would report directly to Groves.

On 16 November 1942 the Columbia University physicist Enrico Fermi and his team began a day and night construction project in the west stands of Staff Field at the University of Chicago. There, in a squash court, Fermi directed the initial assembly of something he had been planning since the previous May, a full-scale chain-reacting atomic pile. Control of the pile was clearly central to the success and safety of the project, and in this pioneering effort, no one really knew what would happen—how much risk was involved—when the neutron fission began in the pile. Fermi intended to control what was happening in the pile with the system of manual and automatic rods he had planned, but despite the staggering calculations done for the project, no one could guarantee that even slow-neutron fission generations, estimated to multiply

Hiroshima on the day after the atomic bomb attack in August 1945.

in thousandths of a second, would not flash the pile to dangerous levels of heat and radiation in a wildly out-of-control scenario.

The team was dealing with a large amount of potentially radioactive material in the pile and the propect of excessive ionizing radiation was terrifying. Ultimately, though, Fermi concluded that the probability of acceptable control of the pile activity was sufficient and the decision was taken to build the first atomic chain-reacting pile, CP-1, there under the stands of the University of Chicago football stadium.

On the bitterly cold morning of 2 December, Fermi and company gathered at the pile in the squash court and began the agonizing, delicate procedure of withdrawing the cadmium rods from their creation. As the work progressed, the results were carefully checked and slide rule calculations were made again and again. The experiment went on through the morning and at 11:30 a safety rod was automatically released with a loud crash when its relay was activated by an ionization chamber because the intensity had exceeded the arbitrary level at which it had been set. Fermi calmly broke for lunch.

In the afternoon the team resumed the experiment where they had left off. By now forty-two people were crowded into the squash court, most of them on the balcony. Fermi called for all but one of the cadmium rods to be removed from the pile, and continued making his calculations. Finally, he asked that the remaining rod be taken out twelve inches, along with the safety rod. In what was certainly one of history's most breathless moments Fermi remarked: "This is going to do it. Now it will become self-sustaining." Eyewitness Herbert Anderson: "At first you could hear the sound of the neutron counter,

clickety-clack, clickety-clack. Then the clicks came more and more rapidly, and after a while they began to merge into a roar, the counter couldn't follow any more. That was the moment to switch to the chart recorder. But when the switch was made, everyone watched in the sudden silence the mounting deflection of the recorder's pen. It was an awesome silence. Everyone realized the significance of that switch: we were in the high intensity regime and the counters were unable to cope with the situation any more. Again and again, the scale of the recorder had to be changed to accommodate the neutron intensity which was increasing more and more rapidly. Suddenly Fermi raised his hand. 'The pile has gone critical,' he announced. No one present had any doubt about it. Everyone began to wonder why he didn't shut the pile off, but Fermi was still calm. He waited another minute, then another, and then when it seemed that the anxiety was too much to bear, he ordered ZIP (the safety rod) in!" The experiment had succeeded. Fermi and his team had achieved the controlled release of atomic energy.

High on the New Mexican mesa where the Manhattan Project lab was sited, Director Robert Oppenheimer had brought together about thirty of the 100 scientists originally hired to work on the design and development of the bomb, for a series of introductory lectures to be given by Robert Serber, a Berkeley theoretician and former student of Oppenheimer's. He briefed the group on the achievements of the fast-fission research activity of the previous year. Many of them now heard for the first time precisely what it was they were there to do. They were told that the object of the project was to produce a prac-

tical military weapon in the form of a bomb in which the energy is released by a fast neutron chain reaction in one or more of the materials known to show nuclear fission. Reducing their problem to its simplest form, then: designing and building a workable bomb. Their deadline: workable bombs ready when enough uranium and plutonium was ready. It was estimated they would have about two years to complete the job.

First came the Serber orientation lectures at Los Alamos. There followed a conference to plan the work of the lab. After that, as more scientists, engineers, senior consultants and experts of the various required disciplines joined the project, it began to appear that General Groves's seemingly intuitive selection of Oppenheimer, the theorist, to head the work of the bomb-design team was most appropriate. Unlike the Fermi chain-reacting pile at Chicago, there could be no laboratory-scale bomb test. The bomb-making effort was to be a supreme challenge to Oppenheimer and the other theorists in the project, for nearly everything that the team would have to understand in the course of developing the weapon would need to be analysed theoretically. In a sense, they were having to shape a new science as they went, devising theory, technology and detailed experiments that would ultimately result in Little Boy and Fat Man, the bombs that would be delivered over Hiroshima and Nagasaki respectively.

They did their jobs very well and at a few seconds before 5:30 a.m. of 16 July 1945, the first man-made nuclear explosion was detonated at the Trinity test site north of Alamagordo, New Mexico. The twelve-pound payload of plutonium released the energy of 18,500 tons of TNT, scoring

CARL L. NORDEN, INC.
80 LAFAYETTE STREET
NEW YORK 13, N. Y.

CONTENTS LIST FOR THIS CRATE

SECRET

Date APR 17 1944

ONE BOMBSIGHT

TYPE Mod 7 -

SERIAL NO. N-6212

– INCLUDING –

1 – DIRECTIONAL STABILIZER

1 – BOMBSIGHT COVER

1 – LOG BOOK AND COVER

1 – PRECESSION CHART

1 – TACHOMETER, SERIAL NO. ——
FURNISHED BY N. I. O.

SECRET

ORIGINAL PACKING LIST FOR THIS LOT
SHIPMENT IN CRATE NO. 1

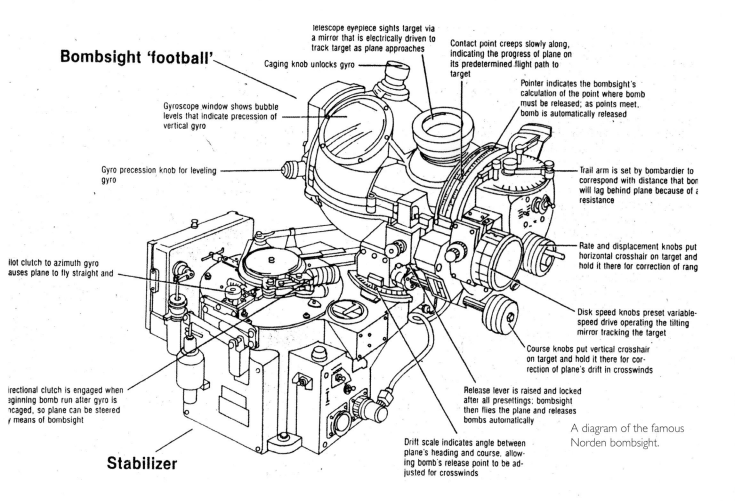

Bombsight 'football'

Telescope eyepiece sights target via a mirror that is electrically driven to track target as plane approaches

Contact point creeps slowly along, indicating the progress of plane on its predetermined flight path to target

Caging knob unlocks gyro

Pointer indicates the bombsight's calculation of the point where bomb must be released; as points meet, bomb is automatically released

Gyroscope window shows bubble levels that indicate precession of vertical gyro

Gyro precession knob for leveling gyro

Trail arm is set by bombardier to correspond with distance that bomb will lag behind plane because of air resistance

Pilot clutch to azimuth gyro causes plane to fly straight and

Rate and displacement knobs put horizontal crosshair on target and hold it there for correction of range

Disk speed knobs preset variable-speed drive operating the tilting mirror tracking the target

Course knobs put vertical crosshair on target and hold it there for correction of plane's drift in crosswinds

Directional clutch is engaged when beginning bomb run after gyro is uncaged, so plane can be steered by means of bombsight

Release lever is raised and locked after all presettings; bombsight then flies the plane and releases bombs automatically

Stabilizer

Drift scale indicates angle between plane's heading and course, allowing bomb's release point to be adjusted for crosswinds

A diagram of the famous Norden bombsight.

a half-mile-wide crater and sending a huge fiery cloud from the desert floor to 38,000 feet in seven minutes. It worked. And it made Oppenheimer recall a line from the *Bhagavadgita*: "I am become Death, the destroyer of worlds."

Through the spring of 1945, B-29 Superfortress bombers of Curtis LeMay's Twentieth Air Force had been fire-bombing upwards of sixty Japanese target cities with a fury and intensity surpassing even that of the Allied attacks on Germany. In early June Lt Col Paul W. Tibbets Jr, who commanded the 509th Composite Group, the B-29 crews charged with delivery of the atomic bomb (or bombs if need be) arrived on

Tinian in the western Pacific Marianas Islands. He met with LeMay and they discussed the progress of the specialized facilities then being prepared on Tinian for the mission of the 509th. On 10 June the first combat crews of the group arrived on the island in new, specially-modified lightweight B-29s that were equipped with fuel-injection engines rather than carburetion, quick-action pneumatic bomb doors, fuel flow meters, and reversible electric propellers. Many other modifications had been made to the planes so they could perform their secret task. The engineer in charge of their procurement later wrote: "The performance of those special B-29s was exceptional. They were without doubt the finest B-29s in the theatre."

By the middle of July, much of the technical facilities for the bomb assembly and test activity had been established on the island base. Before that, the largest airport in the world had been built there, with six runways, each nearly two miles long. Literally hundreds of Superfortresses were in residence on the hardstands of the mammoth complex. Mid-July found the flight crews of the 509th practicing navigation and bombing with standard general purpose bombs.

On 2 July, U.S. Secretary of War Henry Stimson had summed up his assessment of Japan's current position: "Japan has no allies. Her navy is nearly destroyed and she is vulnerable to a surface and underwater blockade which can deprive her of

Examples of patches worn on the A2 leather flying jackets of American bomber and fighter airmen in the Second World War.

Factory-fresh B-29 bombers awaiting delivery to combat units from their Boeing assembly plant.

sufficient food and supplies for her population. She is terribly vulnerable to our concentrated air attack upon her crowded cities, industrial and food resources. She has against her not only the Anglo-American forces but the rising forces of China and the ominous threat of Russia. We have inexhaustible and untouched industrial resources to bring to bear against her diminishing potential. We have great moral superiority through being the victim of her first sneak attack." Stimson felt there might be an alternative to an Allied invasion of Japan after all. He continued: "I believe Japan is susceptible to reason in such a crisis to a much greater extent than is indicated by our current press and other current comment. Japan is not a nation composed wholly of mad fanatics of an entirely different mentality from ours. On the contrary, she has within the past century shown herself to possess extremely intelligent people, capable in an unprecedentedly short time of adopting not only the complicated technique of Occidental civilization, but to a substantial extent their culture and their political and social ideas. Her advance in these respects . . . has been one of the most astounding feats of national progress in history. It is therefore my conclusion that a carefully timed warning be given to Japan."

Through 16 July top officials of the Truman administration had been considering the implications of Stimson's view, and of others high in the Government who disagreed with it. That evening Stimson, in Potsdam with the President for the summit meeting with Stalin, received the following message from Washington: OPERATED ON THIS MORNING. DIAGNOSIS NOT YET COMPLETE BUT RESULTS SEEM SATISFACTORY AND ALREADY EXCEED EXPECTATIONS.

LOCAL PRESS RELEASE NECESSARY AS INTEREST EXPANDS GREAT DISTANCE. DR GROVES PLEASED. It confirmed for Stimson the success of the first test detonation at the Trinity Site.

General George C. Marshall later recalled the situation as he had perceived it: "We regarded the matter of dropping the bomb as exceedingly important. We had just gone through a bitter experience at Okinawa [the last major Pacific island campaign, when the Americans lost more than 12,500 men killed and missing, and the Japanese more than 100,000 killed in eighty-two days of fighting]. This had been preceded by a number of similar experiences in other Pacific islands, north of Australia. The Japanese had demonstrated in each case they would not surrender and they would fight to the death. It was expected that resistance in Japan, with their home ties, would be even more severe. We had the 100,000 people killed in Tokyo in one night of [conventional] bombs, and it had had seemingly no effect whatsoever. It destroyed the Japanese cities, yes, but their morale was not affected as far as we could tell, not at all. So it seemed quite necessary, if we could, to shock them into action . . . we had to end the war; we had to save American lives."

Secretary Stimson learned on 23 July that it might be possible to drop the first atomic bomb after 1 August, and certainly before 10 August. The initial target list, in order of preference, was Hiroshima, Kokura, and Niigata. Nagasaki was added to the list several days later. The target selection was based on factors such as the condition of the city—damage assessment after the strike would be easier with a target that had been relativly untouched by prior bombing attacks; and weather—if one target city was obscured by cloud cover, another might be clear.

Harry Truman recorded in his private diary: "We have discovered the most terrible bomb in the history of the world. It may be the fire destruction prophesied in the Euphrates Valley Era, after Noah and his fabulous Ark. Anyway, we 'think' we have found a way to cause a disintegration of the atom. An experiment in the New Mexican desert was startling—to put it mildly . . . This weapon is to be used against Japan between now and 10 August. I have told the Secretary of War, Mr Stimson, to use it so that military objectives and soldiers and sailors are the target and not women and children. Even if the Japs are savages, ruthless, merciless and fanatic, we as the leader of the world for the common welfare cannot drop this terrible bomb on the old Capital or the new. He & I are in accord. The target will be a purely military one and we will issue a warning statement asking the Japs to surrender and save lives. I'm sure they will not do that, but we will have given them the chance. It is certainly a good thing for the world that Hitler's crowd or Stalin's did not discover this atomic bomb. It seems to be the most terrible thing ever discovered, but it can be made the most useful."

On 25 July a directive drafted by General Groves and Secretary Stimson was approved by General Marshall and Secretary Stimson who, presumably, showed it to Truman. The President's authorization of the directive is not recorded.

To General Carl Spaatz, CG, USASTAF:

1. The 509th Composite Group, 20th Air Force will deliver its first special bomb as soon as weather will permit visual bombing after about 3 August 1945 on one of the targets: Hiroshima, Kukura, Niigata and Nagasaki.

2. Additional bombs will be delivered on the above targets as soon as made ready by the project staff.

3. Dissemination of any and all information concerning the use of the weapon against Japan is reserved to the Secretary of War and the President of the United States.

4. The foregoing directive is issued to you by direction and with the approval of the Secretary of War and the Chief of Staff, USA.

Japan rejected the Allied ultimatum, and on 27 July, in an effort to minimize the loss of life, eleven Japanese cities were warned by leaflets that they would be subjected to intense air bombardment. The following day six of them were bombed. On 31 July an additional twelve cities received the leaflet warnings and on 1 August, four more were attacked. A final warning was issued on 5 August. The crews of the seven B-29s that would fly the first mission, to deliver the bomb Little Boy, were briefed by Col Tibbets at 3:00 p.m. on 4 August. They were shown photographs of the target cities with the exception of Niigata, which was apparently excluded owing to unacceptable weather conditions. Three of the aircraft were assigned to fly ahead on the day of the attack, to assess cloud cover over Japan. Two other B-29s would accompany the bomber flown by Col Tibbets which would actually drop the atomic bomb. Their role was to observe and photograph the event. The seventh bomber was a spare plane which would be available should Tibbets' B-29 develop a problem and be unable to make the trip. The colonel's plane was called *Enola Gay* for his mother.

In the final briefing the crews were told of the weapon they would be taking to Japan. The New Mexico test was described and they were forbidden to write about or discuss the mission even among themselves. Tibbets told them that he was personally honored, and was sure they were, to have been chosen to take part in this raid which would shorten the war by at least six months. That afternoon the first combat-ready atomic bomb was prepared for loading into the bomb bay of the *Enola Gay*. One crew member is said to have described it as looking like "an elongated trash can with fins." It was 10 feet long, twenty-nine inches in diameter and weighed 9,700 pounds.

At 2:45 a.m. on 6 August, Paul Tibbets released the brakes of the bomber and, using nearly all of the two-mile Tinian runway, the B-29 was airborne in just over a minute. He climbed slowly, to preserve fuel and because two crewmen had to complete assembly of the bomb in the unheated, unpressurized bomb bay.

At 7:30 a.m. U.S. Navy Captain William "Deke" Parsons, Scientific Officer for the mission and the man who would arm Little Boy, entered the bomb bay for the final time and Col Tibbets took the *Enola Gay* on the long climb to the bombing altitude of 31,000 feet. Latest reports from the weather airplane over Japan indicated that the primary target city of Hiroshima was the best target, and Tibbets told the crew they would make the bomb run on that city.

The bomber reached 31,000 feet at 8:40 a.m. and the crew, except for the two pilots, put on flak suits and anti-glare goggles. There was no flak or fighters.

The target city was distinctively sited on a wide river delta and was divided by seven tributaries. The bomber approached the city over the Inland Sea on a nearly due west com-

An area of Hiroshima that was devastated by the atomic bomb attack.

pass heading and at a ground speed of about 330 mph.

Major Thomas Ferebee, the bombardier and a veteran of sixty-three bombing missions in the European air war, was now flying the airplane through the Norden bombsight. His aiming point was the Aioi bridge spanning the Ota River in the center of the city. The Headquarters of the Japanese Second Army was located near the bridge.

With her bomb doors open, the Superfortress passed over Hiroshima on course, on time and at the prescribed altitude. As she crossed the aiming point, Little Boy dropped from the bomb bay, dislodging the arming wires that would start its clocks.

Relieved of the bomb's weight, Paul Tibbets banked the *Enola Gay* into an extreme fighter-like turn away from the coming blast. Forty-three seconds after the drop, Little Boy exploded 550 feet southeast of the aiming point and 1,900 feet above the Shima Hospital. Tibbets recalled: "I threw off the automatic pilot and hauled *Enola Gay* into the turn. I pulled anti-glare goggles over my eyes. I couldn't see through them; I was blind. I threw them to the floor. A bright light filled the plane. The first shock wave hit us. We were eleven and a half miles slant range from the atomic explosion, but the whole airplane crackled and crinkled from the blast. I yelled 'Flak!,' thinking a heavy gun battery had found us. The gunner had seen the first wave coming, a visible shimmer in the atmosphere, but he didn't know what it was until it hit. When the second wave came, he called out a warning. We turned back to look at Hiroshima. The city was hidden by that awful cloud . . . boiling up, mushrooming, terrible and incredibly tall. No one spoke for a moment; then everyone was talking. I remember Lewis pounding my shoul-

der saying, 'Look at that! Look at that!' Tom Ferebee wondered about whether radioactivity would make us all sterile. Lewis said he could taste atomic fission. He said it tasted like lead."

"Pushing up through smoke from a world half-darkened by overhanging cloud—the shroud that mushroomed out and struck the dome of the sky, the angry flames—black, red, blue—dance into the air, merge, scatter glittering sparks, already tower over the whole city."
—from *Flames* by Toge Sankichi

"The Reverend Mr Tanimoto got up at five o'clock that morning. He was alone in the parsonage, because for some time his wife had been commuting with their year-old baby to spend nights with a friend in Ushida, a suburb to the north. Of all the important cities of Japan, only two, Kyoto and Hiroshima, had not been visited in strength by B-San, or Mr B, as the Japanese, with a mixture of respect and unhappy familiarity, called the B-29, and Mr Tanimoto, like all his neighbors and friends, was almost sick with anxiety. He had heard uncomfortably detailed accounts of mass raids on Kure, Iwakuni, Tokoyama and other nearby towns; he was sure Hiroshima's turn would come soon. He had slept badly the night before, because there had been several air raid warnings. Hiroshima had been getting such warnings almost every night for weeks, for at that time the B-29s were using Lake Biwa, northeast of Hiroshima, as a rendezvous point, and no matter what city the Americans planned to hit, the Superfortresses streamed in over the coast near Hiroshima. The frequency of the warnings and the continued abstinence of Mr B with respect to Hiroshima had made its citizens jittery; a rumor was going

around that the Americans were saving something special for the city."

"Early that day, August 7th, the Japanese radio broadcast for the first time a succinct announcement that very few, if any, of the people most concerned with its content, the survivors of Hiroshima, happened to hear: 'Hiroshima suffered considerable damage as the result of an attack by a few B-29s. It is believed that a new type of

bomb was used. The details are being investigated.' Nor is it probable that any of the survivors happened to be tuned in on a short-wave re-broadcast of an extraordinary announcement by the President of the United States, which identified the new bomb as atomic: 'That bomb had more power than twenty thousand tons of TNT. It had more than two thousand times the blast power of the British Grand Slam, which is the largest bomb ever yet used in the history of warfare.' Those victims who were able to worry at all about what had happened thought of it and discussed it in more primitive, childish terms—gasoline sprinkled from an airplane, maybe, or some combustible gas, or a big cluster of incendiaries, or the work of parachutists, but, even if they had known the truth, most of them were too busy or too weary or too badly hurt to care that they were the objects of the first great experiment in the use of atomic power, which (as the voices on the short-wave shouted) no country except the United States, with its industrial know-how, and its willingness to throw two billion gold dollars into an important wartime gamble, could possibly have developed."

—from *Hiroshima* by John Hersey

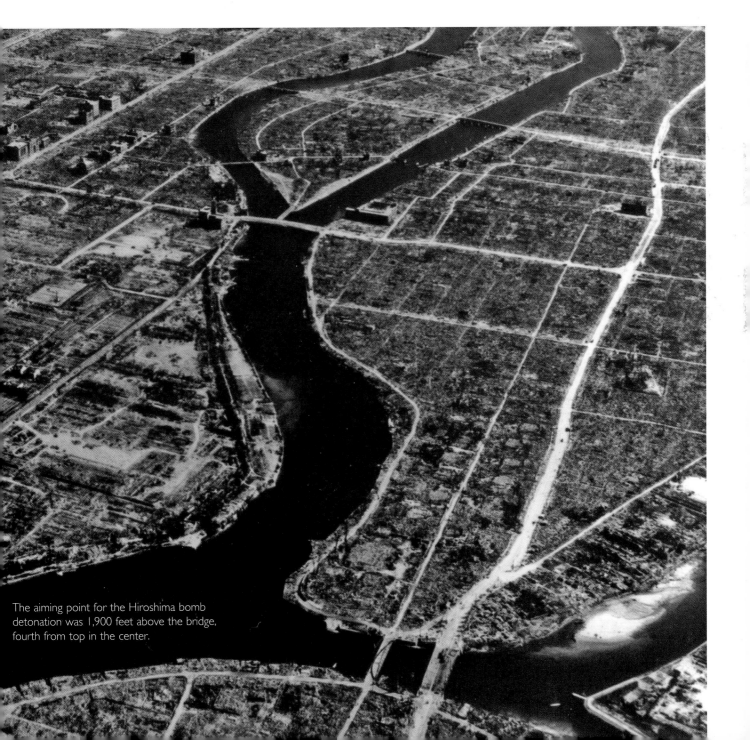

The aiming point for the Hiroshima bomb detonation was 1,900 feet above the bridge, fourth from top in the center.

Some of the great love songs of the Second World War.

Y DREAMS ARE GETTING BETTER ALL THE TIME

FROM THE UNIVERSAL FILM STARRING
BUD ABBOTT AND LOU COSTELLO
"In Society"

SUNG BY MARION HUTTON

BEGINNING TO SEE THE LIGHT

Words & Music by
HARRY JAMES
DUKE ELLINGTON,
JOHNNY HODGES
& DON GEORGE

FEATURED WITH ENORMOUS SUCCESS BY
HARRY JAMES

OU'LL NEVER KNOW

by MACK GORDON   Music by HARRY WARREN

OU'LL NEVER KNOW
VE GOTTA HAVE YOU

PRICE : 1/- NET EACH
HAPPELL & CO. LTD.

Alice FAYE • John PAYNE
Jack OAKIE • Lynn BARI
"Hello, FRISCO, Hello"
TECHNICOLOR

He wears a Pair of Silver Wings

as created by
Miss Frances Day
in:

BLACK VANITIES

George Black's

1/-

AIR BRIDGE

A Douglas C-54 transport landing at Berlin's Tempelhof airport during the great airlift.

It began with Operation Knicker, a British response to the stranglehold that Red Army Forces put on the British, American, and French sectors of West Berlin from the middle of 1947. In April 1948 the Royal Air Force sent sixteen C-47 Dakotas to the airfield at Wunstorf in heart of the British sector to bring supplies to their garrison. They brought in sixty-five tons of urgently needed goods daily.

The Russians had put Berlin under siege. Relations had not been good between Russia and the Western powers in Berlin—the United States, Britain, and France—for some time. Germany, since the end of World War II, had been under their combined military occupation and was divided into four zones. Berlin lay more than a hundred miles deep in the Soviet Zone and was split into four sectors.

At the end of the war, the Russians had claimed they lacked sufficient transport to carry supplies to Berlin, and asked the Western Allies to assume responsibility for providing three-quarters of the food and fuel needed by the three western sectors of the city. At the same time the Russians allowed access to their sector via only a single road, one railway line and a few canals. The Western Allies wanted and needed Soviet cooperation to keep Germany running, and didn't make much of a fuss about the limited access. They believed there was a "gentlemen's agreement" among the four powers and that all would pull together. Clearly, the Russians had a separate agenda for Germany and never intended to relax their restricted access.

From the end of the war Russia's Josef Stalin pursued the domination of western Europe, exploiting the countries that were most weakened by economic depression, hunger, and devastation from that conflict. His brand of Communism thrived amid the ruins of these suffering states. In an effort to

help rebuild the various economies of Europe in June 1947, U.S. Secretary of State George Marshall offered them enormous financial aid. The nations of western Europe gratefully accepted; the Soviet Union, on behalf of her satellites, flatly refused the assistance. The Russians, meanwhile, were systematically plundering their Zone and shipping everything of value, every vital resource, back to the Soviet Union. By the spring of 1948 the "working relationship" between the Western Allies and the Soviets was in tatters. Their patience with the Soviets now exhausted, the British, French, and Americans decided to make Berlin and Germany

work without the cooperation of their Russian ally.

In February 1948 the Western powers proposed to a west European conference in London that the Germans draft a constitution for a semi-independent West German state, designed as an interim measure until there could be agreement with the Russians on a unified, autonomous Germany. To bolster the West German economy the Western Allies announced the introduction of a brand new Deutschmark, a sound currency that would be in use in the western sectors of Berlin by June 1948. It was this move that made Stalin snap.

Through the early part of the year his forces had been interfering with road and rail traffic from the west, creating delays and causing electric power shortages. In March, the Soviet Military Governor quit the Allied Control Council, ending four-power government in Germany. On 5 April, a British European Airways Vickers Viking was harassed by a Soviet Yak-3 fighter that performed aerobatics quite near the airliner as it approached to land at Gatow. Tragically, the Yak pilot collided with the BEA plane and both aircraft crashed, killing the BEA crew and all seven passengers as well as the Soviet

left: A Douglas DC-3, one of the key aircraft in the airlift; below: A British contribution to the massive effort, the Avro York version of the historic Lancaster bomber.

pilot. The Russians attributed the crash to the Viking having rammed the Yak. From that day on, British and American transport aircraft were given fighter escort into Berlin, and the Russians hastened to say that no more interference was contemplated.

In mid-June the Russians pulled their representative from the Allied Kommandatura which was running Berlin, ending the four-power administration of the city. And on 24 June the Russians began a complete blockade of the western sectors of Berlin. More than two million Berliners were at risk. The Russians must have believed that they could starve the western sectors

and take them over, thus destroying the West German recovery.

From the earliest interference by the Russians, U.S. Military Governor General Lucius Clay had threatened that he would instruct his troops to open fire "if Soviet soldiers attempted to enter our trains." His approach, however, was vetoed by President Harry Truman who stated that the USA would never open fire unless first fired upon. The Western Allies had only 12,000 men in their Berlin garrisons. They were surrounded by as many as 300,000 Soviet troops. Even if the Allies had chosen to storm the city from the west, it meant risking a new

war with Russia. They were in no shape to fight such a war, and in fact lacked the strength to prevent the Russians from advancing into western Germany should they have chosen to make that move. The Allies had but a single trump card . . . the atomic bomb, and no one thought that a reasonable option.

It seemed that the only solution to the problem of keeping Berlin supplied with food and fuel was a dramatic expansion of the British airlift. While the Allies did have access from their zones to Berlin via three twenty-mile-wide and 10,000-foot-high air corridors that had been allocated by the Russians in November 1945, the idea

The C-54 Skymaster served the U.S. Army Air Forces in World War II and later in the Korean War, as well as during the Berlin Airlift.

was fraught with complications. Berlin had two available airfields—Gatow and Tempelhof, each had only one runway and in both cases it was merely of temporary pierced-steel planking, a surface never intended to withstand the heavy landings of the laden transport planes that were required. There was the threat that the Russians would block the air corridors with barrage balloons or bring up anti-aircraft batteries in the Soviet Zone. Navigation was a problem, complicated by the fact that the Americans did not have the navigational aids the British used, and had to rely mainly on the radio compass. The primitive ground control facilities at the Berlin fields were not up to dealing with heavy air traffic, and especially not in poor weather. Most worrying to the Allies, though, was the need to bring at least 13,500 tons per day of food and fuels that they had been previously providing by road, rail and canal. Neither the British nor the Americans could quickly provide enough aircraft to mount the airlift on the scale required.

Despite the difficulties, Britain's Operation Carter Paterson, which soon became Plainfare, began on 28 June with an initial RAF Dakota taking off from Wunstorf, the first airlift base and the main feeder airfield in the British Zone, in very heavy weather to bring a maximum 7,500-pound load to Gatow. The American effort, called Operation Vittles, was started on 26 June by twenty-five C-47s operating initially from the Wiesbaden and Rhein-Main airfields in the American Zone. These operations were launched primarily by British Foreign Secretary Ernest Bevin and U.S. President Harry Truman who, to their credit, stood firm in the face of some determined domestic, political and military opposition to the planned airlift. Many generals believed at the time that, rather than expanding the effort to provide the airlift capability, they should be concentrating all efforts on preparing for war with the Soviets. Many of the air crewmen who were to fly the airlift had already seen their share of war, having flown as bomber crew members with the Royal Air Force, the U.S. Army Air Force, the Royal Australian Air Force, the Royal New Zealand Air Force, or the South African Air Force, in World War II. In a great historic irony, some who only a few years earlier had been dropping bombs to destroy Berlin now found themselves delivering supplies to help keep its people alive.

The Berlin Airlift was simply a stop-gap meant to buy time to keep the city supplied. Truman and Bevin hoped to save Berlin from a Russian takeover and to convince the Kremlin of the West's strength and determination. They gambled that the Russians would not risk starting a war by shooting down one of the airlift planes. At the same time Bevin arranged for a force of American B-29 Superfortress bombers, by then well known for their nuclear delivery capability, to be stationed in England.

It was all the Allies could manage to supply about 4,000 tons of food and fuel a day. It was September before they could bring in 4,500 tons daily, and January 1949 before a daily delivery of 5,500 tons was achieved. The Berliners were struggling to survive on this greatly reduced ration. The scope of the problem was simply overwhelming. Even with a massive infusion of York, Hastings and Sunderland aircraft by the British, and C-54s by the Americans, to augment the overburdened RAF Dakotas and USAF C-47s, as well as a mish-mash of civilian aircraft, they were still significantly short of airplanes and load capacity. Most of the crews who flew the airlift were for-

mer RAF and USAAF bomber air crew members.

Spare parts were in short supply, as were personnel for servicing and time to do the work. The state of the Tempelhof and Gatow airfields necessitated their upgrading for landing and unloading, which meant that heavy building equipment and materials had to be flown in, and a third airfield had to be constructed at Tegel in the French sector. The new facility was built by the Americans using mostly German female labor who were paid DM1.20 an hour and one hot meal per shift. The women had to do the work as the majority of German military prisoners of war had still to be repatriated. Work on Tegel was round-the-clock and the new airfield allowed a substantially greater quantity of supplies to be flown into Berlin. All ground control facilities had to be modernized and nine new supply airfields had to be built; seven in the British Zone and two in the American. Much of the rubble used as hardcore for the new fields came from the staggering bombed-out ruin of Berlin and was cleared mainly by women. Air traffic control had to be not just reformed, but revolutionized. Aircraft had to take off in timed departure blocks from the supply airfields, and the flights and landings had to be precisely timed to avoid chaos and collision.

RAF Sunderland flying boats were employed from 4 July to operate from the Havel See, a lake located just five minutes by car from the airfield at Gatow. The Sunderlands were special in that they could bring a 10,000-pound load on each trip and because they were sufficiently corrosion-proofed to carry a cargo of salt to Berlin. The flying boats carried their salt to the city until the winter of 1948-49 ended their role, which was then picked up by converted Halifax bomb-

ers known as Haltons. They stored the salt in externally-mounted belly panniers. Soon more aircraft types were added to the airlift effort, including the Tudor, and the Lancastrian version of the Avro Lancaster bomber.

The U.S. Air Force had established a primary airlift operation at the Tempelhof airport in south-central Berlin. Tempelhof now had three parallel runways, each more than 2,000 yards long. The approaches to it were, however, still pbstructed by the remains of some fairly tall buildings, requiring an attentive, on-your-toes landing. The Americans mainly operated Douglas C-54s capable of carrying a ten-ton load into Tempelhof. They had used C-47s until sufficient quantities of the larger planes were available. They also operated a small number of rear-loading Fairchild C-82 Packet cargo planes, mostly for the transport of vehicles and machinery.

The problem of how to haul coal for the essential fueling of industry, for light and heat, was of great concern to the Allies. This heavy, bulky item had to be properly loaded aboard the planes or it could upset their trim and the dust from the coal could find its way into every area of the aircraft, making controls sticky and unresponsive. Similar problems were encountered with the transport of flour. Vegetables and fruit were dried for lighter shipment. Meat was boned to save on weight, and then tinned or made into sausage to give it a longer life. One such sausage product was evidently so repellent that even the undernourished Berliners could not tolerate it. It is said that a civil servant then had the bright idea that they could be bribed to eat it by offering them a double ration. There were few takers.

Through it all the hungry and courageous people of Berlin carried on, feeling that as long as they could hear the drone of aircraft they had hope. Through it all the Russians continued to hassle and harass the Berliners. They were only allowed four hours of electricity a day and never knew when it would be turned on. There was very little coal for heating in that terrible winter and they broke up their furniture to burn rather than accept Soviet offers of free coal. They endured endless abuse and harassment by the Russians, but held fast to their will to be free. And through it all they retained their sense of humor: "Aren't we lucky? Imagine if the British and Americans were besieging us and the Russians were running the airlift."

The great airlift continued beyond 12 May 1949, when the Soviets officially ended their 318-day blockade of Berlin. Scaled down from their peak days, the British and Americans continued Plainfare and Vittles through 23 September and 1 October respectively, to stockpile supply reserves for the Berliners. In the end the numbers were impressive. Royal Air Force aircraft delivered 394,509 tons, British civil aircraft delivered 147,727 tons, and U.S. Air Force aircraft brought in 1,783,573 tons, for a combined total of 2,325,809 tons. Of the load carried by the British, food amounted to 241,713 tons; coal 164,800 tons; military 18,239 tons; liquid fuel 92,282 tons; and miscellaneous 25,202 tons. Of the total delivered by the USAF, food amounted to 296,303 tons; coal 1,421,730 tons, and liquid fuel 65,540 tons. The British also elected to bring loads back west from Berlin, a total of 35,843 tons. The French delivered 800 metric tons of supplies to the garrison in their sector in 424 sorties. Both British and American aircraft were used to airlift passengers to and from Berlin; the British bringing in 36,218 and carrying out 131,436, while the Americans brought in 24,216 and

A cargo of what may be coal is unloaded from this C-54 in Berlin.

carried out 36,584. In the course of the airlift British and American aircraft made 195,530 sorties to Berlin. The daily average tonnage carried was 4,980. Aircraft used in the Berlin airlift included the Douglas C-47 Skytrain and Dakota, the Avro York, the Handley-Page Hastings, the Handley-Page Halifax, the Short Sunderland, the Fairchild C-82 Packet, the Handley-Page Halton, the Avro Tudor, the Avro Lancastrian, the Douglas C-54 Skymaster, the Avro Lincoln, the Short Hythe, the Consolidated Liberator, The Bristol Freighter, the Boeing C-97 Stratofreighter, the Douglas C-74 Globemaster, and the Vickers Viking. During the airlift there were thirty-one American fatalities, eighteen British military fatalities, and twenty-one British civilian fatalities.

The Berlin Airlift was a kind of miracle. Even the weather seemed to cooperate to some extent, with less frost and ice in Germany than in most winters. As the complex problems of

the effort were gradually resolved, so too did the hoped-for effect occur. Stalin undoubtedly realized that West Berlin would come through his siege to the prospect of a bright and prosperous future thanks to the Marshall Plan and their rescue by the amazing airlift.

February 1949. Germany's political leaders met in Bonn to draft their constitution for a separate West German state. And in light of the burgeoning airlift the Soviet ambassador to the United Nations approached his American counterpart for conversations leading to a settlement of the Berlin crisis. There followed meetings of the Western Allies on the establishment of a new bond of nations to be called the North Atlantic Treaty Organization, in which all members would come to the aid of any member nation that was attacked. The treaty was ratified on 9 May and the next day the Russians announced that they were lifting the Berlin blockade.

German school children watch the departure of a Douglas Skymaster after it delivered its precious cargo of supplies to the people of Berlin in the midst of the airlift operation.

STEALTH

An example of the F-117A stealth fighter-bomber on public display in an airshow at RAF Fairford, England.

Sombre the night is. And though we have our lives, we know what sinister threat lurks there.
—from *Returning, We Hear the Larks* by Isaac Rosenberg

Can you keep a secret? Certainly, the United States Air Force can. For more than a decade it managed to hide the existence of its ultra-low-observable F-117A stealth fighter/bomber from the press, the public, the "other side" and, to a large extent, from the members of the U.S. Congress.

In the mid-1970s the USAF began a serious effort to develop a significantly less visible fighter/bomber aircraft, one that projected a dramatically reduced radar cross section or RCS. The Air Force was looking for an aircraft that would be inherently less visible to enemy radar and thus safer from radar-directed threats than conventional aircraft. It had to be able to approach and attack its target undetected, to minimize the possibility of its being intercepted.

So-called "stealth" technology was developing during this time, and in 1975 two Lockheed engineers, members of Kelly Johnson's Advanced Development Projects Division, known as the Skunk Works group, made the key breakthrough. They solved the problem of predicting how a body of a given shape (an aircraft) would scatter radiation over all feasible angles of incidence, offering an extremely low RCS. That elegant solution came to be known as "faceting." One of these design engineers, Bill Schroeder, produced a drawing of a flyable, controllable aircraft that featured no curved surfaces at all, substituting instead small-radius straight edges on the wings and tail surfaces. The point was to show a finite number of edges and flat

surfaces to the radar wave, and to achieve this, Schroeder sought the help of software engineer Dennis Overholser. Overholser designed a program utilizing the Skunk Works' Control Data mainframe computer, to model the scattering of radiation from Schroeder's faceted shapes and predict their radar cross section relatively quickly.

Through trial and error, the Overholser program ultimately made it possible for the Lockheed designers to produce an aircraft shape which seemed capable of flight as well as the efficient management of incoming radar energy all at once.

Lockheed was then in a position to begin design of a faceted operational stealth combat aircraft that was to be all but undetectable by radar or infrared capabilities. The plane would carry a pair of highly accurate 2,000-pound bombs over a reasonable range and would combine the most effective uses of faceting and radar-absorbent material (RAM) possible in early 1976, when its first drawings were being made.

The people at Lockheed knew then that no one, and especially not the United States Air Force, would be likely to fund their new stealth fighter/bomber development project. So, they opted instead for a "technology demonstration" program; a relatively cheap effort which they expected would prove the viability and near-invisibility of their stealthy baby. They proposed construction of two prototypes scaled to 60 percent actual size and looking a lot like the real projected aircraft. They contained costs in the development of the prototypes by using, whenever possible, off-the-shelf parts from existing aircraft, and brought the two test aircraft in for about $35 million.

In 1976, Ben Rich, then head of the

Skunk Works design team, persuaded the U.S. Defense Advanced Research Projects Agency (DARPA) to pick up the tab for the stealth demonstrator program. DARPA has historically supported relatively high-risk technology projects which appear to offer high potential, and often a multi-service application. The Lockheed project received DARPA funding in early 1977 and was given the code name HAVE BLUE, which probably meant something to someone somewhere.

During the time of the Jimmy Carter presidential administration, security concerns about the highly sensitive stealth project resulted in it being moved from DARPA, with its many civilian employees, to the control of the U.S. Air Force Systems Command. It was set up in a secure project office at Wright-Patterson Air Force Base, Ohio, and the tightest of security nets was thrown over it. The design and fabrication of the two demonstrator aircraft was going ahead at Lockheed's Burbank, California facility. The planes were virtually made by hand, test pilots were selected, and flight testing of the completed scaled-down prototypes began early in 1978 at the top-secret Groom Lake, Nevada, base.

Groom Lake surely heads the list of America's least hospitable tourist attractions. Enclosed in an immense parcel of government-owned land about the size of Switzerland, the complex of hangars and support structures presents a bleak and bleached vista to anyone approaching, not that doing so is advisable. The proprietors are never in the mood to receive callers, and the many prominent official warnings along the hundreds of miles of perimeter fencing make their attitude abundantly clear. Stay out, go away, don't come back. What goes on here doesn't concern

you and if you try to gain entry to the area you'll wish you hadn't. That is the essence of the message from those who run the place where things like stealth aircraft have been tested. Fair enough. National security normally demands one or more layers of secrecy, and how many of us really have a need to know what happens at places like Groom Lake?

Through the detailed test program Lockheed and the Air Force learned about the subtleties of radar cross section reduction and the vital importance of radar-absorbent materials to their wondrous faceted aircraft. As in any test program, there were accidents and failures. But with them came understanding and the pair of HAVE BLUE airplanes proved that an ultra-low-observable aircraft could fly and fly well.

With this proof in hand, the Carter administration moved quickly to fund the next phase of U.S. stealth development. The project, code-named Senior Trend, had as its goal to prove that a stealth aircraft could perform its combat mission. To do so, the program was charged with the final design, development and production of the full-size Lockheed stealth fighter/bomber.

The idea behind the stealth fighter/bomber was that it should be capable of flying its mission, hitting at relatively small but important targets with a high degree of precision and minimal collateral damage, without much need for escort or support aircraft. It was to be developed as a single-seat night strike plane. It had to be deliverable virtually anywhere in the world where it might be needed by means of a giant C-5 transport, the outer wing sections of the stealth plane being removable.

An initial production order for twenty aircraft was placed; it included

five planes designated as test aircraft. The Senior Trend airplanes entered production in 1980 and in August of that year President Carter cancelled the B-1 bomber program (revived in October 1981 by President Reagan). Carter had his reasons, of course, and one of them—the undisclosed key reason—was probably the rapidly growing stealth aircraft technology which seems to have changed a lot of minds in Washington and redirected a lot of 1980 developmental funding by the Congress. It then directed that research should begin immediately into the feasibility and design of a new Advanced Technology Bomber (ATB). The plan was to have the new bird operational by 1987. It was at this point that the Administration decided to disclose the existence of Have Blue, though not by that name. Some of the history of the program was released, but no reference was made to work on the stealth fighter/bomber project which continued in its highly classified status for several years.

"We were like the rabbi who gets a hole-in-one on Saturday"
—Ben Rich, Vice President and General Manager of the Lockheed special projects facility known as the 'Skunk Works,' on why he could not discuss the F-117 stealth aircraft for many years.

The stealth fighter/bomber was ultimately designated F-117 and continued in test at the Groom Lake facility through 1982.

The plane is impressive from any angle. It has the size and weight of the front-line F-15 Eagle. Its delta-like wing delivers low drag at high speed, easy handling at high attack angles and simplicity of structure and assembly. It takes off at about 180 knots and

The F-117A Nighthawk.

comes in on final at a fairly hot 150-175 knots. Most modern fighters are not naturally stable and the stealth is no exception. It flies with a GEC Astronics analogue control system, artificially generating the necessary in-flight stability characteristics through fly-by-wire technology.

With the F-117 becoming operational in the early 1980s, it was clear to the Air Force that the Groom Lake base, while perfectly adequate as a test facility, was no place to house an operational unit. The best option seemed to be a site within Nevada's immense Tonopah Test Range, another restricted area northwest of Las Vegas. Prior to 1983, the range was where the nuclear weapons drop-tests had been conducted, and the

existing airfield built in the 1950s for Sandia Laboratories offered an excellent foundation around which to build a new stealth base. The size of the test range area was to provide ample seclusion for the black jets and the security was so efficient that the location was not reported to the public until nearly two years after the base became operational.

When the Air Force began to comb its files for people to fly the stealth fighter/bomber operationally, it followed a criterion calling for pilots with 1,000 hours of flying time, mainly in fighter aircraft. Most of them would hold the rank of Captain and would have considerable experience flying air-to-ground missions in aircraft like the F-4, the A-10, and the F-111.

The ideal candidate would be a very good pilot who was calm, serious, and mature. When interviewed, the candidates were informed that they would be flying the A-7 aircraft, which, in fact, they would to some extent; that they would be in a location which would require them to be away from their families during the week and that, at the end of the interview, they would only be given five minutes to decide whether to volunteer for the program.

"The young men of the world no longer possess the road: The road possesses them. They no longer inherit the earth: The earth inherits them. They are no longer the masters of fire: Fire is their master: They serve him, he destroys them. They no lon-

ger rule the waters: The genius of the seas has invented a new monster, and they fly from its teeth. They no longer breathe freely: The genius of the air has contrived a new terror that rends them into pieces.
—from *Lament* by F. S. Flint

The first of them were brought into the program in mid-1982, and with no two-seat version of the F-117 to be trained on, each new pilot's first flight was also his solo. Their training progressed and in 1983 the new 4450th Tactical Group took up residence at the Tonopah base where a more formal level of operational training was administered. At this time more and more key members of the U.S. House and Senate armed services and appropriations committees were cleared to be briefed about the stealth program. They liked what they heard, so much that they voted to increase funding for the program and directed the Air Force to buy an entire four-squadron wing of seventy-two aircraft. The final purchase, however, was just fifty-nine.

The continuing security requirement of the F-117 activity made many demands on the pilots in the early months at the Tonopah base. All pilots in the program were required to be housed with their families at Nellis AFB near Las Vegas, 190 miles from the TTR base. They had to commute to and from the job at Tonopah on Mondays and Fridays, flown back and forth in 727s operated by a company called Key Airlines, a charter line that was being kept quite busy by the U.S. Defense Department.

Flying virtually all training missions at night during the week, and then having to adjust to a normal daytime routine on weekends with their families at Nellis, meant that the stealth pilots had to change their body clocks as much as eight or nine hours

a week. Thus many of them were carrying a very high fatigue factor through their training, as well as being chronically jet-lagged. One Thursday night during this period, Major Ross Mulhare admitted to another stealth pilot at TTR that he was tired and "just couldn't shake it." Still, he elected to fly, launching on one of the last missions of that night at 1:13 a.m. At approximately 1:45 Mulhare's aircraft was seen by an accompanying pilot to plunge into a mountainside in the Sequoia National Forest, north of Bakersfield, California. According to the other pilot, Mulhare apparently made no attempt to eject and was killed in the crash. A cloak of secrecy was dropped over the crash site by the Air Force. Firefighters called to the scene were made to sign statements declaring that they would say nothing about what they had seen at the site.

After the Mulhare crash things were different. When armed USAF personnel took charge of the area surrounding the crash site, word of it got out and the press and media were on the scent of something unusual and important by early the next day. Reports about the stealth were beginning to leak now, though the Air Force still did not acknowledge the plane's existence. But the 800 or so civilian employees at TTR who lived in or near Tonopah were seeing the F-117 regularly, as were many residents of other nearby towns. Keeping the secret became more of a challenge to the service and events like the Mulhare crash added to the problem. Members of the Reagan administration believed in maintaining the veil of secrecy around the U.S. stealth activity to the maximum, and resisted pressures to show the fighter/bomber to the press and public.

While continuing to believe that the secrecy was essential to the secu-

rity of the program, the Air Force was at the same time inhibited by its own restrictions on day flying of the stealth fighter/bomber and on the use of any bases for it other than the TTR facility. Finally, on 10 November 1988, after the recent presidential election, the announcement came and with it a rather poor-quality, heavily-edited photo of the plane, released by the Pentagon, which actually revealed very little about the design phenomenon the USAF had kept quiet about for so many years.

Now the news was out. The rumors were proven to be true, and the Air Force was at last able to fly its strange black fighter/bomber at all hours of the day and night from TTR and elsewhere.

16 January 1991. Forty-five combat-ready F-117A stealth fighter/bombers were housed in the brand new hardened and blast-proof aircraft shelters of the Khamis Mushait base, nicknamed Tonopah East, in southern Saudi Arabia. Their deployment to the Gulf had begun on 19 August 1990, when aircraft of the 37th Tactical Fighter Wing's 415th Tactical Fighter Squadron were moved from their Nevada base as a result of Iraq's invasion of neighboring Kuwait on 2 August. In addition to the aircraft, some sixty combat-qualified stealth pilots were on hand at the immaculate Saudi base.

When the Allied Coalition attacks began, the F-117As hit the vital Iraqi communications and command and control sites, which they took out with relative ease. Thereafter, the black jets were shifted to strategic targets, including airfields, bridges, chemical and nuclear facilities, as well as specialized targets within Baghdad. One third of the 1,271 combat missions flown by the F-117As during

A Nighthawk stealth fighter-bomber being towed to the main runway at RAF Fairford.

the Desert Storm campaign were flown over Baghdad, penetrating the fire of an estimated 3,000 anti-aircraft artillery pieces and some sixty SAM missile sites. No hits of any kind were recorded on any of the stealths.

The black fighter/bombers always attacked at night and each aircraft normally flew two missions a night, though each pilot usually flew only once. A mission from their Saudi base averaged 5.4 hours and required a number of in-flight refuelings. The planes flew in pairs but normally attacked singly. A typical stealth mission put the airplane inside Iraqi airspace for about thirty minutes. The stealth pilots flew their missions in radio-silence. The mission routes and altitudes were constantly changed, to keep the Iraqis guessing.

The accuracy of the stealth's imaging infra-red weapons system amazed the world when CNN and other television networks showed the plane's laser-guided bombs targeting and destroying objectives as small as specific windows and ventilation shafts. The stealth's hit rate in the Gulf campaign was 80-85 percent, compared to the 30-35 percent that was typically achieved by other aircraft in the Vietnam War.

In time the stealth became known as Nighthawk. It had been created to bring stealth technology against high-value targets and, in the operations against targets in Baghdad, the airplane proved capable of delivering its load of sophisticated weaponry on such priority

sites with remarkable efficiency, virtual impunity, and with minimal loss of civilian life.

In 2014, the Northrop Grumman B-2 Spirit stealth bomber was twenty-five years old. It was announced that this most formidable of weapons would be receiving a $10 billion upgrade over the next several years to improve its avionics, communications and other systems and keep the amazing bat-winged beast at the forefront of modern bomber capability at least through the middle of the twenty-first century.

In the late 1970s, when Jimmy Carter was President of the United States, development of the B-2 began in the Advanced Technology Bomber

The American B-2 Spirit stealth bomber on display for the first time at RAF Fairford, England.

project and continued through the years of the Ronald Reagan presidency. In the course of those developmental years, as has so often occurred in new technologies, the program was beset with delays and substantial cost increases. The unit cost in 1997 dollars of the B-2 was averaging $737 million, but the total procurement cost per aircraft, including spare parts, was closer to an average of $929 million, pushing the total program cost, including design, development, engineering and testing, to a staggering $2.1 billion per airplane.

The Spirit was a strategic bomber concept taking advantage of low-observable stealth technology, intended to penetrate dense anti-aircraft defenses of Soviet airspace to deliver both conventional and nuclear bombs. But late in the 1980s, with the end of the Cold War, the B-2 project became highly controversial in Washington as both houses of the U.S. Congress, as well as the Joint Chiefs of Staff, debated the need for the aircraft. The debate resulted in a substantial reduction of the original plan to order 132 of the planes, to a new total of just twenty-one. With the loss of a B-2 in a 2008 crash, the U.S. Air Force now operates a total B-2 force of twenty aircraft which it plans to keep in service through at least 2058.

"If the B-2 is invisible, just announce you've built a hundred of them and don't build them."
—John Kasich, Chairman, U.S. House Budget Committee, July, 1995

The U.S. requirement for a major strategic jet bomber force was fulfilled in 1952 with the introduction of the big eight-engine Boeing B-52, a very capable, highly durable and adaptable airplane. As capable as she was, however, by the 1970s, the Air Force began planning a replacement for the Stratofortress, as the B-52 was called. And in the '70s, the developing American stealth technology led to a new approach to the design of the next USAF bomber. The notion that a bomber built with an airframe that could absorb and/or deflect enemy radar and thus be largely undetectable and relatively invulnerable to such types of enemy attack, had become viable. In 1974, the Defense Advanced Research Projects Agency called for expertise from American military aircraft companies on what they believed to be the largest radar cross section of an aircraft that could be built to effectively be invisible to radars.

Northrop and Lockheed aviation corporations were selected by DARPA to pursue early development of such an aircraft; Northrop, for its background in flying wing technology, design and construction; and Lockheed, due to its experience in the design and development of the SR-71 ultra-high performance reconnaissance plane with its various "stealthy" features, and their involvement led to the Have Blue stealth aircraft program. The proof of the stealth aircraft capability, as demonstrated by the Have Blue aircraft, led to the start of the Advanced Technology Bomber program in 1979. Aircraft manufacturer combinations Northrop/Boeing and Lockheed/Rockwell were then awarded research contracts for further work in the ATB program and both of these teams went forward on the basis of flying wing designs.

On 20 October 1981 DARPA chose to proceed with a Northrop design for what would become the B-2 bomber, an aircraft operated by a crew of two, with a cruising speed of 560 mph, a top speed of 630 mph, a

range of 6,000 nautical miles without refueling and over 10,000 miles with one aerial refueling. It has a 336,500-pound loaded weight and a service ceiling of 50,000 feet. The B-2 can carry up to eighty 500-pound JDAM guided bombs, or sixteen 2,400-pound B83 nuclear bombs.

The B-2 was produced through its prime manufacturer Northrop Grumman between 1987 and 2000, with a total run of twenty-one aircraft. The aircraft first flew on 17 July 1989, from Palmdale, California, to nearby Edwards Air Force Base. It was introduced into USAF service in April 1997.

The low-observable B-2 is made mostly of a carbon graphite composite material that is both lighter than aluminum and stronger than steel. It's stealth comes mainly from reduced acoustic, visual, infra-red, and radar signatures, and the ability of the carbon graphite composite material to absorb a lot of radar energy, all resulting in a relatively tiny radar signature. The airplane reportedly does not always fly in its most stealthy mode. When approaching potentially hostile air defenses, the B-2 pilots "stealth up" to absolutely minimize the aircraft's visibility to radar. Unlike the stark, flat surfaces which form all the shapes of the F-117 fighter/bomber, the B-2 is largely designed with curved and rounded surfaces over its airframe to deflect radar beams. Its radar signature is further reduced through the use of special radar-absorbent surface materials (RAM), and through the design of its clean, low-drag wing.

The B-2 fleet is based at Whiteman Air Force Base, seventy miles southeast of Kansas City. The airplane first entered combat in 1999 during the war in Kosovo where it was used to destroy approximately one-third of the Serbian targets in the first two months of American involvement in that conflict. In these operations, the B-2s flew non-stop sorties from Whiteman to Kosovo and back and, in these flights it was the first aircraft to use GPS-satellite-guided JDAM "smart bombs." And in Afghanistan B-2s flew some their longest-ranging missions during Operation Enduring Freedom.

B-2s took part in the Iraq War during Operation Iraqi Freedom, operating from Whiteman as well as from a base on the island of Diego Garcia and one other location.

"The B-2 is a legacy of the Cold War. It was designed to deliver as many as sixteen nuclear bombs inside the Soviet Union by using stealth technology to evade its dense air defense systems. The plane can't shoot to defend itself, but then it shouldn't need to. Its radar-deflecting skin is designed to let it sneak through hostile skies undetected."
—Matt Campbell, *The Kansas City Star*

The North American P-51 Mustang was unquestionably the outstanding escort fighter of the war and, in the opinion of many airmen and historians, the best all-round fighter aircraft as well. German Air Force chief Hermann Goering told an interviewer during the period of the Nuremberg War Crimes Trials that he realized Germany had lost the war when he first saw Mustangs escorting American bombers over Berlin.

above: B-17s of the Horham-based 95th Bomb Group, 8AF being escorted on a raid by P-47 Thunderbolt fighters; right: A P-47 fighter in close-up and probably photographed from an American bomber; far right: Armorers feeding ammunition into the wing-mounted machine-guns of a Thunderbolt on an fighter station in southern England during World War II.

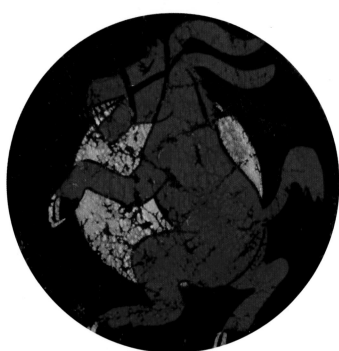

below: American bomber air crewmen prior to a mission; left: Nissen huts remaining at the Steeple Morden fighter base near Cambridge; below: Jacket patches and an 8AF wall painting.

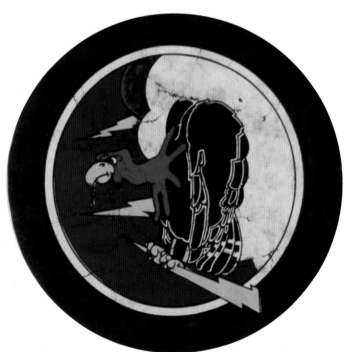

left: Servicing a P-47 fighter on an 8AF station in southern England; right: P-47 pilots Bob Johnson, Hub Zemke, and Bud Mahurin at their Boxted base; bottom right: Former 8AF fighter crew chief Merle Olmsted and the outstanding fighter leader Hub Zemke.

above: An RAF Polish squadron Spitfire escorting B-17s of the Podington-based 92nd Bomb Group, 8AF, on a raid to Germany; right: P-47 pilots Bob Johnson and Bud Mahurin of the 8AF 56th Fighter Group engage in a little hangar flying back at their Boxted base; far right: 56th FG Thunderbolt ace Francis Gabreski with his aircraft.

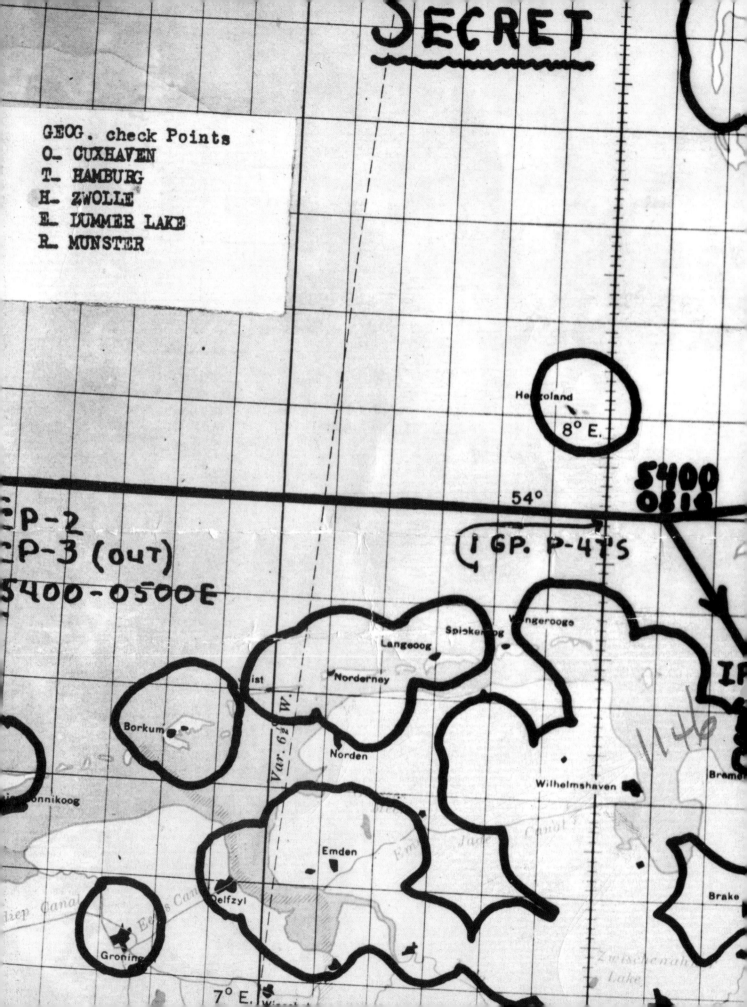

SECRET

GEOG. check Points
O. CUXHAVEN
T. HAMBURG
H. ZWOLLE
E. DUMMER LAKE
R. MUNSTER

Helgoland
8° E.

54°

5400
0818

P-2
P-3 (OUT)
5400-0500E

1 GP. P-47'S

Vangerooge
Spiekeroog
Langeoog
Norderney
ist
Borkum
Norden
Wilhelmshaven
Bremen
onnikoog
Var. 6° W.
Emden
Brake
Delfzyl
Groningen
Zwischenahn Lake
7° E.

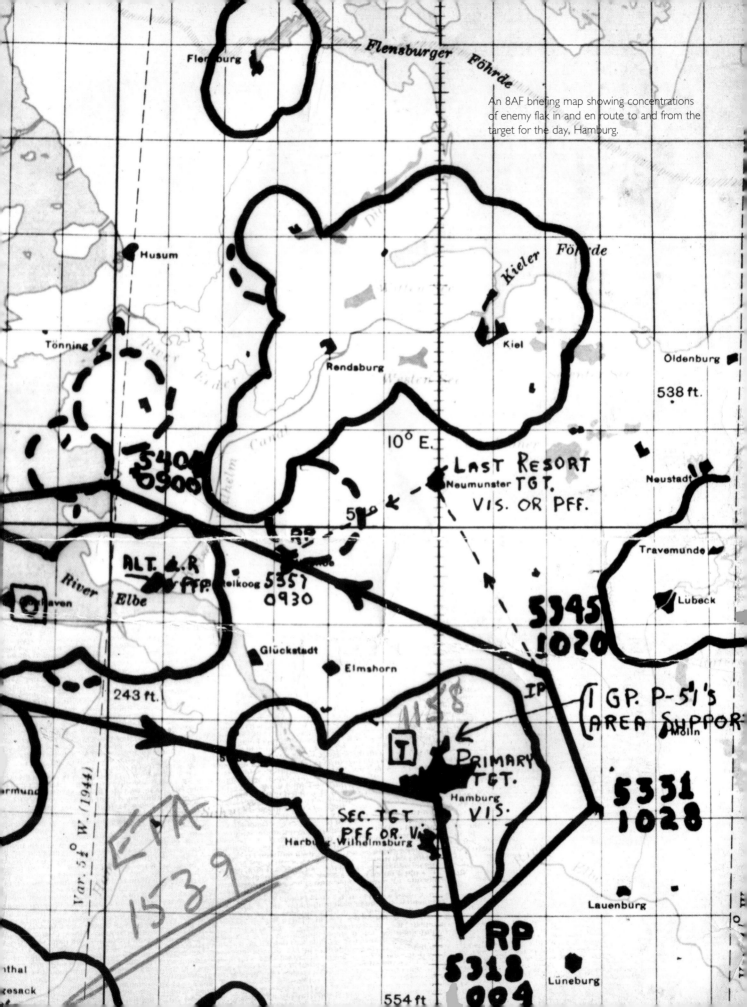

An 8AF briefing map showing concentrations of enemy flak in and en route to and from the target for the day, Hamburg.

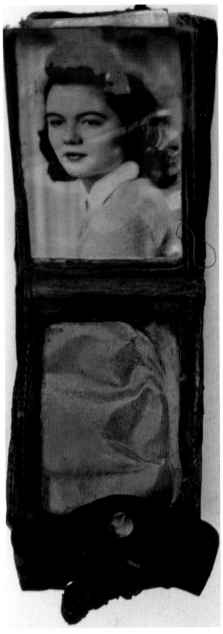

left: Late-model P-47 Thunderbolts in fine formation; above: The wallet of an American fighter pilot was found at the crash site of his aircraft in wartime England.

The Lockheed P-38 Lightning undergoing servicing in Burbank, California during the war.

below: The Lockheed P-38 fighter of Lt Col Jack Jenkins, Commanding Officer, 55th Fighter Group at Wormingford, England; right: A P-38 pilot standing atop his drop-tank-equipped airplane; bottom center: Captain Jack Illfrey and his P-38 Lightning; bottom far right: Captain Ilfrey after being shot down and evading capture in France during June 1944.

A beautifully restored P-51D Mustang escort fighter
still airworthy in the twenty-first century.

Pilots of the 4th Fighter Group at Debden,
England in 1944; right: Captain Don Gentile,
an outstanding ace of the group;.

below: Ralph "Kid" Hofer, 4FG; right: Vermont Garrison, 4FG, bottom right: Colonel Don Blakeslee, Commanding Officer of the 4FG.

Major Winslow "Mike" Sobanski, 4FG, 8AF, shown here with his P-47 Thunderbolt, was killed on D-Day, 6 June 1944, while flying a fighter sweep in northern France when his P-51 Mustang was damaged and then shot down by an enemy fighter. He was credited with five aerial victories in combat; far left: A Lockheed employee at work on a P-38 Lightning fighter at the Burbank, California plant.

EFFECTIVE?

How well have bomber aircraft been employed in the many conflicts since World War I? How effective have campaigns such as the Combined Bombing Offensive against Germany in World War II been, and in what measure did aerial bombing actually contribute to ultimate victory in that and the other wars of the twentieth century?

Throughout World War I, bombing was fascinating to the participants as a concept, but in practice it was not particularly effective. Many attempts were made by the air arms of the combatants to strike decisively at their enemy through aerial bombardment, but nearly all such efforts fell short of acknowledged victory in battle. The relatively fragile and under-powered aircraft of the time were simply incapable of the energy and the bomb-carrying capacity needed to make a significant impact on their targets. With the exception of the attacks aimed at destroying enemy aircraft sitting on their aerodromes, and thus ensuring at least temporary control of the airspace above a battle zone, little was actually achieved by the majority of airmen operating in the pure bombing role.

Bombing did, however, make a powerful psychological contribution to the efforts of the First War combatants. Stark visions of terror bombing in the years to come raised the level of fear in world capitals and many military leaders correctly predicted horrific future raids.

In World War I, the most effective bombing was done by tactical aircraft. Relatively light, small and fast, these machines proved the most successful in support of their ground forces in the battle zones.

While it is true that the bomber was born in World War I, and that its development and evolution gath-

ered momentum in that conflict, so too were its vulnerabilities then identified and exploited. Progress in the development of fighter aircraft and in anti-aircraft defenses was equally impressive. Probably the most interesting portents of the bomber's role in future wars, though, were the early indications that it would be of greatest effect when applied against enemy airfields and other targets relating to the suppression of enemy air power and the control of enemy airspace. Where the planners seem to have erred repeatedly since 1914 is in their assumption that saturation attacks on essentially civilian targets would be as effective as hitting industrial, supply, or communications targets, or enemy airfields. Most evidence to date suggests that bombing civilians invariably fails to destroy their collective morale. Nearly all nations who have mounted significant campaigns of aerial bombardment in all conflicts since World War I have discovered, but failed to learn, that bombing civilians actually tends to harden their resolve.

The Spanish Civil War in 1936 revealed what Germany would soon bring to the air action of World War II. When Nationalist General Francisco Franco requested assistance from Adolf Hitler in the form of Ju 52 transport planes, the German leader not only complied, sending twenty, but also supplied crews to operate and maintain them, as well as reinforcements. In August of that year, he provided the first elements of the Kondor Legion, a force made up of bomber and fighter gruppe, a reconnaissance staffel, three air signals units and a marine gruppe. Kondor was initially led by GeneralMajor Hugo Sperrle, who was later to command Luftflotte 3 in the Battle of Britain. The Kondor Legion was relatively ineffective until the summer of 1937 when

it was re-equipped with the newest Me 109B fighters and the Dornier Do 17 and Heinkel He 111 bombers. Spain became the test bed for the new German bombers as well as the 109. Their strengths and deficiencies were quickly spotlighted and several important tactics were devised in this period. The Heinkel, in particular, performed well, hinting at somewhat more promise that it would actually deliver in the greater war to come.

To their dismay, the Germans found that they had committed one of the major errors of World War II in an early stage of the Battle of Britain in August 1940. They suddenly relented after a week of bombing RAF fighter airfields that were key to the defense of the UK. Instead of continuing to pound these vital bases, they turned their attention to essentially civilian targets and in so doing allowed the RAF precious time to regroup, repair and recharge itself for the rounds to come.

In the period between the two great world wars, opportunities for testing new and improved bomber types, including the Junkers Ju 86 and the Heinkel He 111, came for Germany with the Spanish Civil War. That war exposed dramatic deficiencies in both German aircraft. In the far east, the Sino-Japanese war, which broke out in 1937, afforded the Army Air Force of Japan a chance to put their new Mitsubishi Ki-30, and the Kawasaki Ki-32 single-engine monoplane bombers to the test. These machines, together with the Mitsubishi Ki-21, and the Mitsubishi G3M (built for the Japanese Naval Air Force) were used in a series of highly effective attacks against Chinese airfields, in which most of China's military aircraft were destroyed. They were considerably less successful, however, in 1939 when they went up against the Soviet

A low-level view of the ruins of Munich after the combined Allied bombing offensive against Germany.

Union and a multitude of Russian fighters.

Meanwhile, design and testing of a range of new bombers for the French Air Force, including the Breguet 693-AB2 and the LeO 451, many of them showing promise in their early development, was largely to no avail. By the time they were operational, they were obsolete.

Italy proved to be a significant player, fielding three bombers of impressive quality and performance, all of them emanating from the mid-1930s. Undoubtedly the best of these was one that emerged from its earlier airliner origins to become a superb land-based bomber, the Savoia-Marchetti SM 79. Built mainly of wood and powered by three 750 hp Alfa Romeo engines, this 267 mph lightweight was able to deliver a 2,750-pound bomb load over a range of 1,180 miles, with a service ceiling of more than 21,000 feet. It proved extremely effective in the Mediterranean, the Balkans, and North Africa. Additionally, the Italians produced significant machines in the twin-engined Fiat BR 20 and the somewhat shorter-lived Savoia-Marchetti SM 81, the latter operating successfully in both the Ethiopian campaign and the Spanish Civil War.

The two best Russian bombers of World War II were the long-range Ilyushin Il-4 and the Petlyakov PE series beginning with the Pe-2 tactical bomber. The Pe-2 was an outstanding combat aircraft originally planned as a fighter. It was adapted as a high-altitude bomber which, like the De Havilland Mosquito, evolved through many refinements and, with its clean aerodynamic design, was always fast enough to be difficult for the German fighters to intercept. Speed was its great asset and Russian Hurricanes, flying in the escort role for the Pe-2s, were frequently unable to keep up

with them. The Pe-2 was easily among the most effective, efficient, and high-achieving weapons on the Eastern Front.

Ethical and political issues aside, the argument over the effectiveness of aerial bombardment in war rages on. The most devout advocates of aerial bombing insist that air power alone, properly directed and utilized, can achieve victory. At the other extreme are those who feel that bombing per se, even highly precise bombing of the most legitimate targets, is prohibitively expensive in all ways. They believe that in the end it accomplishes very little and that ground and sea forces are the only real means to a win. While it may be a stretch to suggest that bombing alone won World War II, it is demonstrable that the delivery of two atomic bombs by American B-29s in August 1945 certainly ended it.

Statistically, RAF Bomber Command's bombing accuracy progressed from the early days through 1941 when, using as a measure, bombs striking within three miles of their aiming point, accuracy had risen from almost nil, to 16 percent. It actually increased to 96 percent by late 1944.

Two significant surveys were launched near the end of, and just after World War II, to establish the effects, statistically and in real terms, of the Allied bombing offensive against Germany. The Americans set up the U.S. Strategic Bombing Survey in November 1944 to begin to assess the results of their bombing campaign. By the end of the war in Europe, the USSBS employed some 500 military enlisted men, 350 officers, and 350 civilians who represented a range of disciplines. The British Bombing Survey Unit was administered by the Royal Air Force and was comprised of personnel from the RAF, the British Army and the Royal Navy as well as civil servants and civilians from business and industry.

Both the American and British survey units were viewed with some suspicion and mistrust by some in high places within the American Air Force and the British Air Ministry. In both cases, direct and indirect attempts were made to influence the results in the report of these survey units.

The work of the U.S. survey team, and the publication of more than sixty reports (of more than 200 prepared) went on through the spring of 1947. It involved the responses to questionnaires given to some 8,000 industrial managers in fifty German cities, along with interviews of local and central Government officials, as well as extensive field research in several key locales. According to Norman Longmate in his book *The Bombers*: "Every possible aspect of the effect of bombing was studied, from the suicide rate—people killed themselves just as frequently in the lightly-bombed areas as in the devastated places—to the effect of religious and political background on attitudes to the war. 'The more actively religious cities . . . had a lower war morale', it appeared, than the more Godless districts, while the largest 'incidence of voluntary participation in war activities and . . . the smallest number of people ready to accept unconditional surrender' was in the North Central Region, containing Hamburg and Bremen, which had been more badly bombed than anywhere else in Germany.

"The immensely thorough U.S. survey bore out to a remarkable degree the conclusions of the British team: 'The major cities of Germany present a spectacle of destruction so appalling as to suggest a complete breakdown of all aspects of urban activity. In the

first impression it would appear that the area attacks which laid waste these cities must have substantially eliminated the industrial capacity of Germany. Yet this was not the case. The attacks did not so reduce German war production as to have a decisive effect on the outcome of the war . . . The effects of town area attacks on the morale of the German people were, with the exception of one estimate, very much over-estimated by all other ministries and departments throughout the course of the war . . . There is no evidence that they caused any serious break in the morale of the populations as a whole.' From a report of the U.S. survey: 'Bomb damage to the civilian economy was not at proximate cause of the military collapse of Germany. There is no evidence that shortages of civilian goods reached a point where the German authorities were forced to transfer resources from war production in order to prevent disintegration of the home front.' In its final conclusion statement, however, the U.S. Strategic Bombing Survey report stated: 'Allied air power was decisive in the war in western Europe. Hindsight inevitably suggests that it might have been employed differently or better in some respects. Nevertheless, it was decisive. In the air, its victory was complete; at sea, its contribution, combined with naval power, brought an end to the enemy's greatest naval threat—the U-boat; on land, it helped turn the tide overwhelmingly in favor of Allied ground forces. Its power and superiority made possible the success of the invasion. It brought the economy which sustained the enemy's armed forces to virtual collapse, although the full effects of this collapse had not reached the enemy's front lines when they were overrun by Allied forces. It brought home to the German people the full impact

of modern war with all its horror and suffering. Its imprint on the German nation will be lasting.'

"The decisive facts came from the show-place of area bombing, Hamburg. The 1943 raids left more than 750,000 homeless . . . At the end of 1943 there was still a backlog of 80,000 unfilled requests for housing. Of the 81,000 industrial and commercial buildings in the city . . . more than 48 percent were completely destroyed. But though production dropped by 50 percent in August, it was back to 82 percent of normal by December. Seventy-five thousand of the industrial labor force of 250,000 had 'failed to return to work' by then but 'war industries were least affected and later transfers of workers from non-essential plants . . . were generally sufficient to offset the slight shortage which did exist.' All Bomber Command's most destructive operations had achieved was a loss of 1.8 months of the city's industrial production, about half of which was intended for the German armed forces. The Americans' main conclusion was the same as that already reached by the British: 'Although attacks against city areas resulted in overall production loss estimated at roughly 9 percent in 1943 and perhaps as much as 17 percent in 1944, this loss did not have a decisive effect upon the ability of the German nation to produce war material . . . The direct loss imposed was of a kind which could be absorbed by sectors of the German economy not essential to war production, while the indirect loss fell on industries easily able to bear the burden.' "

In their impressive historical volumes *The Army Air Forces in World War II*, Wesley F. Craven and James I. Cate state: "The air offensive against German oil production was the

Bomb-damaged U-boats in a German harbor near the end of the Second World War.

pride of the U.S. Strategic Air Forces. Initiated through the insistence of its officers, effective immediately, and decisive within less than a year, this campaign proved to be a clear-cut illustration of strategic air war doctrine. In April 1944, Germany possessed barely adequate supplies of crude oil and was producing a growing volume of synthetic oil. In the following year the Eighth Air Force aimed 70,000 tons, the Fifteenth Air Force 60,000 tons, and RAF Bomber Command 90,000 tons at oil targets. By April 1945, when Germany was being over-run by the ground forces, her oil production was 5 percent of the pre-attack figure. She had been starved of oil, as her captured commanders and officials testified, often with genuine emotion, for the last year of the war. Her air force seldom flew after the first concentrated attacks on synthetic oil plants, which produced aviation gasoline. Tanks and trucks had to be abandoned. Toward the last, even the most august Nazis in the hierarchy were unable to find gasoline for their limousines. Germany's industries were badly crippled, and an enormous amount of effort was absorbed in the furious attempt to defend and rebuild oil installations. The Allied oil offensive had been quite as devastating as [General] Spaatz had predicted in March 1944, but it had taken longer than he and the British had expected to produce collapse. The Germans, never easily beaten, used passive and ground defenses skilfully in protecting their oil producers, and they reconstructed their bombed plants faster than the Americans anticipated. Nevertheless, the offensive had gone on as first priority until the desired results were attained."

On morale, the U.S. survey went on to state: "Continuous heavy bombing of the same communities soon led to diminishing returns in morale effects. The morale in towns subjected to the heaviest bombing was not worse than in towns of the same size receiving much lighter bomb loads. War production is the critical measuring rod of the effects of lowered morale in the German war effort. Allied bombing widely and seriously depressed German morale, but depressed and discouraged workers were not necessarily unproductive workers . . . armaments production continued to mount till mid-1944, in spite of declining civilian morale, but from that point on, arms production began to decline and dropped every month thereafter at an increasing rate."

In conclusion the British Bombing Survey Unit report stated: "Three major factors were associated in Germany's defeat. The first and most obvious was the over-running of her territory by the armies of the Allies. The second was the breakdown of her war industry, which was mainly a consequence of the bombing of her communications system. The third was the drying up of her resources of liquid fuel and the disruption of her chemical industry, which resulted from the bombing of the synthetic oil plants and refineries . . . if none of these factors had operated, another less decisive, but nevertheless potential war-winning event was looming on the horizon—the damage to the Ruhr steel plants, which would have shown itself in a decline in the output of armaments in the second half of 1945."

Of the bombing campaign against Germany, Sir Arthur Harris said in his memoirs: "If we had had the force we used in 1944 a year earlier, and if we had then been allowed to use it together with the whole American bomber force and without inter-ruption, Germany would have been defeated outright by bombing as Japan was . . . The Allied war leaders did not have enough faith in strategic bombing . . . We were always being diverted from the main offensive by the demands of other services. Without these diversions, there would have been no need for the invasion." And in Nazi wartime Minister of Armaments Albert Speer's view: "The real success of the bombing of the Royal Air Force is in fact that you succeeded in tying up tremendous forces. Those forces, if they had been free, would have caused great damage to the Russians. I doubt if with them [in action] the Russians would have succeeded in their offensive at all. We had to pile ammunition everywhere, because we never knew where the attacks would take place. We were forced to increase the production of ammunition of the anti-aircraft guns larger than 8.8 centimetres in 1940 to 1944 by 70 million rounds. And this was much more than we could produce for the anti-tank guns, which we could provide only with 45 million rounds. You had a second front already from the beginning of 1944 and this second front was really very effective."

In his book *Bomber Command*, on the RAF bombing campaign against Germany in World War II, Max Hastings takes the view that: "Beyond any doubts, the area offensive punished Germany terribly. It destroyed centuries of construction and of culture, the homes and property of Germans who for the first time experienced the cost of Nazism. At the end of 1942 Göring had said: 'We will have reason to be glad if Germany can keep the boundaries of 1933 after the war.' By the end of 1943 production in every critical area of war industry—

tanks, U-boats, guns, aircraft—was still expanding at a gigantic rate. But it had become apparent to the German people that they were beyond the hope of mercy. After three years of terrible sacrifice, this was the principal achievement of Bomber Command.

"The two great achievements of the Allied strategic air offensive must be conceded to the Americans: the defeat of the Luftwaffe by the Mustang escort fighter, and the inception of the deadly oil offensive."

Albert Speer: "In the burning and devastated cities we daily experienced the direct impact of the war. It spurred us to do our utmost. Neither did the bombings and the hardships that resulted from them weaken the morale of the populace. On the contrary, from my visits to armament plants and my contacts with the man in the street, I carried away the impression of growing toughness." Speer was amazed by what he referred to as "the inconsistency of the Allied air attack" (in ironic similarity to that of the German bombing attacks during the Battle of Britain). He believed that "the vast but pointless area bombing had achieved no important effect on the German war effort by 1944." Referring to the American attacks on the ball-bearing works at Schweinfurt, and the combined raids on Hamburg, he was astonished by the failure of the Allied bomber forces to return to these and other targets of such great importance: "At intervals the bombers had stumbled on a blind spot, a genuine Achilles heel, only to turn aside and divert their attack elsewhere when they had done so."

The great cathdral of Cologne somehow survived most of the Allied bomb damage to the city.

Considered by many to be the most valuable German source on the effects of the strategic bombing, Speer stated emphatically that, in his opinion, such bombing could have won the war without a land invasion. Other notable Germans offered comment and opinion at war's end. Colonel General Alfred Jodl stated that the winning of air superiority altogether decided the war and that strategic bombing was the most decisive factor. Field Marshal Wilhelm Keitel gave credit to the Allied air forces for the victories in the west, and Reichsmarshall Hermann Goering told USAAF Generals Carl Spaatz and Hoyt Vandenberg that the Allied selection of targets had been excellent and that American precision daylight bombing had been more effective than the night raids. Grand Admiral Karl Dönitz said that the air power of the Allies was the decisive element in the failure of the Nazi submarine war, and Field Marshal Gerd von Rundstedt ranked Allied air power first among several ingredients in the triumph of the United Nations.

The cost of the Allied bombing offensive against Germany and German-occupied target areas in pounds sterling and in dollars is all but impossible to calculate, there being so many variables and indirect expenditures involved. The cost in lives of airmen alone: 47,268 RAF Bomber Command aircrew were killed on operations or died in captivity, the total rising to 55,573 when it includes those airmen killed in accidents. In addition, 8,403 airmen were wounded and 9,784 became prisoners of war. RAF Bomber Command lost a total of 10,724 aircraft, of which 6,931 were heavy bombers. It dropped a total of 954,958 tons of bombs on enemy targets in Europe between September 1939 and May 1945.

Forty-four thousand four hundred seventy-two aircrew of the American Eighth Army Air Force were killed in the European air war. The Eighth lost 8,857 aircraft, of which 5,857 were heavy bombers, most of the rest being fighter escorts. It destroyed 9,472 enemy aircraft and dropped a total of 726,923 tons of bombs on German targets. Operating from bases in Italy, the American Fifteenth Army Air Force suffered 2,703 aircrew killed, 12,359 missing in action or captured, and 2,553 wounded. It lost nearly 3,400 aircraft and destroyed 1,946 enemy aircraft. The Fifteenth dropped a total of 303,842 tons of bombs on enemy targets in twelve countries. A total of more than 100,000 Allied aircrew involved in the bombing offensive against Germany lost their lives. The raids on German cities killed upwards of 305,000 people and seriously injured 780,000. More than 25,000,000 Germans experienced the terror of the bombing.

Between the summer of 1940 and the end of the war, the German Air Force dropped a total of 74,172 tons of bombs on the United Kingdom.

In the bombing campaign against Japan, between June 1944 and August 1945, the American Twentieth Army Air Force dropped 178,700 tons of bombs on enemy targets and the combined efforts of the U.S. Navy and Fifth, Seventh, and Thirteenth U.S. Army Air Forces accounted for an additional 13,801 tons of bombs dropped on Japanese targets.

On 14 September 1944, control of the strategic bomber forces in the European Theatre of Operations was shifted to Sir Norman Bottomley, Deputy Chief of Air Staff, RAF, and General Carl Spaatz, Commander of U.S. Army Air Forces, Europe. In a letter to Bottomley on 29 March 1945, Bomber Command's Sir Arthur

The ruins of Nuremburg after the massive RAF raid of March 1944.

Harris wrote: "I have always held and still maintain that my Directive, 'the progressive destruction and dislocation of the German military, industrial, and economic systems,' could be carried out only by the elimination of German industrial cities and not merely by attacks on individual factories however important these might be in themselves. This view was also officially confirmed by the Air Ministry. The overwhelming evidence which is now available to support it makes it quite superfluous for me to argue at length that the destruction of those cities has fatally weakened the German war effort and is now enabling Allied soldiers to advance into the heart of Germany with negligible casualties. I assume that the view under consideration is something like this: 'no doubt in the past we were justified in attacking German cities. But to do so was always repugnant and now that the Germans are beaten anyway we can properly abstain from proceeding with these attacks.' This is a doctrine to which I could never subscribe. Attacks on cities like any other act of war are intolerable unless they are strategically justified. But they are strategically justified in so far as they tend to shorten the war and so preserve the lives of Allied soldiers. To my mind we have absolutely no right to give them up unless it is certain that they will not have this effect. I do not personally regard the whole of the remaining German cities as worth the bones of one British Grenadier."

In his memoirs of World War II, Winston Churchill wrote: "In judging the contribution to victory of strategic air power it should be remembered that this was the first war in which it was fully used. We had to learn from hard-won experience . . . But although the results of the early years fell short of our aims, we forced on the enemy

an elaborate, ever-growing but finally insufficient air-defense system which absorbed a large proportion of their total war effort. Before the end, we and the United States had developed striking forces so powerful that they played a major part in the economic collapse of Germany."

It was 4:00 a.m. Sunday, 25 June 1950 and the weather in Korea was predicted to be fine and hot. The forces of the North Korean Army began moving south across the 38th parallel into the Republic of Korea, the start of a conflict between the two Koreas that would last until 27 July 1953.

As U.S. Air Force General Hoyt Vandenberg put it in a report to the Congress: "The proper way to use air power is initially to stop the flow of supplies and ammunition, guns, equipment of all types, at its source." The problem, in the case of the North Korean People's Army, was that their primary Communist sources of supply lay beyond the borders of Korea and were declared off-limits to the American bomber force. Thus, the B-29s of the U.S. Far East Bomber Command were ordered instead to attack the five major industrial centers of North Korea, which would at least have the effect of denying such direct "local" support to the Red Korean Army.

These industrial targets, with the exception of Pyongyang, were all located on Korea's northeast coast. Within these large complexes lay the petroleum refineries and tank farms, the seaports, rail hubs, rail-repair, manufacturing and locomotive shops, the arsenals and armament plants for the manufacture of weapons, ammunition, and vehicles, as well as the aircraft maintenance and repair facilities, chemical, aluminum, and magnesium production facilities, iron and steel

Severe bomb damage to rail repair facilities
and marshaling yards in Germany.

Oil refinery and tank farm storage facilities after an 8AF attack on Misburg, Germany.

works, explosives plants and their principal naval bases. Also located in this same coastal region were Japanese-built dams and one of the world's major hydroelectric systems.

Yet another consideration remained on the table for the U.S. strategic bombing planners—whether to use incendiary bombs predominantly in attacks on the key northern industrial targets. These fire-bomb raids, the bombing planners believed, would be the most efficient, economical and expeditious means of destroying both the major targets and the adjacent subsidiary facilities as well. It was not to be. The Administration in Washington was concerned that the North Korean Communists would gain propaganda capital which they would exploit on a massive scale if, in the course of such fire-raids, unnecessary civilian casualties resulted. The Far East Air Force bombers were then prohibited from the use of incendiary munitions in their forthcoming raids on the North Korean targets. They were also ordered to fly leaflet missions notifying the civilians to leave the industrial areas before the impending U.S. attacks.

On 10 August 1950, the attack began with a raid on the Wonsan railway repair shops and oil refinery. In his determination to carry on the bombing at the specified rate of sorties and tonnage, General Emmett O'Donnell let his B-29 crews know that he would not wait around for favorable weather conditions to mount his strikes. Instead, he sent an airborne mission commander in a weather aircraft in advance of the striking force, a senior officer with authority over the method of attack. This officer would also decide if the primary target could be bombed by radar or if the bombers should be redirected to an alternate target. By these means the Americans were able to conduct the missions with a minimum of interference from the weather.

By mid-September, Lieutenant General George Stratemeyer, Commander of Far East Air Forces, announced: "Practically all of the major military industrial targets strategically important to the enemy forces and to their war potential have now been neutralized." On 26 September the final attack of the strategic bombing campaign on the northern industrial targets was flown when eight B-29s struck the Fusen Hydroelectric Plant near Hungnam. Following this raid, Washington called a halt to the strategic attacks and ordered that the air forces of the United Nations were to be employed against tactical objectives from that date forward.

According to Robert F. Futrell of the USAF Historical Division, writing in *The United States Air Force in Korea 1950-1953*: "The FEAF Bomber Command strategic air attacks destroyed none but legitimate military targets in North Korea, and the bombing was so accurate as to do little damage to civilian installations near the industrial plants."

There followed a campaign to neutralize North Korea's airfields, utilizing the B-29s with their large bomb load capacity. These were essentially night attacks and by 1952 the North Koreans had developed a well-coordinated radar air defense intercept system which effectively interfered with the bomber missions.

In general, most historians tend to conclude that the various uses of air power employed in the Korean conflict—strategically, in interdiction and in support roles, were never truly decisive. The total air combat losses of the Far East Air Forces were 139, including seventy-eight F-86 Sabre fighters. The total of U.S. Navy and Marine Corps aircraft losses was 1,183. The total of FEAF airmen killed was 1,180; 368 were wounded and 220 became prisoners of war.

Whether you perceive it as a wind-down, a cease-fire, a disengagement, or a defeat, the key results of the Vietnam War when the Americans left it in 1973 included the fact that the North Vietnamese Army remained on the territory of South Vietnam, as committed as ever to a Communist victory. Without a further air and naval campaign by the United States, the armed forces of South Vietnam were simply incapable at that point, of strategic defense, and the fate of the country appeared sealed. Still, fighting continued, mainly in guerrilla and sapper activity, into 1975, ending in a decisive Spring offensive and a Communist takeover.

For seven years, beginning in 1965, the U.S. Air Force B-52 strategic bombers were utilized in a most unconventional way, bringing and delivering millions of iron bombs in a tactical function. The giant bombers operated routinely in support of ground forces, against North Vietnamese bases and offensives, and interdicting the enemy infiltration routes into the South. Finally, in December 1972, they played their most significant role in an operation called Linebacker II in which they achieved spectacular success. The eleven days of bombing attacks against the Hanoi and Haiphong areas of North Vietnam were highly instrumental in persuading the North Vietnamese to return to the Paris peace talks which resulted in a settlement of the lengthy war in January 1973.

In the eleven days of Linebacker II, the big B-52s flew 729 sorties—340 from U-Tapao, Thailand, and 389 from Guam. Fifteen of the bombers were lost, all to SAM missiles, and nine others were damaged. Twenty-nine

The remains of a Heinkel He III bomber after an Allied bombing attack on this German airfield.

crewmen were killed and thirty-three were captured and later returned. A further twenty-six were rescued in courageous post-mission efforts. The bombers struck at thirty-four separate targets, dropping 49,000 bombs with great accuracy amid determined and effective defenses. Many military analysts believe that the costly and prolonged repairs to the targets damaged in this Linebacker operation significantly delayed the North Vietnamese invasion of South Vietnam in 1975.

More than eight years of American bombing in Southeast Asia ended on 15 August 1973 when the U.S. Congress halted funding for the air campaign, which had shifted in January to Laos, and then in April to Cambodia. Two million six hundred thirty-three thousand tons of conventional bombs had been dropped in eight years and two months and 124,532 successful sorties were flown. In all B-52 operations, eighteen of the bombers were lost to enemy action, and thirteen in mid-air collisions or other accidents. In the entire Vietnam and Southeast Asia conflict, from January 1962 through August 1973, the U.S. Air Force lost 2,257 aircraft to combat and operational causes. 2,118 airmen were killed and 3,460 were wounded. Five hundred eighty-six were reported missing or captured. U.S. Air Force operations in Vietnam and Southeast Asia in that period cost the American tax payer $3,129,900,000. Of the B-52's contribution in that war, General William C. Westmoreland, Commander, U.S. Military Assistance Command, Vietnam, later wrote: "The use of this weapon has won many battles and made it unnecessary to fight many more."

In the spring and early summer of 1982 South-Atlantic conflict usually referred to at the Falklands War,

the Argentine forces lost a total of 100 fixed-wing and helicopter aircraft, while the aircraft losses of the United Kingdom numbered thirty-four. The action, known as Operation Corporate, saw significant contributions in the areas of low-level ground attack, reconnaissance and air interdiction on the part of the RAF Harrier GR.3s, which also proved tough against the small arms fire of the Argentine defenses. Prior to the Falklands conflict, the Royal Navy's Sea Harrier had been perceived by some in the British military establishment as not really up to the tasks it was intended to perform. The airplane rose to the challenge, however, and operated in the South Atlantic with distinction. Its reliability and high state of readiness was exceptional among combat aircraft, and the level of confidence it inspired in its pilots was unparalleled.

Avro Vulcan B-2 bombers from RAF Waddington participated in sorties, mainly runway denial attacks, operating from Ascencion Island during the campaign. The initial Vulcan sortie on 30 April took a load of twenty-one 1,000-pound bombs to hit the Stanley airport runway, thus beginning the six-week British air action. The attack was only marginally successful, and was followed on 3 May by another of equally unremarkable result. The big RAF bombers were then modified to carry Shrike missiles and were redeployed to Ascencion to begin anti-radar missions. They finished up with a final raid on the Stanley airport facilities on the night of 11 June. While the results of this last attack were considered good, the overall performance of the Vulcans in the Falklands arena was not impressive.

The level of technology brought to bear on Iraq in the Gulf War, which was triggered when Saddam Hussein's

Republican Guard entered Kuwait on 2 August 1990, must have been startling and unimaginable to him and his people. The ferocity of the air campaign mounted against him and his forces by the United Nations coalition was historically unprecedented.

The Gulf War may have been the most interesting proving ground for aircraft, tactics, weapons, and technologies since the Spanish Civil War. The Iraqis found themselves blind-sided in attacks by the world's deadliest helicopter, the AH-64 Apache, which was turned loose on Iraqi armor with utterly devastating effect, unseen from stand-off range. For the first time, the F-117A stealth fighter/bomber appeared in combat and in 1,271 sorties, all of which were flown at night from the Khamis Mushait base in Saudi Arabia, proved itself beyond any doubt. The black jets, or "ghosts" as the Iraqis called them, drew the most difficult and dangerous assignments of the conflict, attacks on heavily defended command and control targets in downtown Baghdad. They also struck at airfields, bridges, chemical and nuclear sites, and evaded the Iraqi SAM and triple-A defenses so well that not a single F-117A was even damaged during the entire conflict. More than 2,000 laser-guided GBU-10 and GBU-27 Paveway bombs were delivered by the stealths.

A literally ground-breaking assignment for the Royal Air Force and Royal Saudi Air Force Tornados was the dropping of runway-cratering bomblets and anti-personnel mines to discourage the repair of the runways, thus denying Saddam facilities from which to launch aircraft against those of the coalition. Flying at a height of 180 feet, the the JP-233-equipped Tornados scattered their bomblets with great effect and made a major contribution to the ultimate result for the coalition force.

U.S. Navy A-6 Intruders and U.S. Marine Corp F/A-18 Hornets were employed in an iron-bombing role against Iraqi railyards, airfields, bridges, and a power plant, performing creditably, while French and RAF Sepecat Jaguars carried their share of ordnance to war in the coalition cause with distinction. The vital "Scud-hunting" mission was the province of the magnificent F-15E Strike Eagles. It proved how effectively they could surround the enemy missile launch units with very destructive cluster bombs, when they weren't busy taking out Iraqi bridges.

From RAF Fairford in southern England, from airfields in Egypt, Saudi Arabia, and Spain, elderly B-52 Stratofortresses were once again pressed into service as the coalition's pre-eminent haulers of bomb tonnage. The planes regularly brought up to fifty-one 750-pound bombs each on their sorties from as far away as the UK, targeting the Iraqi leader's elite Republican Guard personnel in saturation attacks. The B-52s operated in "cell" units of three aircraft, dropping their combined total of 153 iron bombs silently, from a high altitude, causing maximum terror and psychological trauma among the targeted troops when the weapons arrived without warning. The effect on the morale of those on the receiving end was undoubtedly profound and resulted in many of them surrendering by the start of the ground offensive in late February 1991.

In the Gulf War coalition losses to all causes, combat, non-combat, and accident, came to eighty-eight aircraft of various types. 106 airmen were killed; fifteen were rescued; twenty-six were captured and later released, and five were missing in action.

In spring 1999 a major air campaign was conducted by the nineteen member nations of the North Atlantic Treaty Organization. They were engaged in a series of conventional, cruise, and other missile attacks on Serbian targets in the Albanian province of Kosovo and in Yugoslavia. The effort was intended to degrade and ultimately end the ability of the Serb leader, Slobodan Milosevic, to threaten, displace, terrorize, and murder Kosovars in his program of so-called "ethnic cleansing" in the region.

Argument raged around the world about the wisdom and morality of the NATO bombing raids, and, after seventy-nine days of concerted attacks (the majority of the sorties were flown at night), Milosevic yielded and agreed to abandon the Serb positions within Kosovo. NATO forces began to occupy the province and several hundred thousand Kosovar refugees, who had been forced to flee their homes and villages in the wake of the Serb terror, began their journey home.

Whether or not NATO's detractors were correct in their condemnation of the air campaign, whether or not some alternative approach to halting the activities of Milosevic's army and police forces might have been employed, the debate continues. It seems clear, however, that the cumulative effect of the bombing campaign did, ultimately, cause the Serbs to give up.

Bombing and aerial attack may or may not be perceived as an ethical and appropriate means of warfare; it may or may not prove effective when applied in particular situations, but since the first time it was tried it has been perpetuated and has continued to evolve. It is simply a fact of warfare.

The extreme bomb damage inflicted on the city of Bremen in American and British raids.

An American bombing attack on the German
U-boat pen shelter at La Pallice on the Brittany
coast of France. Penetrating the massive walls
and roofs of the submarine pens along the
coast from Bordeaux up to Brest was all but
impossible and the great pen shelters still stand
today having survived the worst the Allies
could do to bring them down in the war.

PICTURE CREDITS
Photos from the collection of the author are credited: AC; photos by the author: PK; photos from the U.S. National Archives and Records Administration: NARA; photos from the Imperial War Museum: IWM. P3 both: PK, PP4-5: NARA, P7: NARA, P8: Toni Frissell-Library of Congress, PP10-11: AC, PP12-13: AC, PP14-15: PK, P17: AC, P18: AC, P19: NARA, PP20-21: AC, P22: AC, P23 both: AC, P27: AC, P29: NARA, P30: courtesy Quentin Bland, PP32-33: NARA, P34: AC, P35: IWM, PP36-37: courtesy Tiny Cooling, P38: AC, PP40, 41, 42, and 44: courtesy Tiny Cooling, P46: AC, P47: PK, PP48-49: PK, P50: PK, P51 top: AC, bottom NARA, P52 top: AC, bottom: NARA, P55: PK, P56 both: NARA, P57: PK, PP58-59 all: PK, P61: NARA, P62: AC, P63: PK, PP64-65: AC, PP66-67: IWM, P68: AC, P71: AC, PP72-73: AC, P74: AC, P75: AC, P76: Charles E. Brown, PP78-79 all: Mark Brown, P81: AC, PP82-83: AC, P84: AC, P85: AC, P86: AC, P88: IWM, P89: AC, P90 top: PK, P91 top left: PK, top right: Mark Brown, bottom: PK, P92: NARA, P93: AC, PP96-97: NARA, P99: AC, PP100-101 all: AC, P102: AC, P103: AC, PP104-105: Mark Brown, P107: NARA, PP108-109: AC, PP110-111: NARA, P113: AC, P114 both: Toni Frissell-Library of Congress, P116 both: AC, P118: AC, P119: RAF Museum, P120: NARA, P121: AC, P123: NARA, P125: courtesy Adolf Galland, P126: AC, P127: PK, P128: AC, P129 both: AC, PP130-131 both: PK, P132 top: Mark Brown, bottom: AC, P133 top: PK, bottom: courtesy Albert Tyler, PP134-135: Associated British Picture Corporation, PP136-137: AC, P138: AC, PP140-141: AC, P142: IWM, P143: AC, PP144-145 all: AC, P147: RAF Museum, PP148-149 all: PK, P151: AC, P152: AC, P154: NARA, P156: NARA, P158: AC, P159: AC, P160-161 all: PK, P162: NARA, P165: NARA, P167: NARA, PP168-169 all: AC, PP170-171: AC, P172: PK, P173: AC, PP174-175: PK, P177: AC, PP178-179: AC, P180: PK, P185: PK, P186: PK, P188: PK, PP190-191: AC, P192 both: AC, P193: AC, P194 top: PK, bottom both: PK, P195 top: AC, bottom both: PK, P196: AC, P197 top: AC, bottom: PK, P198 both: AC, P199: USAF Academy, PP200-201: PK, PP202-203: AC, P203 right: PK, PP204-205: AC, P206: AC, P207 all: AC, PP208-209: Mike Durning, P210: AC, P211: AC, P212: AC, P213 both: AC, P214: AC, P215: AC, P216: AC, P218: USAF Academy, P221: AC, P223: AC, P225: AC, P227: AC, P228: USAF Academy, P230: AC, P233: AC, PP234-235: AC.

ACKNOWLEDGMENTS
The author is particularly grateful to the following for their generous help in the development of this book: Joseph Anastasia, Robert Bailey, John M. Bennett, Jr., Johgn S. Bennett, Quentin Bland, JoAnne Bromley, Piers Burnett, Paul Connolly, R. D. Cooling, Robert F. Cooper, Kate and Jack Currie, Sir John Curtiss, Dan DeCamp, Mike Durning, Ella and Oz Freire, Bill Graham, Nick Grey, Stephen Grey, Brian Gunderson, Bill Harvey, Don Haines, Larry Henderson, Dave Hill, John Howland, Claire and Joe Kaplan, Hargi and Neal Kaplan, Margaret Kaplan, Ruth and Fred Kaplan, Karen King, David C. Lustig, Missy Marlow, Judy and Rick McCutcheon, James McMaster, Tilly McMaster, Michael O'Leary, Merle Olmsted, Robert Owen, Douglas Radcliffe, Duane Reed, Dale O. Smith, Lloyd Stovall, Ann and John Tusa, Ray Wild, Mary K. Wiley, Frank Wootton, Hub Zemke. The author greatly appreciates the kind assistance and inspiration of Fred Allen, Mark Aragon, Roger Armstrong, Philip Avery, Ian Bain, Ray Beckley, Charles Bednarik, Mike Benarchik, Gordon Bennett, Larry Bird, Oscar Boesch, Morfydd Brooks, Nick Brown, Wilfred Burnett, Geoffrey Butcher, M. A. Clarke, Don Clement, Jack Clift, Verne Cole, Harry Crosby, James Dacey, Scotty and Clayton David, Harold Davidson, Louis DelGuidice, Lawrence Drew, Jonathan Falconer, Ray Fletcher, W. W. Ford, Roger A. Freeman, Royal Frey, Bill Ganz, Peter Geraghty, J. R. Goodman, Kenneth Grantham, Sol Greenberg, Ed Haggerty, David Harper, John Hersey, Larry Hewin, John Hill, John Holmes, Alfred Huberman, John Hurd, Frank Isla, Markus Isphording, Walter Ketron, John Kirkland, Walter Konantz, Nick Kosciuk, Edith Kup, John Lamb, E. F. Lapham, Ed Leary, Curtis E. LeMay, Sylvan Lieberthal, Walter Longnecker, Walter Lybeck, Ron MacKay, Roger MacKenzie, Ken Manley, Nelson McInnis, Brian McMaster, John McQuarrie, Edgar Moore, Douglas Newham, Keith Newhouse, Steve Nichols, Geoffrey Page, Greg Parlin, David Parry, John Pawsey, Reg Payne, Len Pearman, Horst Petzschler, Gerald Phillips, R. H. Powell, George Reynard, Ted Richardson, J. G. Roberts, Ken Roberts, Lynn Seabury, Dave Shelhamer, Cliff Shirley, Robert Silver, Jerome Solomon, Stan Staples, Ken Stone, Robert Strobell, Stephan Stritter, Alfred Tarry, Leonard Thompson, Robert Thompson, John Turnbull, George Unwin, John Vietor, Douglas Warren, A. I. Wilson, Robert White, Jack Woods, Sam Young.

Grateful acknowledgment is made to the following for the use of their previously published material:
Ian Allen Ltd for excerpts from Bomber Pilot 1916-1918, by C. P. O. Bartlett.
Frederick Muller Ltd for an excerpt from Pathfinder by D. C. T. Bennett.
Goodall Publications Ltd for excerpts from No Moon Tonight by Don Charlwood.
Hutchinson & Co. Ltd for an excerpt from Bomber Pilot by Leonard Cheshire.
Houghton Mifflin Company for an excerpt from The Second World War by Winston S. Churchill.
The University of Chicago Press for an excerpt from The Army Air Forces in World War II by Wesley F. Craven and James I. Cate.
Macdonald & Co. for excerpts from Yesterday's Gone by N. J. Crisp.
Kate Currie for an excerpt from Lancaster Target by Jack Currie, reprinted by permission.
Harper and Row for an excerpt from Bomber by Len Deighton.
Victor Gollanz Ltd for excerpts from Bomber's Moon by Negley Farson.

Duell, Sloan, and Pearce for an excerpt from *The United States Air Force in Korea 1950-1953* by Robert F. Futrell. Goodall Publications Ltd for excerpts from *Enemy Coast Ahead* by Guy Gibson.

McClelland and Stewart Ltd for an excerpt from *Boys, Bombs and Brussels Sprouts* by J. Douglas Harvey.

Michael Joseph for an excerpt from *Bomber Command* by Max Hastings.

John Hersey for excerpts from *Hiroshima* by John Hersey.

Alfred A. Knopf Inc. for excerpts from *The War Lover* by John Hersey.

McGraw Hill for *The Fighters Queued Up Like a Bread Line and Let Us Have It* by Beirne Lay, Jr.

Ballantine Books for an excerpt from *12 O'Clock High!* by Beirne Lay, Jr. and Sy Bartlett.

Random House for excerpts from *Thirty Seconds Over Tokyo* by Ten W. Lawson.

Doubleday for an excerpt from *Mission With LeMay* by Cirtis E. LeMay and MacKinlay Kantor.

Hutchinson & Co., Ltd for excerpts from *The Bombers* by Norman Longmate.

Missy Marlow and John S. Bennett for excerpts from *Letters From England* by J. M. Bennetts, Jr., reprinted by permission.

Special acknowledgment to Richard Rhodes, author of *The Making of the Atomic Bomb* published by Simon and Schuster for the reference it has provided.

The Viking Press for excerpts from *Once There Was A War* by John Steinbeck.

Leo Cooper for excerpts from *The Eighth Passenger* by Miles Tripp.

J. B. Lippincott for an excerpt from *Heritage of Valor* by Budd J. Peaslee.

Wartime News for an article on No. 617 Squadron reproduced by kind permission of Wartime News and Robert M. Owen.

BIBLIOGRAPHY

Armstrong, Roger W., *USA The Hard Way*, Quail House, 1991.

Barker, Ralph, *The Thousand Plane Raid*, Chatto and Windus, 1965.

Bartlett, C. P. O., *Bomber Pilot 1916-1918*, IanAllen, 1974.

Bekker, Cajus, *The Luftwaffe War Diaries*, Doubleday, 1968.

Bennett, D. C. T., *Pathfinder*, Frederick Muller, 1958.

Bennett, John M., Jr., *Letters from England*, 1945.

Bowyer, Michael J. F., *The Stirling Bomber*, Faber & Faber, 1980.

Brown, G. I., *The Big Bang*, Sutton, 1998.

Caidin, Martin, *Black Thursday*, E. P. Dutton, 1960.

Campbell, James, *The Bombing of Nuremberg*, Doubleday, 1954.

Charlwood, Don, *No Moon Tonight*, Angus & Robertson, 1956.

Cheshire, Leonard, *Bomber Pilot*, Hutchinson, 1943.

Collier, Richard, *Eagle Day*, Hodder & Stoughton, 1966.

Crisp, N. J., *Yesterday's Gone*, Viking Penguin, 1983.

Crosby, Harry, *A Wing and a Prayer*, Harper Collins, 1993.

Cumming, Michael, *Pathfinder Cranswick*, William Kimber, 1962.

Currie, Jack, *Lancaster Target*, New English Library, 1977.

Currie, Jack, *Mosquito Victory*, Goodall Publications, 1983.

Currie, *The Augsburg Raid*, Goodall Publications, 1987.

Deighton, Len, *Bomber*, Harper and Row, 1970.

Farson, Negley, *Bomber's Moon*, Victor Gollanz, 1941.

FitzGibbon, Constantine, *The Blitz*, Allan Wingate, 1957.

Frankland, Noble, *The Bombing Offensive Against Germany*, Faber & Faber, 1965.

Freeman, Roger A., *The Mighty Eighth*, Macdonald, 1970.

Futrell, Robert, *The United States Air Force in Korea 1950-1953*, Duell, Sloan and Pearce, 1961.

Harvey, J. Douglas, *Boys, Bombs and Brussels Sprouts*, McClelland and Stewart, 1981.

Hastings, Max, *Bomber Command*, Michael Joseph, 1979.

Hersey, John, *The War Lover*, Alfred A. Knopf, 1959.

Hersey, John, *Hiroshima*, Alfred A. Knopf, 1946.

Holder, Bill, *Northrop Grumman B-2 Spirit*, Schiffer, 1998.

Jablonski, Edward, *Flying Fortress*, Doubleday, 1965.

Kaplan, Philip and Smith, Rex Allen, *One Last Look*, Abbeville, 1983.

Kaplan, Philip and Currie, Jack, *Round The Clock*, Random House, 1993.

Lay, Beirne, Jr., and Bartlett, Sy, *12 O'Clock High!*, Ballantine Books, 1965.

Lawson, Ted, *Thirty Seconds Over Tokyo*, Random House, 1943.

Longmate, Norman, *The Bombers*, Hutchinson, 1983.

Lyall, Gavin, *The War in the Air*, Willam Morrow, 1968.

McCrary, John and Scherman, David, *First of the Many*, Simon and Schuster, 1944.

Middlebrook, Martin, *The Nuremberg Raid*, Penguin, 1973.

Morris, Eric, *Blockade Berlin & the Cold War*, Hamish Hamilton, 1973.

Pearcy, Arthur, *Berlin Airlift*, Airlife, 1997.

Peaslee, Budd, J., *Heritage of Valor*, J. B. Lippincott, 1964.

Reynolds, Quentin, *A London Diary*, Random House, 1941.

Rhodes, Richard, *The Making of the Atomic Bomb*, Simon and Schuster, 1986.

Robertson, Bruce, *Lancaster-The Story of a Famous Bomber*, Harleyford, 1964.

Saward, Dudley, *"Bomber" Harris*, Cassell, 1984.

Sloan, John, *The Route As Briefed*, Argus Press, 1946.

Smith, Dale O., *Screaming Eagle*, Algonquin Books, 1990.

Steinbeck, John, *Once There Was a War*, Viking, 1958.

Stiles, Bert, *Serenade To the Big Bird*, W. W. Norton, 1947.

Tripp, Miles, *The Eighth Passenger*, William Heinemann, 1969.

Truman, Harry S., *Memoirs-Year of Decisions*, Doubleday, 1955.

Vietor, John, *Time Out*, Richard R. Smith, 1951.

Verrier, Anthony, *The Bomber Offensive*, B. T. Batsford, 1968.

INDEX